MEDIA AND MINORITIES

Representing Diversity in a Multicultural Canada

**RELATED TITLES FROM
THOMPSON EDUCATIONAL PUBLISHING**
~ ~ ~

Communications in Canadian Society, 5th Edtiion
Edited by Craig McKie and Benjamin D. Singer
ISBN 1-55077-118-3

Understanding Diversity:
Ethnicity and Race in the Canadian Context
Wsevolod W. Isajiw
ISBN 1-55077-102-7

Seeing Ourselves:
Exploring Race, Ethnicity and Culture, 2nd Edition
Carl James
ISBN 1-55077-103-5

Racism and Social Inequality in Canada:
Concepts, Controversies and Strategies of Resistance
Edited by Vic Satzewich
ISBN 1-55077-100-0

The New Poverty in Canada:
Ethnic Groups and Ghetto Neighbourhoods
Abdolmohammad Kazemipur and Shiva S. Halli
ISBN 1-55077-108-6

Canadian Social Trends, Volumes 1, 2, and 3
Statistics Canada
ISBNs 1-55077-010-1 , 1-55077-062-4 , 1-55077-105-1

For information on these and other titles:
www.thompsonbooks.com

MEDIA AND MINORITIES

Representing Diversity in a Multicultural Canada

Augie Fleras

University of Waterloo

Jean Lock Kunz

Human Resources Development Canada

THOMPSON EDUCATIONAL PUBLISHING, INC.

Toronto

Information on how to obtain copies of this book may be obtained from:

Web site: www.thompsonbooks.com
E-mail: publisher@thompsonbooks.com
Telephone: (416) 766-2763
Fax: (416) 766-0398

National Library of Canada cataloguing in publication data

Fleras, Augie, 1947-
   Media and minorities : representing diversity in a multicultural Canada

Includes bibliographical references and index.

ISBN 1-55077-123-X

1. Mass media and minorities - Canada. I. Kunz, Jean Lock. II. Title.

P94.5.M552C33 2001   302.23'089'00971   C00-933244-8

Copy Editing: Elizabeth Phinney
Cover Design: Elan Designs
Text Design: Danielle Baum

Reader's Comments: If you have suggestions or information that might improve future editions of this book, the authors and publisher would be pleased to hear from you. Please send your comments to: author@thompsonbooks.com

The publisher acknowledges the support of the Government of Canada through the Book Publishing Industry Development Program for our publishing activities.

The authors thank the Department of Canadian Heritage for providing funding for their project on media-minority relations in Canada. The views expressed are of course their own.

Every reasonable effort has been made to acquire permission for copyright materials used in this book and to acknowledge such permissions accurately. Any errors or omissions called to the publisher's attention will be corrected in future printings.

Printed in Canada.

ISBN 1-55077-123-X 1 2 3 4 5   06 05 04 03 02 01

Table of Contents

PREFACE, VII

SECTION I: MEDIA, RACISM, AND MULTICULTURALISM, 1

1. Multicultural Canada, *3*
2. The Media and Racism, *29*
3. The Mainstream Media: Discourses in Defence of Ideology, *47*

SECTION II: MISCASTING MINORITIES, 63

4. Newscasting: "Problematizing" Minorities, *65*
5. "Who's On?": Programming Minorities, *87*
6. Advertising and Minorities, *103*
7. Filming the "Other", *121*

SECTION III: RECASTING THE MOULD, 139

8. Miscasting Minorities: Patterns and Causes, *141*
9. "Multiculturalizing" the Media, *157*
10. Re-Priming the Relationship, *171*

REFERENCES, 181

GLOSSARY, 189

INDEX, 197

Dedication

To: Luo Zhao-tian, Chen Pei-zhen, Thomas H. Kunz

Preface

Canada is a paradox. Messages about its progressive stature are conflicting, and none is more striking than that found in the oft-quoted aphorism about Canadian society as a "solution in search of a problem." Consider this paradox: a United Nations (UN) Developmental Agency has declared that Canada is the best country in the world in which to live for the seventh consecutive year, yet criticism is mounting over Canada's mistreatment of aboriginal peoples and continued discrimination towards minority women and men. Or ponder the list of Canada's many firsts: Canada was the first and remains the world's only official multicultural society, the first and only country to have constitutionally entrenched aboriginal rights, and the first and only jurisdiction to receive a UN award (the Nansen Medal in 1986) for assisting international refugees (Fleras 2001). But glowing praise for the progressive "management" of race, ethnic, and aboriginal relations has not exempted Canada from being criticized as a "racist" society, with a penchant for denying or excluding those who fall outside the mainstream (Henry et al. 2000). Such discontinuities cannot continue unchallenged: certainties and myths of the past are dissolving under pressure from the demands of a changing, diverse, and interconnected world, resulting in emergent new fictions for making sense of a contested and uncertain reality.

Of those social and cultural forces at the forefront in the construction and comprehension of these realities, few have been as formidable or controversial than the mainstream media. Mainstream media have proven complicit in fortifying the cultural hierarchy and moral authority at the heart of an existing social order. Media constructions have also proven pivotal in shaping public consciousness over how social differences should be conceptualized or assessed. Yet the mainstream media have been subjected to endless criticism over the miscasting of minorities because of their centrality in framing issues, establishing agendas, setting priorities, and codifying realities. Media representations of minorities border on the questionable at best, reprehensible at worst, and the structural nature of this miscasting process both complicates and compromises prospects for improvement. To the extent that the mainstream media images have mis/under/over/represented minorities, minority concerns and contributions to society continued to be de-politicized. Inasmuch as media minority images do not necessarily embrace the postulates of an official multicultural society, despite a mounting urgency to improve the representational basis of media-minority relations, the prospects for living together with differences are recklessly compromised.

Thirty years of official multiculturalism in Canada have confirmed what many would prefer to ignore: Initiatives for constructively engaging diversity within Canada's institutional framework are proving the process to be complex and perplexing. The politics of institutional inclusiveness are fraught with ambiguity and contradiction as competing forces struggle to protect interests, resist unwelcome incursions, score public relations points, or advance hidden agendas. At the cutting edge of Canada's multicultural wars are the mainstream media who, collectively, have been impugned for compromising minority interests with respect to different media processes. Mainstream media have endured criticism as being a kind of thought control in democratic societies, with the intent or effect of "framing" minorities as a threat to the status quo, a risk to national interests, inconsistent with core values and institutions, and inimical to a united and prosperous Canada. For what amounts to be a virtual smear campaign that stigmatizes minorities as fringe players in Canadian society—interesting and colourful, at best, but menacing or consequential at worst—media miscasting of minority women and men has come under fire for irresponsible and stereotypical coverage (Tator and Henry 2000). Media minority miscasting continues to reflect mediacentric agendas and institutional dynamics. This miscasting remains rooted in Westocentric notions of universality or normalcy, anchored in the imperatives of a capitalist economy, and inseparable from a broader framework of diversity, change, and uncertainty. To be sure, the mainstream media rarely set out to demean or diminish minority women and men. However the one-sidedness of negative media messages has had a demeaning effect by "miniaturizing" minorities as inferior or irrelevant. In that this "otherizing" effect is systemic rather than personal, the mainstream media have evolved into a complex yet contradictory site of cultural politics. Insofar as mainstream images of minority women and men remain profoundly anti-democratic and contrary to the principles of a multicultural Canada, notwithstanding modest improvements in the quantity and quality of media minority representations, the politics of inclusiveness continue to be riddled with paradox and perplexity.

The inception of Canada's official multiculturalism has compelled all federally regulated institutions to deliver a culturally sensitive service that is pluralistic in objectives, equitable in outcome, and representative in composition. Canada's mainstream media are hardly exempt from these pressures to advance minority women and men as positive role models and legitimate contributors to Canadian society. Yet the same mainstream media appear to have acted irresponsibly in confronting the challenge of engaging diversity, and it is precisely this very slack between the real and ideal that has prompted this examination of the relationship between media and minorities in a multicultural society.

Media and Minorities: Representing Diversity in a Multicultural Canada proposes to analyze and assess changes in the representational basis of media-minority relations against the backdrop of Canada's commitment to multiculturalism. This text argues that media images of minority women and men continue to be couched in compromise; that is, improvements in the quantity of minority media representations are often offset by continued misrepresentation of minorities as "invisible," "problem people," "stereotype," and "adornment." It also contends that the cumulative effect of slanted coverage has had the effect of "miniaturizing" minorities as the "other," unworthy of serious attention or equitable treatment and inconsequential in contributing to Canada's society-building project. The "racialization" of minority women and men as inferior or irrelevant is neither random nor personal but systemic and structural, since media bias is constructed by consent rather than coercion, without recourse to open prejudice and overt discrimination, and in ways consistent with securing media interests rather than those of Canadians at large. In short, media minority miscasting constitutes an integral component of "doing business," rather than any egregious departure from conventionality. The systemic nature of this (mis) representation makes it exceptionally difficult to detect or reform.

Media and Minorities grapples with the contradictory and increasingly contested relationship between the mainstream media and Canada's multicultural minorities at the level of visual and verbal representation. Using the notion of the media as discourses in defence of ideology, either by intent or by consequences, this book examines the representational politics of media-minority relations in a multicultural Canada. The focus is not intended to be descriptive, however deplorable media minority representations may be; nor is the book about race, ethnic, and aboriginal relations per se. Rather, the text examines how constructions of race, ethnicity, and aboriginality are interpreted by the mainstream media and translated into public discourses that are then consumed by millions. Emphasis is on analyzing the rationale behind media misrepresentation of minorities. It involves "going against the grain" by interrogating media power in formulating ideologies of domination that shape public understanding of diversity (Hubbard 1998). The following themes provide an organizational framework: (a) media coverage of minority women and men by way of visual and verbal images, (b) the degree to which misrepresentations are the result of conscious manipulation or inadvertently reflect the organization of power in society at large, (c) the persistence of media racism and systemic institutional bias, and (d) the proposed characteristics of an inclusive and multicultural media (Jakubowicz et al. 1994). Initiatives that have empowered minority women and men to challenge the representational basis of media-minority relations are also addressed. Media initiatives to improve minority representations are discussed as well, thus confirming minority demands to (re)claim public recognition of those images by which to define themselves, assume their rightful place in public debates, and attain full and equal participation in society (Salee 1998).

The conclusion is as ambiguous and contradictory as it is hopeful. That is, the process and the politics of representing diversity continue to be couched in compromise despite modest gains in portrayal of minorities, largely because proposed improvements are (a) inconsistent and contradictory, (b) ignore the systemic biases at the heart of media dynamics, (c) undermined by commercial imperatives, (d) eroded by institutional inertia, (e) plagued by mixed messages and diverse publics, and (f) confused by uncertainty over what to do and how. Advances in media minority representations are also compromised by coverage that is selective, reflective of certain media channels rather than others, and often achieved by accident rather than design. And a dangerous dialectic is established when media falsely stereotype minority women and men while the public, in turn, encourages such caricatures as a basis for relating to the world at large. Not surprisingly, the mainstream media are routinely subjected to double standards and contradictory expectations, including a vulnerability to criticism regardless of what they do or don't do. Just as many have hopelessly unrealistic expectations of the media, so too are the mainstream media equally anxious to be highly regarded even as they slip away from their traditional notions of public service—thus further imperilling progress in multiculturalizing both society and media (Sandford 1999).

This book is organized around three sections. Section 1 is concerned with framing the issues for study and analysis. This section looks at the relationship between minorities and the mainstream media when refracted through the prism of Canada's official multiculturalism. Attention is directed at the multicultural context in which the mainstream media operate, the pervasiveness of racism in a multicultural society, the logic and dynamics of the mainstream media in engaging diversity, and the barriers that preclude inclusiveness. A framework is established for operationalizing key concepts such as "media as discourses in defence of ideology," "multiculturalism as principle and practice," "media racism," "systemic propaganda," and "mediocentrism."

Section 2 explores the politics of media minority misrepresentations. Our conclusions reflect what many suspect: the representation of minority images in newscasting, advertising, TV, and film continue to elicit mixed messages whose cumulative impact has had the effect of miscasting minorities as invisible, problem people, stereotypes, and adornments.

Section 3 deals with the challenges of "recasting the mould." The principle and practices of institutional inclusion are sharply contested around the politics of diversity within contexts of power and inequality. Media miscasting of minorities are not necessarily an error of perception involving deviation from institutional norm, but rather systemic, integral to conducting media business, and intrinsic to a commercially driven enterprise. The book concludes by exploring accomplishments to date in "multiculturalizing" the media through both institutional reforms ("mainstreaming diversity") and establishment of a separate ethnic and/or indigenous media. But until the issue of power is resolved in re-defining the representational basis of minority-majority relations, depictions of minorities as active subjects rather than passive objects will continue to be an elusive grail.

Two explanatory frameworks are employed to anchor the argument. First, the representational basis of media-minority relations in a multicultural society is interpreted as relations of inequality (Elliott and Fleras 1991). A coherent framework for "theorizing" about the politics of media minority representations is secured by exploring how this inequality is created, expressed, sustained, challenged, and transformed by way of institutional policy, collective action, and minority resistance. The centrality of power is critical in acknowledging media minority relations as a contested site of competing agendas. Second, a social problem perspective is applied. Such a perspective is not intended to stigmatize the mainstream media as a social problem per se. Under a social problem perspective, media minority representations are problematized as social constructions that vary over time and place, as a convention constructed by individuals who make choices albeit not in contexts of their own choosing, and as amenable to criticism and reform. Central to the social problem perspective are the following: What is the problem? How is this problem expressed? Who says media miscasting of minorities is a problem? Why, on what grounds, and by what criteria? Who or what is responsible? Why does miscasting persist? What is its impact on individuals and its implications for society? What is being done or what can be done to improve media-minority relations? Responses to each of these questions will yield insights into the contestation at the heart of representational politics.

Any book is informed by an underlying set of assumptions that shape the problem at hand, questions asked, answers given, burden of proof required, corresponding methodology, and pattern of findings and conclusions. This study on the representational politics of media-minority relations in a multicultural Canada is no exception. First, and foremost, this book revolves around a commitment to the principles of a critically informed political economy (Curran and Gurevitch 1994). A critical political economy approach provides an explanatory framework for analyzing institutional philosophies, policies, and programs, based on the premise that the complex web of political and economic relations impose a constraining but not determining context for organizing institutional action (Saggers and Gray 1998). According to the principles of a critical political economy, the mainstream media exist in the first instance to generate revenue, primarily by massaging the message of more to the many. Yet the mainstream media are more than a marketing tool despite the aphorism that "advertisers want an audience, media provide the link." As socially constructed, yet socially constructing, the mainstream media are loaded with ideological assumptions about what is acceptable, right, or normal. In short, both commercial and ideological imperatives have proven relevant in shaping the complex and contested relationship between the mainstream media and representational politics of minority images.

Second, the mainstream media are no longer portrayed as monolithic institutions with dictatorial powers to bully or control. Contemporary readings interpret the mainstream media as "sites" of contestation involving a struggle among competing interests for privileging priorities or controlling agendas. A similar line of reasoning applies to media representations of minorities. Media mistreatment of minority women and men remains compromised at best, deplorable at worst. Nevertheless, the representational basis of media-minority relations is complex, often confusing or inconsistent, and subject to continuous challenge and change. Moreover, oppositional readings provide a fertile if contested site for articulating a vision of "minorityness" that simultaneously advances yet contests minority interests within the context of an official multiculturalism that prefers a "pretend" pluralism over taking differences seriously.

Third, media messages, images, and symbols are refracted through a prism of whiteness. That is, the mainstream media automatically and routinely interpret the reality from a media perspective as natural and normal, while dismissing dissenting viewpoints as inferior or irrelevant. Minority women and men are defined by what they are not in relationship to the mainstream, rather than in terms of who they are. However unconsciously or inadvertently, such mediacentrism has the effect of naturalizing social reality by normalizing mainstream meanings as superior or universal and in the process reinforcing the view of media as discourses in defence of ideology. To be sure, media effects on individuals or society are neither direct or causal nor uniform and consistent but rather negotiated, contradictory, and indirect. Minority women and men routinely resist the imposition of meanings, preferring instead to subvert media images as one way of controlling, affirming, or re-imagining a preferred identity. Nevertheless, the cumulative effect of this mediacentrism fosters a social climate and cultural frame of reference at odds with minority aspirations.

Fourth, the representational basis of media-minority relations may be interpreted as forms of systemic propaganda—propaganda, because of media values and structures in massaging the message of what is socially acceptable or desirable, and systemic, because these messages are absorbed without drawing attention to the consensual character ("hegemony") of this persuasiveness. In consenting to be controlled rather than being coerced, people's attitudes are changed without their awareness of attitudinal change. Institutionalization of this "hegemonic" bias not only compromises minority prospects for full and equitable involvement in society, but such systemic propaganda also de-politicizes minority contributions to society by diminishing the social status of minority women and men to the level of tokens and embellishments—to be pitied as victims, played for laughs, or demonized as menacing threats to society.

In working through these assumptions, we, the authors, hope to break with conventional studies in this area. To date, most studies have ignored the interactional dynamics involving the interplay of minority demands and media agendas within a broader socio-political framework. Existing studies also suffer from an overconcentration on one medium rather than several, an overdependence on a single methodological approach and set of methods, excessive reliance on minority perspectives to the exclusion of media perspectives, and one-sided criticism of media as offensive to Canada's social and cultural fabric. By contrast, our approach seeks to be comprehensive, contextual, interactionist, and critically informed. Only readers of *Media and Minorities* will determine our success in expanding our understanding of the representational politics of media-minority relations in a multicultural Canada.

The onset of the twenty-first century has made it more important then ever to re-think the representational grounds of media relations with minorities in rapidly changing and increasingly diverse contexts. The demographics say it all: nearly half of Canadians now claim some non-French, non-English background while nearly 12 percent of all Canadians claim to have visible minority status. Close to 50 percent of the population in Toronto is foreign born, while nearly one-third of Toronto residents are classified as visible minorities. Such numbers speak volumes of the need for constructive engagement. Failure to acknowledge this diversity at media levels undermines minority contributions to Canada. The self-esteem of minority women and men is sabotaged by a mediacentric process that "miniaturizes" minorities as irrelevant, "racializes" minority women and men as inferior, "otherizes" them as people removed in time and remote in space, privileges the "whitestream" as normal and preferred, and glosses over the "systemic biases" that complicates and constrains minority life. To be sure, even measuring the magnitude and scope of media mistreatment has proven a complex endeavour, given the difficulties of "defining" ("operationalizing") those indicators that miscast media representations of minority women and men. Nevertheless, media minority representations are not only reflective of some objective reality, but are indicative of conventions socially constructed by those with the power to create and enforce such labels. As a result, depiction of minority women and men may often say more about the mainstream "us" rather than the minority "them."

There is yet another compelling reason for accepting the challenge: Canadians take considerable pride in envisaging themselves as part of a multicultural society that privileges both tolerance and inclusiveness as integral components and definitive characteristics. Those institutions that deny or distort diversity are not only offensive to minority women and men, but also compromise the challenge of crafting a progressive Canada. The implications are staggering: However contrived the appearance of normalcy or neutrality, the mainstream media wield potential sufficient to set agendas, codify realities, reality construct, and frame issues. Such power has proven to be both a strength and drawback. In defining what is acceptable and desirable in society, the mainstream media may well provide the elusive ingredient for our learning to live together with our differences. And this is where this text falls into place. By drawing attention to the perils and pitfalls as well as the potential and promise of reconfiguring the representational basis of media-minority relations, we hope to make a modest contribution in advancing the cause of a multicultural Canada that is both inclusive and equitable, yet workable and fair. Anything more would be presumptuous; any less would be unconscionable.

SECTION I

MEDIA, RACISM, AND MULTICULTURALISM

Accolades abound in proclaiming Canada as a universally admired pace-setter in living together with differences. Few societies have ventured as far as Canada in capitalizing on multicultural principles as an official framework for constructively engaging minority women and men through the removal of discriminatory barriers or the creation of cultural space. Fewer still have formalized a multicultural agenda as a template for society building, in the process legitimating Canada's claim as the world's first and only official multicultural society. However flattering this effusiveness in the multicultural "engagement" with diversity, some of which is deserved, some not, these kudos gloss over certain contradictions that obscure discrepancies between rhetoric and reality. Multiculturalism has been taken to task as irrelevant or divisive by a host of critics, from academics (Bibby 1990, Bannerji 2000) and politicians (Manning 1994) to leaders of national organizations (Thobani 1995) and popular authors (Bissoondath 1994). Even supporters have expressed dismay over those aspects of official multiculturalism that are subject to abuse, public relations, or hidden agendas (Kymlicka 1998; Fleras 1998). Institutions have proven particularly attractive targets because of a seeming indifference to engaging multiculturally with minority women and men.

Few institutions, with the possible exception of education or policing, have attracted as much vitriol or vexation as the mainstream media. Mainstream media have been singled out as visibly negligent in responding positively to Canada's diversity (Fleras 1995). Such an allegation comes as no surprise: Contemporary media represent one of the more contested domains for grappling with issues over race relations, identity politics, and the politics of difference (Gray 1995; Gillespie 1996). As preliminary points of contact for understanding and relating to the world "out there," the power of the media reflect their ability to define and transmit messages about minorities that have the intent or effect of swaying public opinion (Tator and Henry 2000).

In theory, the mainstream media in modern democratic societies are expected to reflect diverse viewpoints, maintain some degree of neutrality and objectivity, and provide equitable access to everyone. In reality, the mainstream media appear to do the opposite when minorities are involved. By circulating mainstream-dominated discourses, metaphors, images, symbols, meanings, and unstated assumptions and subtexts, the mainstream media are known to select those race-related incidents that are deemed newsworthy. They then frame these in a stereotypical fashion, and contrast them with the behaviour and standards of "whiteness," in effect reinforcing a discourse of the "mainstream" as normal or superior while conflating minorities as dangerous or deviants (Henry et al. 2000). Such a controlling effect is accomplished in different ways; namely, through (a) negative stereotypes, (b) racializing certain activities such as crime, (c) asserting Eurocentric judgements that reinforce the normalness of whites while demonizing others as inferior or irrelevant, and (d) imposing double standards. To be sure, commercial concerns related to a growing ethno-demographic base have been pivotal in fostering improvements. Media personnel point to an array of inclusiveness initiatives in "recasting the mould" that, arguably, deserve applause rather than scorn or scepticism. Nevertheless, minority women and men continue to accuse the media of everything from racism to tokenism in "whitewashing" the representational basis of media-minority relations.

The cumulative impact of such discriminatory behaviour (either real or perceived) cannot be casually discounted. In an image-conscious world where appearances count for everything and people are judged on how they measure up, debates over diversity and minority relations are inseparable from identity politics and the politics of difference. Individual and collective identities are formed by interaction with others who provide recognition through assessment and responses (Taylor 1994). When these identities are mis-shapened by others, such misrepresentation may instil a crippling sense of self-hatred through internalization of depreciatory images—often incapacitating minority women and men from taking advantage of new opportunities, even with the removal of discriminatory barriers. Not surprisingly, media miscasting of multicultural minorities has left much to be desired. Even in an avowedly multicultural society such as Canada, systemic distortions in portraying minority women and men as invisible, problems, adornments, or stereotypes have elicited such animus as to fundamentally compromise the prospect of living together with our differences. Mainstream media are shorn of their credibility as a progressive force within minority communities, while the racializing of minorities as "other" compromises the mainstream media of their role in advancing a multicultural society. Failure to "recast the mould" reinforces the need for analyzing how and why the media continue to promulgate images incommensurate with Canada's official multiculturalism (Fleras 2001).

This section sets out to frame the issues for the rest of the book. Put succinctly, while the mainstream media have taken steps towards greater inclusiveness, as might be expected in a multicultural society, only modest improvements in the representational basis of media-minority relations can be discerned. Chapter 1 establishes the framework for analyzing media minority representations in a multicultural Canada. Chapter 2 addresses the concept of racism and how racism in the media precludes the establishment of institutional inclusiveness and a multicultural media. Chapter 3 explores the logic and dynamic of the mainstream media as discourses in defense of ideology. That debate over media minority miscasting draws attention to the mainstream media as systems of persuasion is accurate enough. Yet core questions remain: Who is doing the persuading? Why? How? And with what impact and implications?

CHAPTER 1

MULTICULTURAL CANADA

Framing the Issue

Canada represents one of several democratic societies that have taken advantage of ethnic heterogeneity as a basis for securing official state support (Harles 1998). Since 1971, multiculturalism has served as a formal means for defining government policy and programs at both federal and provincial levels. Originating in part to ensure social harmony among competing ethnicities but without risking control of the overall agenda, official multiculturalism has been perpetuated for a variety of political and economic considerations related to state functions, private interests, and electoral survival. Official multiculturalism has also been associated with re-defining the relational status of minority women and men in the same way that the principles of assimilation or segregation once offered alternative frameworks for "managing" race, ethnic, and aboriginal relations. A combination of demographic and political upheavals in recent years has also helped to re-define the government's multicultural agenda in ways scarcely conceivable even a generation ago.

However much multiculturalism is revered or vilified, there is no escaping a paradox that complicates the dynamics of Canada's multiculturalism. Put bluntly, if official multiculturalism is the solution, what precisely is the problem? Pluralistic societies such as Canada confront a paradox in grappling with the question of how to make society safe "for" diversity, yet safe "from" diversity (see Schlesinger Jr. 1992; Vasta and Castles 1996; Fleras and Spoonley 1999). Consider the dilemma of implementing multiculturalism (Fish 1997): too much diversity may prove fatal in de-stabilizing a society to the point of dismemberment; too little diversity can create a one-size-fits-all society that stifles and standardizes. The challenge lies in establishing a social and political framework that can engage diversity as different yet equal, without eroding national unity and social coherence in the process. Implementation of official multiculturalism is endorsed as one way of solving the riddle of living together with differences. Yet staunch support for multiculturalism as principle or practice has not congealed into any consensus over definition, attributes, or applications (Editorial 1997).

Both championed yet maligned, idealized as well as demonized, the term multiculturalism has absorbed such a broad range of often conflicting social articulations that many despair of any clarity or consensus (Caws 1994). Contradictions compound the search for definition. Multiculturalism simultaneously evokes a two-edged preference for consensus as well as criticism and change; of conformity yet diversity; of control yet emancipation; of exclusion yet participation; of compliance yet creativity (see Vasta 1996). Compounding the disarray are different levels of meaning, including reference to the notion of multiculturalism as (a) fact (what is); (b) ideology (what should be); (c) policy (what is proposed); (d) process (what really happens); (e) critical discourse (what is being contested); and (f) social movement (collective resistance) (Fleras and Elliott 1999). Failure to distinguish between these different levels of meaning has generated more multicultural muddles than many would like.

Two questions seem particularly relevant. First, what does it mean to constructively engage diversity in a society that is officially multicultural? Second, what precisely is involved in establishing an inclusive and multicultural media? Responses to these questions establish a framework for analyzing official multiculturalism as a principle and practice for advancing the representational basis of media-minority relations. This chapter explores the concept of multiculturalism by providing a working definition, examining different levels of meaning associated with multiculturalism, and analyzing the diverse perceptions and reactions towards official multiculturalism in Canada. Emphasis is directed at (a) how Canada is multicultural in terms of demography; (b) the endorsement of multicultural ideals in Canadian society; (c) the entrenchment of multiculturalism as official policy, including a shift in emphasis from ethnicity to equity and civic; (d) the practices associated with official multiculturalism at political and minority levels; and (e) comparisons with the critical multiculturalisms in the United States. This chapter argues that official multiculturalism is properly interpreted around a society-building framework, that is, the role of multiculturalism in creating a progressive and prosperous Canada in which differences are incorporated as a basis for living together. It also argues that efforts to make multiculturalism safe for Canada in addition to being safe from Canada has profound implications in restructuring the relationship of media to minorities.

Conceptualizing Multiculturalism

Multiculturalism can mean whatever people want it to mean, and it is precisely this ambiguity that is proving to be both a strength and a weakness when applied to the representational basis of media-minority relations. The protean quality of multiculturalism yields diverse definitions. Popular versions of multiculturalism tend to dwell on the celebrating of differences as differences, as valuable in their own right or in challenging for cultural space. Other definitions focus on multiculturalism as a process for promoting an inclusive society by constructively engaging diversity in a manner both workable and fair (Fleras 1994). Still others prefer a political dimension: multiculturalism provides a political framework and official policy for advancing the related goals of cultural differences, social equality, societal integration, and national unity (Wilson 1995). Definitions may incorporate a dynamic and contested component. Too static an interpretation of multiculturalism, such as that conveyed by the terms stew or *quilt* or *smorgasbord*, cannot capture what is formative and evolving. References to multiculturalism as a "mosaic" are also unhelpful if they reinforce a view of society as a series of compartmentalized cultures separated by grouting (Gates Jr. 1994). A preferred metaphor for multiculturalism is that of a kaleidoscope with its emphasis on the re-combining of elementary pieces into novel configurations depending on the luck of the turn.

In general, then, multiculturalism can be defined as a process of constructively engaging diversity as different yet equal. More specifically, Canada's official multiculturalism can be approached as a set of policies and programs for "integrating" minority women and men into the institutional framework of society, without losing sight of national interests pertaining to unity, identity, and social order. With multiculturalism, a framework is established that proactively promotes the full and equal participation of minority women and men through the removal of discriminatory institutional barriers (both cultural and structural). Cultural space is created that confirms a minority right to be the same ("equal") yet different, depending on the circumstances or consequences, while acknowledging differences as a basis for recognition, reward, and relations. Furthermore, a social and political climate is fostered in which diversity initiatives can be introduced without inciting a backlash or social turmoil. Inasmuch as multiculturalism engages with diversity by challenging society to move over and make space without losing the interconnectedness at the core of society, multiculturalism indeed represents a bold if somewhat flawed experiment in making society safe for diversity, and safe from diversity.

Consider the different dynamics and debates associated with operationalizing the concept of a multicultural Canada:

1. Is multiculturalism about emphasizing differences or focussing on our similarities? Is a multicultural society one in which ethnocultural differences are unequivocally endorsed even if such endorsement culminates in relatively independent ethnic enclaves or tramples over the rights of other ethnic groups? (see Fish 1997). Or does a multicultural society consist of one in which differences are deemed irrelevant as a basis for special treatment to ensure that everyone is valued or treated the same, regardless of race or ethnicity? Or is a multicultural society one in which cultural differences are expected to fuse into each as paints in a bucket, thus creating a new cultural amalgam from the commingling of differences?

2. Is multiculturalism about diversity or disadvantage? Is a multicultural society one that focuses on celebrating cultural differences or is it one that emphasizes the removal of discriminatory barriers to ensure inclusion of those minority women and men whose differences have proven disadvantageous? Is it one that acknowledges the diversity of

differences—a kind of ethnocultural smorgasbord for sampling by consumers—or is it one that endorses a diversity of ways of belonging for minorities? (Taylor 1992).

3. Is multiculturalism about colour-conscious or colour-blind equality? Is a multicultural society one in which ethnocultural differences are taken into account as a basis for fair and equitable treatment within the institutional framework of society? Or is it one that denies the relevance of differences as a basis for treating everyone the same? Will recognition of diversity increase the risk of otherizing differences as irrelevant or inferior? If differences are dismissed in the drive to treat everyone alike, does ignoring disadvantage increase the risk of perpetuating inequality by freezing the status quo?

4. Is multiculturalism about cultural space or institutional inclusiveness? Is a multicultural society one in which society is re-structured in such a way that everyone is guaranteed the right to full and equal participation because of or despite their cultural differences? Is the essence of a multicultural society one that does not allow minorityness to stand in the way of full and equal incorporation ("melting pot")? Or, does the essence lie in privileging differences as a basis for recognition, reward, and relationships?

5. Is multiculturalism about universality or particularity? Is a multicultural society one that upholds the liberal pluralist principle that what we have in common as rights-bearing, equality-seeking, and freedom-loving individuals is more important than what divides us as members of a group? Or is it one that acknowledges the primacy of distinct group membership as preceding any commonality as basis for entitlement or engagement?

To the extent that no consensus prevails, debates over "what constitutes a multicultural society" will remain endlessly fascinating.

Criticism of multiculturalism is often misplaced, largely because of the failure to appreciate the simultaneity of its strengths and weaknesses. Canada's multiculturalism operates at two levels. First, it acknowledges the right of each individual to identify with the cultural tradition of their choice, as long as this ethnic affiliation does not interfere with the rights of others, violate the laws of the land, or infringe on core values or institutions. Everyone has the right to be treated the same irrespective of his or her ethnicity; everyone also has the right to be treated differently because of ethnicity without incurring a penalty in the process (Breton 1998). Cultural differences are thus transformed into a discourse about social inequalities in need of government intervention (McLaren 1994; Hesse 1997). Second, official multiculturalism is concerned with society-building functions. Multiculturalism does not set out to celebrate ethnic differences per se or to promote cultural diversity; nor does it condone the creation of segregated ethnic communities with parallel power bases and special collective rights. The objective of an official multiculturalism is to create a cohesive society in which differences are incorporated as legitimate and integral without undermining either interconnectedness or distinctiveness. Diversity is endorsed, to be sure, but only to the extent that all differences are equivalent in status, subject to similar treatment, and comply with the state's self-proclaimed right to define the limits of permissible differences (see Johnson 1994). Reducing all differences to the same level by sanitizing their salience may sully multiculturalism's reputation as a progressive force. Yet this very de-politicization of ethnicity is precisely the reason behind its political popularity.

Multiculturalism in Canada

The de-politicization of diversity under official multiculturalism raises some interesting questions. How would you respond to the question, "Is Canada a multicultural society?" Any response will depend on how diversity is defined in relationship to society, with the result that multicultural outcomes will vary significantly depending on the frame of reference employed. Responses to whether Canada is multicultural will also vary with the level of meaning that is employed. Multiculturalism can be interpreted at the level of (a) empirical fact of what is, (b) an ideology with a corresponding array of ideas and ideals, (c) an explicit government policy and programs, (d) a set of practices for promoting political and minority interests; and (e) a critical discourse that invites challenge and resistance. Failure to separate these different levels of meaning will invariably foster misunderstanding as communicants literally talk past each other. The table below (1.1) provides a brief overview.

Table 1.1:   Levels of Meaning of Multiculturalism

AS FACT	AS IDEOLOGY	AS POLICY	AS PRACTICE	AS CRITICAL DISCOURSE
descriptive and empirical statement of what is	prescriptive and projective statement of what ought to be in terms of ideas and ideals	explicit government initiatives to foster social equality, cultural diversity, and national interests	putting multiculturalism into practice at two levels: (a) political and (b) minority women and men	challenge, resist, and transform the distribution of cultural power in society

I.   Multiculturalism as Fact

As fact, multiculturalism makes an empirical statement about "what is." It may be stating the obvious but the obvious is sometimes overlooked for precisely that reason. Most countries are ethnically diverse, composed of people from a variety of different backgrounds who speak, think, worship, and act differently. Nearly all countries comprise different racial and ethnic groups whose identities are stoutly defended and demanding of recognition or resources. Many of these minority groups wish to remain culturally distinct, yet are equally anxious to enjoy the benefits of full societal involvement.

Employed in the descriptive sense of the term, few would dispute the notion of Canada as a multicultural society. The existence of aboriginal, charter, and multicultural minorities attests to this empirical fact (Elliott 1983). Adding to this variety is the realization that Canadians have been drawn from 170 different countries and speak over one hundred different languages. Canada embraces a diverse collection of immigrants and refugees from different parts of the world. The first wave was inaugurated by East Asian populations who travelled across the Bering Strait as long as 50,000 years ago. Both French and English traders, adventurers, and explorers comprised the second wave of immigrants. These colonizers eventually displaced the aboriginal populations and unilaterally assumed official status as the foundational ("charter") members of Canada. The third wave consisted of various non-English- and non-French-speaking immigrants who arrived "en masse" during the twentieth century as part of Canada's society-building commitments. In recent years, the magnitude and nature of immigration has undergone a significant shift, thus profoundly altering Canada's demographic profile while establishing a new set of dynamics and demands for living together with differences.

Canada's demographic composition has experienced a complete reversal since 1867. Nearly 92 percent of Canada's population were of either British or French ancestry at the time of Confederation (Palmer 1975). Between 1896 and 1914, the balance began to shift with the arrival of nearly three million immigrants—many of them from Central and Eastern Europe—culminating in the entry of 400,000 new Canadians in 1913. Another wave of Eastern European immigrants during the 1920s brought the non-British and non-French proportion up to 18 percent. The period following the Second World War resulted in yet another influx of refugees and immigrants from the war-torn European theatre. Sources of immigration since the 1980s have also shifted. So-called non-conventional countries such as Asia, the Caribbean, and South and Central America are primary sources as the percentage of immigrants from Europe and the United States continues to shrink. This infusion of visible minority immigrants has rekindled controversy over the direction of Canada's immigration policies and programs. It has also fostered considerable debate regarding the role of foreign-born multicultural minorities in forging the demographic basis of Canadian identity and unity (Avery 2000).

How does Canada's multicultural reality stack up at present? Of Canada's total population of approximately thirty million, about 50 percent of all Canadians report having some non-British or non-French ancestry, including 11.2 percent who, in the 1996 census, identified themselves as visible minorities. (The term *visible minority* refers to an official government category of native- and foreign-born, non-white, non-Caucasoid individuals, including blacks, Chinese, Japanese, Koreans, Filipinos, Indo-Pakistanis, West Asians and Arabs, Southeast Asians, Latin Americans, and Pacific Islanders. This Employment

Equity Act-driven administrative category does not always square with popular perceptions of what constitutes visibility (Worthy 1996). A breakdown of those reporting non-British and non-French ethnic origins reveals interesting patterns. Total responses from 1990s surveys indicated that those of German background rank highest (with 2,793,780), followed by Italians (1,147,775), Ukrainians (1,054,295) and aboriginal peoples (1,002,675). With the exception of Quebec and Ontario where Italian-Canadians dominate, those of German descent are the most frequently reported ethnic origin in the other provinces. Those of Chinese origin are the most populous of Canada's 3.2 million visible minorities, with a total of 860,000 persons or 26.9 percent of the visible minority population, followed by South Asian with 671,000 or 21.0 percent, and black with 574,000 or 17.9 percent.

Canada is home to approximately five million foreign-born Canadians. The proportion of immigrants relative to the population at large (17 percent) has remained relatively stable since 1951, despite ebbs and flows in immigration totals. The top 10 source countries for immigration since 1996 continue to be from various regions of Asia (including Russia), suggesting that Canada's population will continue to be ethnically diverse (Citizenship and Immigration 1999). Regional and municipal variations in ethnic composition are noticeable. Ontario has the largest number of persons with non-British or non-French origins, with over five million. This is followed by British Columbia and Alberta, with just over two million each, and Quebec, with just over one million. The Atlantic provinces have relatively small totals.

The distribution of visible minorities continues to be uneven. In the early 1990s, 52.6 percent of all visible minorities lived in Ontario, 20.7 percent, in British Columbia, 13.6 percent, in Quebec, and only 2.3 percent lived in Saskatchewan and the Atlantic provinces combined. By 1996, visible minorities comprised 17.9 percent of British Columbia's population, 15.8 percent of Ontario's population, and 10.1 percent of Alberta's population, but only 1.1 percent of the population in New Brunswick and Prince Edward Island, and 0.7 percent in Newfoundland. The proportion of persons with non-British or non-French origin are higher among the young than among those who are older. Nearly one in two Canadians aged 25 years or younger are of non-French or non-British ancestry, according to the 1996 Census, compared to over one in three among those aged fifty-five years and over (Mata and Valentine 1999).

Multicultural minorities continue to reside in large urban regions. Both absolute numbers and relative percentages make Montreal, Toronto, and Vancouver more diverse than provincial or national averages. In 1996, according to Statistics Canada, 85 percent of all immigrants, including 93 percent of those who arrived between 1991 and 1996 lived in Census Metropolitan Areas. Toronto, Vancouver, and Montreal accounted for about three-quarters of all arrivals. These three metropolitan regions are also important centres for visible minorities. The percentage of Toronto's visible minority population by Census Metropolitan Area in 1996 stands at 31.6 percent, Vancouver's, at 31.1 and

Calgary's, at 15.6 percent. Compare this with the total percentage in Trois Rivières at 0.9 percent and in Chicoutami-Jonquiere at 0.4 percent. The vast majority of visible minorities reside in major urban centres for reasons related to opportunity, sociability, and transition. That concentration, in turn, proves to be an irresistible magnet for the next wave of immigrants and refugees (Hiebert 2000). Arguably, then, Canada can be best described as a moderately heterogeneous society, with relatively concentrated pockets of urban multicultural diversity interspersed with vast stretches of ethnically monochromic hinterland.

II. Multiculturalism as Ideology

Unlike its descriptive counterpart, multiculturalism as an ideology refers to a prescriptive ("normative") statement of "what ought to be." It prescribes a preferred course of thought or action with respect to how a society should be organized. This prescriptive state of affairs is modelled after liberal virtues of freedom, tolerance, and respect for individual differences. As an ideology, multiculturalism embraces a constellation of ideas and ideals about Canada's multicultural mosaic that many Canadians appear to endorse over the American "melting pot." Canadians have long taken pride in themselves as a tolerant society, with numerous national polls demonstrating consistent support for the principles of multicultural tolerance. To be sure, this endorsement varies with time and place, especially when political and economic costs are perceived to be excessive when compared to the anticipated benefits. Nevertheless, multiculturalism is endorsed as a defining cultural value, and living in a multiculturalism society allows for a more varied and richer experience than in a monocultural society (Poole 1996). This notion of "inclusiveness" is nicely captured by the noted British ethnicist, Bhikhu Parekh.

> Multiculturalism doesn't simply mean numerical plurality of different cultures, but rather a community which is creating, guaranteeing, encouraging spaces within which different communities are able to grow at their own pace. At the same time it means creating a public space in which these new communities are able to interact, enrich the existing culture, and create a new consensual culture in which they recognize reflections of their own identity (cited in Giroux 1994, 336).

Several assumptions underlie a multicultural ideology. First, and foremost, is a belief that minority cultures constitute living and lived-in realities that impart meaning and security to adherents at times of stress or social change. Ethnocultural affiliation does not imply an element of mental inferiority, stubbornness, or lack of patriotism. Rather these differences can be woven into a workable national fabric with a common set of overarching values ("unity-within-diversity"). Universalizing the right to a particular identity acknowledges that people are more than individuals; they are social beings whose well-being depends on a shared identity within the cultural framework of an ethnic community.

Second, multiculturalism does not downgrade diversity as contrary to the goals of national unity or socio-economic progress. Cultural differences are not disparaged as being incompatible with national goals, but are endorsed as integral components of a national mosaic, a reflection of the Canadian ideal, and a source of enrichment and strength. Towards that end, multiculturalism points to a utopian state of affairs whereby the integration of minority differences coalesces into a unique but unified whole as people become aware of each other's differences. More importantly, multiculturalism endorses the ideal that these differences can coexist and prosper. As Robert Hughes writes in his otherwise scathing indictment of multiculturalism *The Culture of Complaint*,

> [the premise of multiculturalism is] that people with different roots can co-exist, that they can learn to read the image banks of others, and they can and should look across the frontiers of race, gender, language, and age without prejudice or illusion.... It proposes—modestly enough—that some of the most interesting things in history and culture happen at the interface between cultures (Hughes 1994).

Third, a multicultural ideal builds upon the principles of cultural relativism. Multiculturalism fosters an open-minded philosophy around the principles of tolerance and mutual respect. This doctrine holds that the worth and meaning of all cultural practices are relative to a particular time and place. No cultural lifestyle is regarded as superior to another. If anything, cultural relativism reinforces the equality of diversity when examined in a specific historical and environmental context. This is not to say that everything is equally good; nor is anyone espousing the philosophy of "anything goes." Rather, diversity must be treated *as if* it were an equally valid expression of the human experience. Secure in the knowledge of thoughtful relativism, a commitment to multiculturalism endorses the premise that those confident in their cultural background will concede a similar tolerance to others (Berry et al. 1977). Or, as the late Pierre Elliott Trudeau explained back in 1971, if national unity is to mean anything in the deeply personal sense, it must be anchored in confidence in one's own identity, for it is out of this that respect for others grows (in Roy 1995). This notion, that if people are respected for who they are, they, in turn, will be loyal to the state, was put to the test when the so-called "ethnic vote" in the 1996 October referendum temporarily derailed separatist aspirations in Quebec (see also Cardozo and Musto 1997).

III. Multiculturalism as Policy

Policy considerations are central to any official multiculturalism. By capitalizing on a mix of idealism and self-interest, governments throughout the world have embarked on official strategies for controlling immigration, managing ethnic relations, accommodating differences, and integrating ethnocultural minorities into the mainstream. Multiculturalism represents but one of the policy options open to central authorities for engaging diversity. Other policy frameworks, such as assimilation or integration, have proven inadequate in balancing societal needs with minority demands. Two policy levels can be discerned with respect to official multiculturalism. One, multiculturalism consists of specific government initiatives to transform multicultural ideals into official programs and practice that acknowledge diversity as different yet equal. A new symbolic order, along with a corresponding mythology, is constructed under multicultural policies that helps to paper over any inconsistencies at odds with present realities (Breton 1984; Harles 1998; Helly 1993). As a political principle, government must be seen to protect this diversity, minimally by preventing discrimination, or maximally by positively promoting and sustaining these differences as legitimate and integral to society building (Poole 1996). Two, multiculturalism can also be interpreted within a broader policy framework that justifies the design and implementation of diversity-driven programs without fear of inciting public concern over the possibility of creeping socialism or cultural apartheid. This framework may not be openly articulated; nevertheless, it supplies the "underlying agenda" that justifies specific decision making.

To say that Canada is officially multicultural is stating the obvious, yet the irony is improbable. From its inception in 1971 when it barely garnered a paragraph in Canada's national paper, official multiculturalism has evolved to the point where it constitutes a formidable component of Canada's national identity, having profoundly altered how Canadians think about themselves and their relationship to the world. Three decades of official multiculturalism have been instrumental in orchestrating a national consensus around majority acceptance of minority participation. The policy of multiculturalism did not originate to dismantle the culture and structure of Canadian society, but to modify people's thought and behaviour in hopes of re-defining relations among all Canadians regardless of ethnicity. In other words, multiculturalism as policy originated around the quest for integrative society-building functions; it continues to persist for precisely the same reasons, namely, the "containment" of ethnicity by the modification of the rules of engagement and entitlement in a modern democratic society (Kobayashi 1999). Only the means for "managing" diversity have evolved in response to demographic upheavals and political developments, with cultural solutions giving way to structural reforms and, more recently, the promotion of shared citizenship (Annual Report 1997). An initial ethnicity focus on "celebrating differences" as a means of eradicating prejudice and securing acceptance was superseded by an equity emphasis on "accommodating diversity" through institutional inclusiveness and removal of discriminatory barriers. The ground has again shifted in recent years to embrace a civic commitment by way of inclusive citizenship, full and equal participation, and a sense of belonging by living together with differences. For the sake of simplicity these shifts can be partitioned into three policy stages, including ethnicity, equity, and civic—keeping in mind that overlap among these analytical constructs is the rule rather than exception.

First, a brief look at cultural politics in the pre-multiculturalism era.

A. Ethnicity Multiculturalism ("Celebrating Differences"; 1971–)

Multiculturalism arose in the aftermath of the publication of the Report of the Royal Commission on Bilingualism and Biculturalism in 1969. Various ethnic minority groups, especially the Ukrainians and Germans, had lobbied vigorously in arguing that their language and culture were as vital as Quebec's to Canadian society building (Wilson 1993). Pre-Second World War governments in Canada did not seriously address the issue of ethnic diversity as a basis for entitlement or engagement. Central policy structures overlooked ethnic heterogeneity as inimical to broader interests. The Canada of this era was predominantly of French and English heritage, and the intent was to keep it that way. To be sure, religious and cultural differences were tolerated as private matters, but deemed divisive or dangerous when foisted on the public. Governments instead relied on time-honoured strategies that embraced a commitment to conformity as essential for national unity and prosperity. Expressions of assimilation reflected a commitment either to Anglo-Canadian conformity or to a melting pot (or "fusion") in the American sense of the term (Hudson 1987). Anything that departed from the standards of God, King, and Empire was contemptuously dismissed as incompatible with national interests or loyalty to the Dominion.

But, national consensus and commitment to Anglo-American ideals began to erode with the intake of immigrants from Europe and, later, from developing world countries (Hawkins 1989; also Castles et al. 1988). If only to assist in the integration of immigrants and to foster community harmony, successive governments sought to modify the existing concept of Canada in line with new demographic realities. Passage of the first *Citizenship Act* in 1947 announced Canada's willingness to sever its colonialist identification with the United Kingdom. Changes of such magnitude forced a re-thinking of Canada's character and the place of the "other ethnics" in the evolving configuration of Canadian society. A commitment to recognize diversity, the need for equality, and duty to protect the disadvantaged arose in response to these shifts. Pressure to create a new symbolic order was further heightened by the forces of Québécois nationalism in the aftermath of the Quiet Revolution (Breton 1989). The multicultural nod to ethnic minorities was envisaged as a potential counterbalance to neutralize (or de-politicize) an excessively bicultural focus of Canada (Webber 1994). Its twinning with official bilingualism emerged as part of a new national unity strategy based on a new vision of Canada—not as a bicultural partnership between founding peoples, but as a multicultural mosaic of equality-seeking individuals (McRoberts 1997).

A compromise solution was eventually struck to take "into account the contribution made by the other ethnic groups to the cultural enrichment of Canada" (see Jaworsky 1979). A commitment to multiculturalism within a bilingual framework was articulated by the Liberal government when the late Prime Minister Pierre Elliott Trudeau rose in Parliament and declared his government's intentions on October 8, 1971. Eventually an all-party agreement sought to integrate new Canadians into the mainstream through cultural adjustments on both sides. According to the government, multiculturalism would "strengthen the solidarity of the Canadian people by enabling all Canadians to participate fully and without discrimination in defining and building the nation's future." Four major principles prevailed in this commitment to re-sculpt a new Canada based on the equality of individuals and freedom from the tyranny of culture (MacLeod 1983; McRoberts 1997):

1. Equality of status; Canada does not have an official culture; all cultures are equal to each other.

2. Canadian identity; diversity lies at the heart of Canadian identity.

3. Personal choice; the ability to choose lifestyles and cultural traits is a positive factor in society.

4. Protection of individual rights; to be free of discrimination that precludes equality and participation.

In order to put these principles into practice, the government proposed initiatives to (a) assist those cultural groups that have demonstrated a desire and effort to continue to develop, a capacity to grow and contribute to Canada, as well as a clear need for assistance; (b) assist the members of all cultural groups to overcome cultural barriers to full participation in Canadian society; (c) promote creative encounters and interchange among all Canadian cultural groups in the interests of national unity; and (d) assist immigrants in acquiring at least one of Canada's official languages to ensure full and equal participation in Canadian society. It seems apparent, then, that multiculturalism did not focus exclusively on cultural preservation—at least not beyond an initial period when powerful ethnic lobbyists prevailed. Emphasis instead continues to focus on fostering involvement, cultural exchanges, and individual freedom of choice (McRoberts 1997; Cardozo and Musto 1997).

B. Equity Multiculturalism: Institutional Accommodation (1981-)

Federal multiculturalism had undergone a discernible shift in focus by the early 1980s. Initially, multiculturalism involved the introduction of government programs to protect the distinct ethnic identities that immigrants brought with them while expanding the mainstream mindset through removal of cultural prejudice and discriminatory practices. Pre-1970s immigrants shared with their hosts a broad commitment to Eurocentric values and priorities, notwithstanding superficial differences, thus facilitating assimilation into the mainstream. But the focus of multiculturalism shifted correspondingly to embrace the more equity-driven concerns of non-European immigrants. The often different cultural values of new immigrants from non-conventional sources proved more perplexing and precluded minority integration because of the disadvantages associated with these differences (Fleras 1993). For new immigrants, the need for dismantling racial barriers to opportunity or inclusion was more important than the celebration of their cultural differences (McRoberts 1997). The earlier emphasis on ethnicity and culture was subsequently replaced by a commitment to equity, social justice, and institutional inclusiveness through the removal of discriminatory barriers at structural levels. Funding disbursements corresponded with this reversal in mandate: rather than simply doling out money to ethnocultural organizations or events as had been the case, authorities channelled multicultural spending into pragmatic goals. For the 1993/94 fiscal year, for example, grants from federal multiculturalism totalled $25.5 million, with $13.3 million earmarked for community support and participation (to assist in the settlement of new Canadians), another $6.5 million for public education and anti-racism, and $5.5 million to promote the principle of heritage cultures and languages (Thompson 1994).

Subsequent developments further advanced the political profile of official multiculturalism. The Charter of Rights and Freedoms, which came into effect in 1985, constitutionally entrenched multiculturalism as a distinguishing characteristic of Canadian life. Its emergence as a tool of interpretation at the constitutional levels of national decision making reinforced a fundamental multicultural right in Canadian society—that is, the right to be different (culture) as well as the right to be the same (equality)—without foreclosing either the right to identity or the right to equality. Its prominence was further advanced when Canada became the world's first and only official multiculturalism with passage of the *Multiculturalism Act* in 1988. In consolidating the advances and shifts of the previous decade, the Act sought to promote cultures, reduce discrimination, and accelerate institutional inclusiveness through the "preservation and enhancement of Canadian multiculturalism." The Act obligated federal institutions to address diversity in a manner consistent with Canada's multicultural character, thus compelling state institutions to incorporate Canadians increasingly on ethnic grounds rather than on a geographical or functional basis (Srebrnik 1997). The implications for multiculturalizing the mainstream media will be explored in later chapters.

C. *Civic Multiculturalism: Belonging through Inclusion (1991–)*

Official multiculturalism continues to acknowledge the importance of celebrating differences. Its commitment to engaging diversity is no less important, and is manifest in the mainstreaming of diversity to ensure minority access, representation, and equitable treatment. Equally evident is a trend towards equating multiculturalism with citizenship, a relationship that was consummated under the short-lived Department of Multiculturalism and Citizenship. Multiculturalism remains aligned with the Citizenship and Canadian Identity portfolio, albeit within the broader superministry of Canada Heritage. This downgrading of official multiculturalism from government department to program is not insignificant. The government may remain officially committed to official multiculturalism; nevertheless, its support is increasingly muted, it reflects a disturbing trend towards complacency or expediency, and it is not beyond the pale of axing costly multicultural programs.

Civic multiculturalism is oriented towards society building in emphasizing the ideal of a commonly shared citizenship. It is based on fostering a sense of belonging and a shared sense of Canadian identity as one way of enhancing national unity without forsaking those differences that enrich or empower. Emphasis is on what we have in common as rights-bearing and equality-seeking individuals rather than on what separates or divides us. Policy objectives under civic multiculturalism include a commitment to the society-building goals of social justice, an emergent Canadian identity, citizenship and national unity, and increased civic participation (Annual Report 1998/1999). Objectives tend to focus on inclusion and integration, with points of emphasis that vary from integrating diverse cultures into a uniquely Canadian identity, to removing those barriers such as discrimination that preclude the incorporation of all Canadians into a civic culture, to integrating minorities into a shared civic culture on terms other than those established by old dominant groups (Kymlicka 1998). In contrast to the past, when multiculturalism was ostensibly directed at racial and ethnic minorities, according to the Minister for Multiculturalism, the scope of civic multiculturalism is aimed at "break[ing] down the ghettoization of multiculturalism." Platitudes notwithstanding, however, it may prove difficult to implement an inclusive and civic-oriented multiculturalism when economic realities appear to be eroding those very initiatives for advancing a civic society (Rivzi 1994). It remains to be seen whether a social justice policy can be comfortably located within an economic agenda that is more interested in improving Canada's competitive advantage than in securing social justice.

In short, official multiculturalism must be interpreted as a complex and contested policy that has evolved over time in response to social and political changes. To be sure, its commitment has remained the same, that is, to integrate minority women and men through the removal of prejudice and discriminatory barriers. Only the means have changed, with an ethnicity focus giving way to an equity focus, and current emphasis on a civic dimension. Table 1.2 compares and contrasts the different stages in the evolution of Canada's multiculturalism policies, while recognizing the difficulties of comparing ideal-typical categories.

Table 1.2:   Multiculturalism Policies

	Ethnicity Multiculturalism (1970s)	Equity Multiculturalism (1980s)	Civic Multiculturalism (1990s)
Focus:	Celebrating Differences	Managing Diversity	Constructive Engagement
Reference Point:	Culture	Structure	Society Building
Mandate:	Ethnicity	Race Relations	Citizenship
Magnitude:	Individual Adjustment	Accommodation	Participation
Problem Source:	Prejudice	Systemic Discrimination	Exclusion
Solution:	Cultural Sensitivity	Employment Equity	Inclusiveness
Key Metaphor:	"Mosaic"	"Level playing field"	"Belonging"

IV. Putting Multiculturalism into Practice

Platitudes about celebrating and sharing cannot disguise what many have long suspected: the implementation of multiculturalism as ideology or policy does not always translate into practices that are consistent with principles. Multiculturalism as practice refers to its use by both political and ethnic sectors to promote respective goals and ambitions. Politicians and bureaucrats look upon multiculturalism as a resource with economic or political potential that can be exploited at national or international levels for practical gain. For minority women and men, a commitment to multiculturalism provides a political platform for articulating their concerns and drawing attention to grievances that reflect gaps between multicultural ideals and institutional practices. This focus on putting multiculturalism to work secures its status as a key component in the ongoing reconstruction of Canadian society. Such a focus will also demonstrate how the implementation of multicultural principles into practice at institutional levels does not always coincide with the policy ideals.

A. *Political Gain/Commercial Advantage*

If politics is the art of conflict resolution (Van Loon and Whittington 1981), then multiculturalism is indeed political because of its inseparability from government management of conflicting interests. The politics behind Canada's official multiculturalism origins are widely known: Multiculturalism originated from the customary interplay of good intentions and political opportunism (Gwyn 1994). It was hoped that the inception of official multiculturalism would formulate a new founding myth of Canada as land of opportunity and equality for all Canadians, thus uniting all Canadians at a time of political turmoil, yet doing so without any fundamental redistribution of power (Helly 1993). It was also hoped that it would shore up electoral strength in urban Ontario, counterbalance western resentment over perceived favouritism towards the Québécois, preempt the encroachment of American cultural imperialism, and thwart potential difficulties from changes to both numbers and sources of immigrants (see Burnet and Palmer 1988). The governing apparatus of the Canadian state also relied on multiculturalism to fulfil a variety of legitimating functions involving national unity, economic prosperity, and electoral survival.

In the final analysis, then, official multiculturalism is first and foremost a political program to achieve political goals in a politically astute manner (Peter 1978). It had no pretensions of promoting radical change but, simply, to rearrange social relations within the existing system (Fleras 2001). By making a virtue of necessity, in other words, multiculturalism would parlay a potential weakness into a strength without necessarily revoking a commitment to social cohesion, national identity, domestic peace, economic advantage, and global status (Kurthen 1997).

At its crassest level, multicultural politics are animated by a belief in ethnic support as relevant for (re-)election. The vast majority of Canada's multicultural minorities are concentrated in major urban centres such as Toronto, Montreal, and Vancouver—a trend likely to be amplified by future immigration patterns. The growing heterogeneity of Canada's population has prompted all political parties to pursue the multicultural vote through promises of increased representation, funding, and affirmative action at federal levels. At another level is the preoccupation with the commercial potential of multiculturalism. Former Prime Minister Brian Mulroney outlined this challenge in his "Multiculturalism Means Business" speech at a Toronto conference in 1986:

> We, as a nation, need to grasp the opportunity afforded to us by our multicultural identity to cement our prosperity with trade and investment links the world over and with a renewed entrepreneurial spirit at home.... But our multicultural nature gives us an edge in selling to that world.... Canadians who have cultural links to other parts of the globe, who have business contacts elsewhere are of the utmost importance to our trade and investment strategy (Report, Secretary of State 1987).

By enhancing Canada's sales image and competitive edge in a global economy—particularly by cultivating and tapping into the lucrative Asian market (Hage 1998)—official multiculturalism is touted as having the potential to harness lucrative trade contracts, establish international linkages and mutually profitable points of contact, and penetrate export markets (Multiculturalism/Secretary of State 1993). According to Katharyne Mitchell in her 1993 article "Multiculturalism, or the United Colors of Capitalism?", multiculturalism has been actively deployed by Canada to attract members of the transnational elite and wealthy global citizens. Attention is directed towards Canada as a welcoming country of many different cultures—"Hey, look at us, we're multicultural!"—rather than as one possessing a single, exclusive national culture as is the case with Britain.

The re-working of multiculturalism around an ideology of racial harmony and co-operative coexistence, without fears of racist friction and ethnic conflict, as Mitchell (1993) says, provides a degree of reassurance for nervous investors and fidgety capital. As the globalization of capitalist market economies continues to expand, multiculturalism may well provide the mindset for confronting the challenges of a shifting and increasingly borderless life that may be our lot in the twenty-first century (see Woodley 1997).

B. Multiculturalism for Minorities

Multicultural minorities are inclined to see multiculturalism as a resource for attaining practical goals (Burnet 1981). Needs are basic: many want to become established, to expand economic opportunities for themselves and their children, to eliminate discrimination and exploitation, and to retain access to their cultural heritage without loss of citizenship rights. Multiculturalism is employed as a tool for meeting these needs by opening up economic, social, and cultural channels through the elimination of discriminatory barriers in employment, education, housing, and criminal justice (Report, Equality Now 1984). The resource value of multiculturalism is evident in other ways. Multicultural minorities are often unable to influence central policy structures because of geographical dispersal, cultural heterogeneity, and negligible negotiatory powers. With multiculturalism, an otherwise powerless sector now possesses the leverage to prod, embarrass, and provoke central policy structures by holding them accountable for the failure to practice what they preach. Issues over power sharing, resource distribution, and meaningful decision making take precedent over food courts, folk dancing, and ethnic festivals. A new moral authority has evolved that portrays minorities as legitimate contenders in the competition for power and resources. Minority women and men are now empowered with yet another resource in staking out their claims while articulating their demands alongside those of the first and second force. Appeals to official multiculturalism are thus calculated to extract public sympathy and global sympathy—in the same way that aboriginal peoples in Canada have relied on appeals to international fora (such as the United Nations) as a bargaining chip against the federal government.

V. Multiculturalism as Critical Discourse

Many have said that Canadians and Americans use the same words but speak a different language. Nowhere is this antimony more evident than in references to multiculturalism. Multicultural principles and practices continue to animate the cultural politics in Canada and the United States, albeit in fundamentally different ways. References to Canada's official multiculturalism embrace a commitment to consensus by way of "conformity" and "accommodation." Attainment of these multicultural goals is varied, but generally include fostering tolerance towards diversity, reducing prejudice, removing discriminatory barriers, eliminating cultural ethnocentrism, enhancing equitable access to services, expanding institutional engagement, and improving intergroup encounters. In other words, Canada may claim to be a multicultural mosaic but its multiculturalism is geared towards absorbing ethnic Canadians into the mainstream—albeit on terms different from the past. By contrast, the e *pluribus unum* of the United States may seem conducive to conjuring up the melting pot, but the emergence of an "insurgent" (or critical) multiculturalism has precipitated cultural wars involving identity politics and ethnic identities that threaten a coherent national vision (Simpson 1998). The magnitude of these differences is such to suggest the appearance of a new "postmulticulturalism" turn, in contrast with the modernist multicultural project in Canada.

Multiculturalism in Canada is primarily a political program for pursuit of national interests. In shifting from monoculturalism to pluralism as a basis for a new moral order, Canada's official multiculturalism represents a form of state legitimacy rather than a vehicle for radical social change (see also Goodman 1997). The focus is more concentrated on drawing people into the framework of an existing Canada rather than on protecting social and cultural rights of minority women and men (see also Vasta 1993). This hegemonic discourse in defence of the dominant ideology endorses those policies and initiatives that subordinate minority needs to the "greater good" or to "national interests." Multicultural principles and practices are inseparable from a neo-assimilationist commitment to consensus and commonality as keys to social harmony. The potential disruptiveness of diversity is dispelled by homogenizing differences around a singular commonality so that everyone is similarly different, not differently similar, under a "monocultural" multiculturalism (Eisenstein 1996).

By contrast with Canadian consensus multiculturalism, the postmodernist discourses that animate America's critical multiculturalism subvert as they resist. Critical multiculturalism transcends the constraints of official policy initiatives since it is not compromised by the demands of political engineering or electoral pandering. Under critical multiculturalism, discourses of resistance are advocated instead that contest and challenge Eurocentricity by relativizing the white capitalist patriarchy with its exclusionary designs on the "other" (Giroux 1994; Stam 2000). In contrast with liberal multiculturalism's emphasis on individual diversity, a critical multiculturalism addresses the issue of group differences and how power relations function to secure inequities and structure identities. Unlike consensus multiculturalism, which connotes a pluralism that is devoid of historical context and specificities of power relations, a critical multiculturalism signifies a site of struggle around the reformation of historical memory, national identity, self- and social representation, and the politics of difference (Giroux 1994, 336).

Canadian multiculturalism differs from its American counterpart at several points of contrast (Canadian multiculturalism is featured first in each set of contrasts). One multiculturalism is directed at transforming the mainstream without straining the social fabric; the other multiculturalism is concerned with empowering minorities by eroding the monocultural firmament of society. One is officially political, yet seeks to de-politicize diversity for society-building purposes; the other falls outside the policy domain, but politicizes differences as a catalyst for minority empowerment and entitlement. One is rooted in the modernist quest for unity, certainty, and universality; the other is geared towards embracing a postmodernist zeal for differences, provisionality, and fragmentation. Of particular note is how the one transforms cultural differences into a discourse about social inequality; the other reformulates social inequalities into a discursive framework of cultural differences and public culture. One is based on outward-looking public goals; the other is derived from the inward-looking needs of victims for self-esteem, recognition, compensation, and role models—all of which are difficult to measure and impossible to challenge (Higham 1993). There is nothing inherently right or wrong in conceding the multiplicity of multicultural discourses. Difficulties arise when varying discourses are employed indiscriminately or interchangeably, resulting in predictably distorting effects on expectations and communication.

In other words, official multiculturalism in Canada is essentially a society-building exercise that seeks to de-politicize differences through institutional accommodation. Official multiculturalism is grounded in the liberal pluralist credo that what we have in common as rights-bearing, equality-seeking individuals is more important than what divides us through placement in an exclusive ethnic heritage. Compare this with more militant multiculturalisms, in which group differences and identity claims are politicized by challenging the prevailing distribution of cultural power for moving over and making cultural space. A "playful" inversion is called for in juxtaposing duelling discourses: rather than making society safe from diversity, safe for diversity, as is the case in a multicultural Canada, the underlying logic of critical multiculturalism is to make diversity safe from society as well as safe for society.

Is Canada a multicultural society? Is Canada a society that abides by the principles of multiculturalism? It should be obvious that the degree of "multiculturalness" will vary depending on the level of meaning that is employed. Canada is multicultural by virtue of its ethnic heterogeneity, which is empirically real, persistent, and shows no signs of easing in light of prevailing immigration flows. Canada is multicultural when assessed at ideological levels, thanks to high levels of support for multicultural principles and tolerance of diversity. Canada is multicultural in policy. Canada's status as the world's first and possibly only official multiculturalism is enhanced by the constitutional entrenchment of multicultural principles, statutory legislation, and government policy since 1971. In practice, Canada is a multicultural society in light of how both the political and ethnic sectors have put multiculturalism to work to achieve a variety of national or personal goals. Only the idea of multiculturalism as critical discourse may not apply to Canada. While such a discursive framework is not altogether absent, multiculturalism discourses tend to focus on consensus through society building and inclusiveness rather than on challenge, resistance, and transformation. Failure to distinguish among these different levels of meaning often leads to conflicting perceptions and diverse reactions.

Perceptions and Reactions

Of the trip wires and cultural landmines laid across the Western landscape in recent years, few have triggered as much vitriol or controversy as has multiculturalism (Possner 1997). Timing in particular has played politics with official multiculturalism in Canada. The inception of multiculturalism as an official framework may have originated in an era of optimism and reform but falls under scrutiny at a time of discontent and retrenchment (Cardozo and Musto 1997). What started out as a society-building idea with noble intentions (to assist newcomers into Canada) has evolved into a flashpoint for tension between multiculturalism advocates (Levitt 1997) and those who recoil at the very prospect of foisting still more government on an unsuspecting public (Field 1994). Not surprisingly, public perception of multiculturalism in Canada is varied. Some Canadians are vigorously supportive; others are in total rejection or denial; still others are indifferent; and yet others are uninformed (see Musto 1997). The majority appear to be caught somewhere in between, depending on their reading of multiculturalism and its legitimacy in advancing a new vision of a pluralistic Canada (see also Goot 1993). Variables such as age, income, levels of education, and place of residence are critical in gauging support, with higher levels of approval among those who are younger, more affluent, better educated, and urban. To the extent that most Canadians are unsure of what Canada's official multiculturalism is trying to do, and why, there is much to gain in comparing public attitudes to multiculturalism with what multiculturalism sets out to do (both articulated and hidden agendas) and what it can realistically accomplish in a liberal pluralist society.

I. National Attitudes

The extent to which Canadians support official multiculturalism is open to debate. Opinion polls are known to provide different answers depending on the kind of questions asked (Poole 1996). Nevertheless, national surveys on multiculturalism suggest a solid base of support, often in the 60-70 percent range (Angus Reid 1991; Berry 1993; Musto 1997). Yet these results are not as transparent as the data would suggest. First, support is not the same as enthusiasm. Canadians appear to embrace multiculturalism as a reality to be tolerated rather than an ideal to be emulated. The idea of multicultural tolerance is widely supported, in that a mix of cultures is thought to make Canada a more interesting place, but there is little enthusiasm for its implementation. Approval persists only as long as costs are low and demands reasonable when (a) assisting new Canadians to settle into Canada without revoking their identities, (b) removing discriminatory barriers, and (c) promoting tolerance (Gwyn 1996).

Second, support is conditional; that is, people are prepared to accept different levels of multiculturalism. Multiculturalism is acceptable if it means that everyone has a right to their culture in Canada. Support vanishes when multiculturalism is seen to endorse a mishmash of different but equal cultures, with no centre and in a constant state of tension because of inner contradictions. Multiculturalism is okay if it means learning about other cultures or eliminating discriminatory barriers to improve minority access and participation. Multiculturalism may be rejected when its endorsement is thought to be eroding Canada's sense of national identity, challenging authority or core values, encouraging separation or division, or fixating on demonizing the mainstream.

Third, support or rejection of multiculturalism tends to be selective. Most Canadians support some aspect of multiculturalism; for example, a tolerance towards diversity and acceptance of pluralism are proudly endorsed as a definitive attribute of Canada (Gwyn 1996). But support is revoked when multiculturalism is perceived to be encouraging minorities to challenge cherished symbols of Canadian identity. In other words, resentment is directed not at multicultural diversity per se but at those aspects of multiculturalism that entail excessive government intervention, erode national unity, or contravene core Canadian values.

Official multiculturalism is unevenly supported across Canada. Residents of Ontario and western Canada appear receptive, yet the Québécois (Bourassa 1975; Ryan 1975) and First Nations (Sanders 1987) have demonstrated less enthusiasm. For both national minorities, official multiculturalism is seen as a device to undermine their special status as fundamentally autonomous political communities in exchange for immigrant status. Many observers of Canada's political scene have also criticized government initiatives in this area, admittedly on different grounds (Peter 1978; Kallen 1982; Burnet 1984; Bibby 1990; Das Gupta 1994; Kobayashi 1999; Sugunasiri 1999). Robert Fulford (1997) does not mince words in denouncing multiculturalism as thinly veiled racism:

> Pluralism, the side-by-side existence of many forms of human association, is an essential quality of modern life. Official multiculturalism, the automatic classification of citizens according to race and ancestry, was a bad idea in the beginning, and in time will probably be seen as one of the gigantic mistakes of recent public policy in Canada.

Others are no less contemptuous of multiculturalism, viewing it as little more than politically correct racism, given its perceived inclination to define an individual's worth and identity on racial terms while mistakenly asserting the equal worth of all cultures regardless of their views on individuals, reason, progress, or science (Ayn Rand Institute 2000).

Scholarly opinion has been equally dismissive of or divided over multiculturalism. The paradoxes and ambiguities implicit within multiculturalism make it an easy target: is official multiculturalism a revolution in reshaping the constitutional basis of majority-minority relations or simply a clever political move in managing and marginalizing differences while preserving the status quo behind a facade of platitudes about respect, diversity, and equality? Multiculturalism is portrayed as a colossal hoax perpetuated by vested interests to ensure minority co-operation through ideological indoctrination ("false consciousness") (Duncan and Cronin 1997/98). Critics on the left have pounced on multiculturalism as ineffective except as a mantra for politicians and industry leaders to trot out for dignitaries or public relations; those on the right repudiate it as a costly drain of resources. Those in the middle concede that multiculturalism is a form of ideological indoctrination or symbolic redress, but whose social control functions are inseparable from society building. Those on the left dismiss multiculturalism as a capitalist ideology to divide and distract the working classes; on the right are those who condemn multiculturalism for diluting core values, unity, and identity; and in between are the liberals who believe cultural solutions cannot solve structural problems. In reflecting its unthreatening status for those in positions of power and privilege, official multiculturalism may sound good in theory but is extremely difficult to implement because of the difficulties in integrating differences without undermining the integrity of the whole. The challenge of fostering minority integration without capitulating to mainstream assimilation remains a basic paradox of multiculturalism (Harles 1998).

Others have argued that government is willing to lavish funds on folk festivals and ethnic performing arts, but is reluctant to support minority demands for collective rights or socio-economic enhancement (Kallen 1987). Minorities are ghettoized instead into certain occupational structures and residential arrangements, thereby preserving the prevailing distribution of power and wealth (Porter 1965; Matthews and Lian 1998). The public awareness of cultural diversity may be bolstered under multiculturalism, critics contend, yet cultural solutions cannot possibly solve the structural problems of discrimination and systemic racism (Bolaria and Li 1988). The charge that multiculturalism is the last refuge of the racist raises questions as to whether multiculturalism represents an authentic policy alternative or an interim measure for easing minorities into the mainstream—a kind of "assimilation by slow motion" behind a slurry of diversity intentions. Finally, criticism of multiculturalism is directed at its consequences for society at large, either deliberate or inadvertent. According to Kenneth McRoberts (1997), Trudeau's endorsement of multiculturalism has eroded national unity, despite its avowed promotion as part of a national unity strategy, in part by alienating francophone Quebeckers whose vision of Canada as a partnership is at odds with official multiculturalism. Gina Mallet (1997, D-2) captures a sense of this "good gone bad" when she writes,

> Although the drive to honour diversity through official multiculturalism was originally undertaken in order to promote tolerance, it is accomplishing the opposite. By setting Canadians against one another and emphasizing our differences rather than the many things we have in common, diversity has, in fact, gone too far.

In its role as the appointed catalyst for social engineering, multiculturalism has attracted its share of criticism. National shortcomings for some reason tend to polarize and be magnified around minority relations. But much of this criticism tends to be misguided in that it glosses over the multidimensional nature of multiculturalism. Those who stoutly defend multiculturalism at all costs are as ideological as those who disparage multiculturalism for lacking any redeeming value whatsoever. Multiculturalism is neither all good nor all bad; rather it is both good and bad depending on the context and frame of reference. Multiculturalism can be liberating yet marginalizing, unifying yet divisive, inclusive yet exclusive (Vasta 1993). On the one hand, multiculturalism provides minorities with a platform for participating in society without the imposition of heavy-handed government tactics. On the other, minorities are lured into the dominant culture since measures to improve access or participation often have assimilationist consequences. Even efforts at resistance are perceived as self-defeating exercises that have the effect of absorbing minorities into the very system they are rejecting (Pearson 1993).

II. Putting Multiculturalism into Perspective

Canada's official multiculturalism is double-edged in impact and implication (Fleras 2001). In the same way that ethnicity can empower or divide depending on a particular frame of reference, so too can multiculturalism enhance yet detract. Positive and negative effects coexist uneasily, with one prevailing over another only because of circumstances. To one side, the existence of counter-hegemonic multicultural discourses cannot be discounted, thus reflecting the ability of the powerless and dispossessed to convert the very tools for controlling them into levers of resistance and change (Pearson 1994). Minority women and men are not passive victims in the political arena, but have dissembled official multiculturalism into sites of struggle for access to symbolic and material resources (Pearson 1995). To the other, official recourse to multiculturalism has proven a politically workable strategy for de-radicalizing ("de-politicizing") ethnicity, in part by legitimizing state-approved differences as integral to society, and by transforming institutions into public spaces where minorities can participate without ethnic entanglements. Far from being a threat to the social order, in other words, Canada's official multiculturalism constitutes a discourse in defence of ideology by circumscribing the permissible range of acceptable behaviour (Thobani 1995). No voice shall predominate in creating a community of communities under multiculturalism, the saying goes, except the voice that says no voice shall predominate (James 1997). In defining which differences count, what counts as difference, the controlling effect of official multiculturalism could hardly be more artfully articulated.

A sense of perspective is useful. Multiculturalism is not the cause of Canada's problems, any more than it can be the cure-all. There is no risk of Canada unravelling because of multiculturalism: the politics of "distinct society" and the "nations within" will see to that first. Nor should we get worked up over the absence of a common culture; multiculturalism has not destroyed what was not there in the first place. Perhaps Canada's core value is the absence of any common culture—in the same way that Canada's identity is rooted in the constant quest for identity—except for core shared values, including a basic decency, a respect for rule of law, and a commitment to individual equality, with the result that the only thing we have in common, culturally speaking, is our differences (see Sajoo 1994). Diversity, not uniformity, is Canada's strength. To expect otherwise is unrealistic in a society organized around the overlapping citizenships of First Nations, Québécois, and multicultural minorities (Kaplan 1993; Kymlicka 1994). Disagreement and conflict are inevitable in such a context. Just as shared ethnicity does not entail a unanimity of vision, as Bissoondath (1994) reminds us, albeit in a different sense, so too can a multicultural society survive on a "multiplicity of voices and visions, or the interplay of conflicting views," provided that, within limits, we agree to disagree.

Multiculturalism: The Canadian Way

Canada's commitment to multiculturalism has contributed to its image as an open, secular, and largely tolerant society. Some measure of proof is gleaned from Canada's lofty status (as deemed by various UN panels) as a socially progressive society with an enviable standard of living. Multiculturalism has proven to be a beacon of tolerance in a largely intolerant world. A social framework has evolved for balancing diversity with unity—even if that balancing act is not to everyone's liking. How do we gauge the success of multiculturalism? In contrast with the alternatives that it has replaced, including racism and exclusion, multiculturalism starts to look a lot better than its critics would credit (Keohane 1997). When compared to a utopia of perfect harmony, Canada's multiculturalism falls short of the mark; when compared with the grisliness of reality elsewhere, it stands as a paragon of virtue. The fact that Canada has avoided much of the ethnic strife that currently convulses many countries speaks well of its stature in proactively engaging differences.

The world-wide reputation for tolerance that Canada enjoys is largely deserved (Kurthen 1997). The majority of Canadians, especially the younger and the well educated, are relatively open to diversity and proud of our multicultural heritage, despite undercurrents of fear and hostility towards certain newcomers. Even whole-hearted support, however, is no excuse for glossing over its imperfections. However potent a mechanism for engaging diversity, the principle and practice of official multiculturalism remains riddled with inconsistencies. Multiculturalism embraces contradictions that strike at the discordancy of contemporary society, while raising a host of troubling questions about working through differences as a basis for belonging. Multicultural discourses reflect a Foucaldian theorization of power and meaning, that is, multiculturalism establishes a framework of symbols, rules, and priorities that constitute a reality for both the powerful and powerless (Gunew 1999). Debates over multiculturalism have unmasked a number of political or economic agendas, many of which may compromise minority concerns for national interests. Everyone agrees that there are enough loopholes in federal multiculturalism to dishearten even the most optimistic. Few would deny its vulnerability to manipulation by politicians and minority leaders. Fewer still would dismiss its potential to deter, divide, diminish, or digress. Ambiguity and conflict are likely to prevail in these contested situations, as both political and minority sectors apply different spins to multiculturalism by improvising self-serving lines of action.

But criticism is one thing; proposals for alternatives to multiculturalism are quite another. Critics may be relentless in their attacks on multiculturalism as regressive or irrelevant, but most critiques rarely offer constructive criticism. Many are fond of pulling down multiculturalism, but they are less skilled at proposing positive alternatives that are workable and fair. Our stand is unequivocal: Multiculturalism is hardly an option in a modern Canada with deep diversities and competing citizenships. There are no alternatives to multi-culturalism (see also Sajoo 1994). Neither assimilation nor segregation stand much chance of survival in a globalizing era. A much-touted return to traditional values as a glue for cementing Canadians into a unified and coherent whole sounds good in theory (Bibby 1990; Bissoondath 1993, 1994). In reality such wishful thinking may camouflage a hidden agenda for a return of the so-called "good old days" when minorities knew their place in society, and acted accordingly.

Has it been worth it? On balance, yes. Multiculturalism has resulted in the establishment of a policy and a corresponding set of initiatives for advancing minority interests that strike many as being consistent with Canada's liberal-democratic framework. This may not sound like a lot to those with unrealistically high expectations, but the contributions of multiculturalism should not be diminished by unfair comparison with utopian standards. A sense of proportion and perspective is required: just as multiculturalism cannot be blamed for everything that is wrong in Canada, so too should we avoid excessive praise. The nature of its impact and implications prevails somewhere between the poles of unblemished good and absolute evil. Multiculturalism is neither the root of all Canada's social evils, nor the all-encompassing solution to problems that rightfully belong to political or economic domains. It is but one component—however imperfect—for engaging social diversity, while at the same time seeking to balance the competing demands of individuals, minority groups, national unity, and society building.

Multiculturalism, in short, remains the policy of necessity if not of choice for a changing and diverse Canada. As policy or practice, it symbolizes an innovative if imperfect social experiment for engaging with diversity within the framework of post-colonial society building. Multiculturalism has excelled in rescuing Canada from its colonialist past, to its much ballyhooed status as a trailblazer in engaging with diversity. The Canada of today no longer consists of a British (or French) mainstream with ethnically related tributaries (Burnet and Palmer 1988). In many parts of urban Canada, minorities are the mainstream, and this revolutionary shift holds the promise and the perils of re-shaping our institutions, priorities, and mindsets. Under the circumstances, it is not a question of whether Canada can afford multiculturalism. More to the point, Canada cannot afford not to embrace multiculturalism in its constant search for political unity, social coherence, economic prosperity, and cultural enrichment. The final word goes to Michael Adams, president of Environics Research Group, in acknowledging that what once was seen as a multiculturalism-inspired weakness (lack of strong distinct identity) may in fact prove to be multiculturalism-inspired strength in the twenty-first century: "Ours is a population that is resigned to—and may even take some pride in—the relatively weak attachments that bind us to each other. It is my feeling that we will continue on much as we have ... forever pragmatic, forever flexible, forever Canadian."

CHAPTER 2

THE MEDIA AND RACISM

Framing the Issue

Canada is widely regarded as a socially progressive society whose initiatives for engaging diversity are second to none. Yet there is growing concern that things are not what they seem, and that racism continues to flourish in certain institutions, albeit in ways that rarely reflect conventional modalities. Emphasis is shifting from classic conceptions that equate racism with (a) formally prescribed boundaries between groups; (b) opportunity structures denied because of inherited racial attributes; (c) codification of prejudice and discrimination into openly discriminatory laws against identifiable minorities; and (d) deliberate exclusion of others from full and equal participation (Holdaway 1996). Emphasis instead is on perceptions of racism as being covert and subtle, embedded within institutional structures and cultural values, intrinsic to normal organizational operations, reflective of forces beyond individual control, and a label applied after the fact rather than pre-existing in social reality. Racism is no longer regarded as a static and fixed entity, with clearly demarcated properties, but as evolving and situational, and increasingly defined around consequence and context rather than intent or essences. Such elasticity may sharpen our understanding by broadening our horizons; it also complicates the challenge of detection and eradication. This shift in focus may also elude any consensus over the degree of racism in society, thus compromising both institutional inclusiveness and the prospect of living together with differences.

Even determining the magnitude and scale of racism can be problematic. Just as some Canadians tend to underestimate the scope of racism in Canada, so too can its pervasiveness be overestimated by conflating all criticism of minorities as racially motivated. Negative comments are not necessarily racist, but may more accurately reflect a combination of ignorance, bad manners, greed, fear, or laziness on the part of the speaker. For example, resentment towards employment equity or immigration policy may symbolize a complex and conflicting array of concerns about society building, government involvement, or core values, in which race or racism is but one of many dimensions (Satzewich 1998). Conversely, seemingly neutral or complimentary comments about minority women and men may be interpreted by others as patronizing at best, racist at worst. Racism as a smokescreen may divert attention from the issues at hand; likewise, it may prompt people to cower in silence for fear of being branded a racist. Repeated references to racism as the precipitating cause of discriminatory behaviour may gloss over the complexity of motives in shaping actions (Palmer 1996). Blaming racism for everything when race is irrelevant may be racist in its own right, insofar as doing so may draw attention to racial rather than social causes of minority problems, in effect, contributing to perceptions of minorities as victims or villains. Constant and repetitive use of the term also runs the risk of collapsing racism into a harmless cliché, thus trivializing its consequences for victims at large.

The accusation that Canada's mainstream media is racist is widely invoked (Henry et al. 2000). Mainstream media continue to be accused of racial discrimination against minority women and men by way of images that deny, demean, or exclude (Fleras 1994). Yet such charges are not as clearcut as many would expect. Rather, responses to media racism are contingent on how racism is defined—as race or culture or power. Much will also depend on the level of analysis that is employed, including racism at interpersonal, institutional, or societal levels. Finally, different types of racism are discernible based on the degree of intent and scope of expression, with polite and subliminal counterposed with the systemic and systematic. The following vignettes provide a glimpse into the complexity of racism when applied to media representations of minority women and men.

1. Do mainstream papers provide balanced coverage of minority issues? Not according to a major study of three Toronto newspapers (*Globe and Mail*, *Toronto Star*, and *Toronto Sun*) conducted by Francis Henry between 1994 and 1997. Of the 2,622 articles that mentioned Jamaican-Canadians, 45 percent of the references were about sport or entertainment while 39 percent referred to crime, justice, immigration, and deportation. Only 2 percent were positive.

2. Diversity rules? On the basis of 114 hours of TV viewing by a *Toronto Star* television critic, minorities remain underrepresented in relation to their population and relative to whites. Advertisers justify this discrepancy on the grounds that minority images may offend their mainstream customers.

3. Prime-time segregation? Of the 26 series that were to premier on the top four U.S. networks in 1999 (CBS, ABC, NBC, and Fox), none featured a person of colour in a major role. Some modest changes resulted when the NCAAP voiced its outrage and threatened a boycott. Of the 21 new sitcoms that premiered in 1997 in the United States, 16 were white cast, 4 were all black casts, and only 1 was mixed cast. Factor in the 27 returning all-white sitcoms with the 12 all-black sitcoms, and allegations of prime-time segregation become difficult to refute (Weintraub 2000).

4. A six-month study of five major Canadian papers confirmed how the mainstream media routinely stereotype Muslims as barbaric fanatics. Muslims were repeatedly typecast as violent persons or terrorists who happen to believe in a fundamentalist religion that condones acts of inhumanity.

5. Stereotyping as racism? A high profile *Toronto Star* journalist was criticized for filtering her perceptions of South Pacific cultures through the perspective of a white Eurocentric gaze. According to critics, her articles (including narratives, anecdotes, languages, and images) tended to embrace images of the West as civilized and superior while exoticizing Melanesians as primitive or inferior.

6. Reverse racism? The introduction of the Aboriginal Peoples Television Network APTV) as part of the basic cable package is seen by some as providing aboriginal peoples with an opportunity to authenticate themselves to each other and to other Canadians. Others are not so sure, preferring to criticize APTV as a racist concession to a special interest group.

7. The Ku Klux Klan and other racist groups are increasingly relying on the Internet to spread hate messages. It has become the propaganda venue of choice for scapegoating minorities as social problems, while allowing Klansmen and Klanswomen to access millions rather than hundreds as was the case in the past. They are also shifting their target audiences from street thugs to college-bound teens, according to Atlanta's Southern Poverty Law Centre.

8. When Paul Bernardo tortured and killed two young women, no one in the media asked, "What's wrong with blue-eyed, blond-haired men of Italian descent?" When people of colour commit a crime, including the widely publicized shooting of a white woman in the Just Desserts Café, collective responsibility is imposed on an entire race. Meanwhile, white criminal violence is a matter of individual responsibility, with the result that the "race" card stays in the deck no matter how horrific the crime.

9. A CTV newscaster accidentally blurted out a self-deprecating employment equity "joke" about lesbians, Blacks, people with disabilities, and stutterers. She was subsequently fired for her impertinent remarks. For some, this incident was proof that racism is alive and well in Canada's mainstream media; for others, the draconian response simply confirmed the degree of political correctness that was compromising society, despite Canada's reputation as one of the world's most tolerant countries. For still others, the issue was not about the derisive attitude of one broadcaster, but reflection of a bias that pervades the structure and culture of media organizations (Tator and Henry 1999).

What do these vignettes have in common? In each of these media-related incidents, media has been accused of reflecting, reinforcing, and advancing mainstream racism. Yet the racist dimensions behind each of these accusations is neither entirely transparent nor self-explanatory: Exactly what is meant by racism in media? Are media racist and how so? Is it more accurate to say that media are the sites of racist incidents by racist individuals? Or are media racist by definition, given their priorities, agendas, operational values, and practices? Is there a distinction between racist media and media racism? What is the source of racism in media? Is media racism the result of human miscalculation or is it something embedded within media structures, values, and operations? What would a non-racist media look like? In that responses to these questions remain as baffling as ever, the prospect of a racism-free media appears to be remote (Fleras 2000).

This chapter explores the concept of racism in Canada's mainstream media, with particular emphasis on the impact of media racism in shaping the representational basis of media-minority relations. It argues that racism is no longer what it appears to be, but has assumed a variety of guises that complicate the process of analysis or challenge. The acknowledgement of the multidimensionality of racism as biology, as culture, and as power is shown to yield different types of racism, namely, polite, systematic, systemic, and subliminal, each of which is based on varying degrees of intent and level of expression. Expanding the concept of media racism to include the systemic and subliminal has sharpened our understanding of institutional bias, not as something that is done by "bad" people, but as something intrinsic to institutional logic, structure, and operations. Such an awareness has proven both a strength yet a weakness—a strength, in sharpening our understanding of media racism as systemically institutionalized; and a weakness, in drawing attention to the formidable barriers that preclude attainment of Canada's multicultural commitments with respect to institutional inclusiveness.

Unmasking Racism

Media in Canada have long been accused of being racist. Awareness is mounting that media racism is an intrusive reality for many Canadians, that racist practices affect individuals in very real ways, and that racism is not some anachronism but resonates with meaning and menace in contemporary society (Satzewich 1998). In spite of government measures to level the playing field, minority women and men continue to be excluded from the "inner circle" of power because of racism (Kunz et al. 2000). In the public service, minorities remain underrepresented, especially at decision-making levels, while those in positions of power argue that minority women and men do not know how to make the best of opportunities (Task Force 2000). Yet there is no consensus regarding a definition of racism, much less any agreement over its characteristics, origins, or dynamics. Rather than sitting still or staying put, racism more closely resembles a moving target that is difficult to pin down or push aside. Instead of a tangible thing with definitive properties, racism is increasingly conceptualized as an attribute that is applied to "something" after the fact, depending on context, criteria, and consequences. Racism can span the spectrum from the openly defamatory to the polite, with the systemic and subliminal in between (Fleras and Elliott 1999). Certain expressions of racist behaviour are unplanned and unpremeditated, often expressed in isolated acts and at irregular intervals because of individual impulse or insensitivity. Other expressions are less spontaneous or sporadic, but are systemic or subliminal, and manifested through discriminatory patterns that may be unintentional in motive, yet no less real in consequences.

In other words, racism means whatever people want it mean. Expressions of racism can be wilful, intentional, or conscious; alternatively, they can be involuntary, inadvertent, or unconscious. Racism may reflect an exaggeration of differences for positive or negative treatment, or, conversely, be invoked by a denial of difference as a basis for recognition or reward. Such elasticity may be helpful in casting the net wide. However, it may also intensify confusion or needless provocation. Part of the problem in securing a working definition stems from the definitional process itself. What happens when the phenomena under study are expansive, with such an array of meaning from context to context that there is little hope of extracting a common meaning in the conventional sense of a word? Racism, too, represents an omnibus concept with an remarkable capacity to bend, elude, twist, and conceal according to the demands of the situation. Definitional difficulties are compounded by an indiscriminate use of the term itself, with people pouncing on the "r" word to confuse, distract, label, or silence. What should be included in a definition? Doctrines? Power? Structures? Prejudice? Discrimination? Intent? Consequences? Biology? Culture?

For our purposes, then, *racism* is defined as a set of ideas and ideals ("ideology") that asserts or implies the superiority of one social group over another on the basis of biological or cultural characteristics, together with the institutionalized power to put these racialized beliefs into practice in a way that has the intent or effect of denying or excluding minority women and men. Generally speaking, this definition of racism is multidimensional: It acknowledges references to racism as a perceived inferiority of others (biology or race), a dislike of what they do (culture), and a discriminatory bias within the broader scheme of privilege and power. It also acknowledges the existence of diverse types of racism, from the polite or the systematic to the systemic or subliminal. These distinctions are analytically useful for conceptual purposes but often are mutually interrelated in reality.

I. Racism as Biology ("Racism as Race")

This dimension of racism is derived from the root word *race,* with its attendant notion that biology is destiny. Racism as biology (or race) can be use in four ways. First, racism entails a belief that people's behaviour is determined by genes or biology. For example, it is racist to assert that Blacks are natural born athletes while the Japanese are naturally gifted scientists. Second, related to this is the use of racism as a basis for any kind of entitlement or evaluation of others (Ayn Rand Institute 2000). For example, to include visible minorities as an employment equity target is racist regardless of the intent or outcome since it assigns privilege or preference on the basis of appearance rather than need. Paradoxically, others would argue that it is racist to refuse to take race into account as a basis for levelling the playing field. Third, racism as biology refers to the process of attaching an evaluative and moral quality to racially ranked differences. Racism alludes to an ideological belief that people can be divided into "races" and assessed or treated accordingly. The human world is partitioned into a set of fixed and discrete categories of population. Each of these racial categories contains a distinctive and inherited assemblage of social and biological characteristics that can be arranged in ascending or descending orders of superiority and inferiority. Unequal treatment of others is then justified on the grounds of innate and unequal differences between races. That is, certain races are judged as inherently unequal because of social or mental deficiencies and are subsequently denied rights and opportunities for full participation because of these imputed differences.

A newer slant on racism as race entails a process of racialization. Racialization begins with the notion that there is no such thing as race relations involving discrete biological races in relationship to each other (Holdaway 1997). What prevails instead are relations that have been racialized through a process by which imputed racial differences are conferred social significance and used as a basis for denial, exclusion, and control. With racialization, the negativity associated with race is transferred to particular practices or assigned to objects, for example, the racialization of crime and the criminalization of race because of negative media coverage (Henry et al 2000).

II. Racism as Culture ("Racism without Race")

The biological focus of racism has shifted in recent years from preoccupation with pigment-focused inferiority to incorporate assumptions about cultural inferiority. Racism is no longer perceived as a universalist discourse of biological dominance as was the case with colonialism. Under cultural racism, ethnic minorities are not necessarily dismissed as racially inferior. The new racism is rooted in a dislike towards the "other," not only because of who they are ("biology"), but also because of what they do ("culture"), with the result that minority cultural differences are racialized as a basis for denial or dislike. Conversely, dominant sectors are defined as culturally appropriate or universally valid rather than as racially superior (Stolcke 1999).

Cultural racism prevails when people of one culture assume their way of doing things is normal and necessary, and possess the power to impose these beliefs and practices on others (Wievorka 1998). A coded language that links social cohesion with national identity by way of culture is critical to this racism (Jayasuriya 1998). Racism as culture is predicated on the principle that the cultural "other" poses a danger or threat to the mainstream. Cultural differences are racialized or vilified to marginalize a group as inferior or irrelevant. Conversely these differences are subject to intense assimilationist pressure in hopes of preserving a preferred way of living (Modood and Berthoud 1997). Culturally different migrants are defined as the source of a society's social problems, thus making a multicultural co-existence impossible, with dominant groups drawing on racial definitions that combine biology with culture to criticize the "other" on the grounds they are too aggressive, too "uppity," too demanding, too successful, or not successful enough. In more extreme cases, those who threaten the purity of mainstream culture are expelled or eliminated.

III. Racism as Power ("Racialized Structures")

Another dimension focuses on the notion of racism as power. Racism is ultimately based on patterns of power involving relations of dominance, control, and exploitation. Those in positions of power are able to invoke a doctrine of race or cultural differences to enforce social control over those deemed inferior in the competitive struggle for scarce resources. This broader definition not only goes beyond racism as a set of ideas or individual actions, but racism is defined as virtually any type of exploitation or exclusion by which the dominant group institutionalizes its privilege and power at the expense of others (Bonilla-Silva 1996). bell hooks (1995, 154-155) reinforces the notion that racism is not about prejudice but about power when she writes,

> Why is it so difficult for many white folks to understand that racism is oppressive not because white folks have prejudicial feelings about blacks ... but because it is a system that promotes domination and subjugation. The prejudicial feelings some blacks may express about whites are in no way linked to a system of domination that affords us any power to coercively control the lives and well-being of white folks.

Racism as power also entails the capacity for some to establish agendas regarding what is normal, necessary, desirable, or acceptable, thus reinforcing the superiority of one group over another. Intent and motive may be less important than the ability to impose definitions and structures on those without the resources to deflect or defuse them.

Racism, then, is not about pigmentation or prejudice (Khayatt 1994). Racism is concerned with power and the historically constituted relations of domination and subdomination that are embedded within the institutional structures of society, buttressed by a coherent system of ideas and ideals and perpetuated by vested interests. In contrast with the perception of race as prejudicial ideas, racism as power points to the primacy of structures, values, and institutions in defence of a racialized social order that allocates resources and rewards by race (Bonilla-Silva 1996). Racism has the intent or effect of reproducing a racially unequal social structure by essentializing racial identities or naturalizing perceived differences (Winant 1998). To be sure, power is not used in the sense of a static resource, with white people monopolizing all the power in some kind of zero-sum game. Power is perceived as a component in social relations that is subject to competition, negotiation, and compromise (Holdaway 1996). Minorities are not powerless; people of colour may tap into pockets of power to resist, remove, redefine, or renew. Still, only white power is institutionalized within the structures, values, and institutions of society, and it is these institutionalized power relations that empower some groups to advance their interests at the expense of others.

References to racism may depend on where we stand in society. Racism cuts across all social and economic boundaries, according to Fontaine (1998), with violence against minorities by certain classes of the mainstream, while others might deny the relevance or rightness of diversity or cultural differences. A racial divide is also acknowledged: Whites may not deny the existence of racism but define it as an irrational aberration from the normal functioning of society that can be isolated and eradicated. Racists are perceived as a small bunch of "bad apples" in an essentially sound social "barrel." Minority women and men, by contrast, tend to see this barrel as fundamentally "rotten" to the core, with the "bad apples" simply the most obvious manifestation of this rot. For minorities, racism is a central and normal aspect of racialized society in which patterns of power and privilege are reproduced in overt and covert ways. The racism that minorities are likely to experience is rarely of the "in-your-face" variety. The experience of racism is more "polite" or indirect than in the past. Racism is also conveyed by power imbalances that otherize people of colour as inferior or irrelevant. Not unexpectedly, white refusal to endorse power sharing in pursuit of equal outcomes may be perceived as self-serving and racist, inasmuch as such a stance may have the controlling effect of perpetuating a racialized status quo. This perceptual gap between whites and people of colour makes it difficult to agree on a definition of racism that meets with everyone's approval.

Re-Thinking Racism

Not long ago everyone had definite ideas about racism. Racism was usually seen as an open and deliberate attempt to insult, hurt, deny, or exclude someone on the basis of their race or ethnicity. Not surprisingly, Canada's racism was colour-coded with red, white, and blue: racism as red-necked in orientation, white folk as carriers, and blue collar in composition (see Fiske 1994). But contemporary racism can no longer command such conceptual clarity, that is, a uniform concept reflecting a singular experience or common reality. On the contrary, different modes of racism can be discerned that embody variations in intent, levels of awareness, magnitude and scope, styles of expression, depth of intensity, and consequences. This variation has culminated in the recognition of diverse types of racism, including (a) *interpersonal* (including red-necked and polite), (b) *institutional* (including systematic and systemic), and (c) *societal* (including everyday and cultural) (Fleras 2001). Nevertheless, a slight adjustment to this typology may provide a better fit for analyzing media racism. For our purposes, racism can be analyzed along two axes: Deliberate expressions of racism are positioned at one end of the continuum and inadvertent expressions at the other end. Individual levels of expression of racism are positioned at one end of the other continuum and institutional expressions at the other. The intersection of these two continua create the possibility of four types of racism: (a) polite (individual + deliberate = polite racism); (b) subliminal (individual + inadvertent = subliminal racism); (c) systematic (institutional + deliberate = systematic racism); and (d) systemic (institutional + inadvertent = systemic racism). The table below (2.1) demonstrates this four-fold typology in schematic form.

Table 2.1:   Typology of Racism

	INDIVIDUAL	INSTITUTIONAL
DELIBERATE	Polite	Systematic
INADVERTENT	Subliminal	Systemic

I. Polite Racism

Few Canadians will currently tolerate the open expression of racial slurs. At one time, both personal and institutionalized racism were socially acceptable and politically condoned. There was no need for pretence—everything was up front and openly visible, given the unquestioned superiority of whites over non-whites (Griffin 1996). But racism is less about jackboots and Nazi slogans than about an unconsciously mapped-out strategy of domination that has had the effect of reinforcing the prevailing distribution of power and privilege (hooks 1995, 108). Open intolerance is no longer acceptable, even if tolerated in private and among friends. The risk of social or legal consequences, not to mention the potential for physical retaliation, has seen to that. The passage of constitutional guarantees such as the Charter of Rights and Freedoms and Human Rights Codes have banished red-necked racism from public discourse. As a result, contemporary racism is unobtrusive, often implicit, obliquely phrased, restricted to private domains, embedded in codes, and hidden behind appeals to higher ideals such as procedural fairness.

As a racism both individual and deliberate, polite racism then can be seen as a contrived attempt to disguise a dislike of others through behaviour that is outwardly non-prejudicial in appearance. Such mutedness is often manifested through the use of coded or euphemistic language to disguise personal attitudes. In contrast with the open bigotry of the past, racist attitudes are coded in a way that "rewards" those looking for a racist message but whose politeness render it difficult to prove or disprove (Wetherell and Potter 1993). This politeness is especially evident when people of colour are turned down for jobs, promotions, or accommodation (Henry and Ginzberg 1985). For example, an employer may claim that a job is filled rather than admit "no Blacks need apply" when approached by an undesirable applicant. Or consider how a general principle may be invoked to deny the legitimacy of a specific instance as when refugees are criticized for "jumping the queue." In maintaining a veneer of civility that conceals a streak of dislike, polite racism may appear more sophisticated than its red-necked equivalent; nevertheless, the sting of this politeness is no less damning or discriminatory.

II. Systematic Racism

Canada's mainstream institutions have long relied on racism as a way of sorting out who gets what. Universities once limited the entry of Jews, people of colour were routinely barred from certain theatres or restaurants because of colour-coded restrictions, and access to employment was restricted by signs that read "No Jews or Catholics need apply" (see Walker 1998). The existence of such systematic and institutional racism is declining because of powerful sanctions to stop it and incentives to improve institutional access, equity, and representation.

Systematic racism involve rules and procedures that directly and deliberately prevent minorities from full and equal involvement within society. This institutionalized racism appears when discriminatory practices are legally sanctioned by the state and formalized within its institutional framework, thus reflecting the values and practices of the dominant sector. It consists of formal rules and official procedures that are embedded within organizational design (structure and function) to preclude minority entry or participation. It can take the form of harassment from supervisors or co-workers—often defended as unintentional or not meant to harm—by way of ethnic jokes or racial graffiti. Or, systematic racism refers to the way in which organizations deliberately manipulate rules or procedures that deny minority access or participation. Consider how employment placement agencies in Toronto resorted to "colour-coded" terms to screen out undesirable applicants of colour. Although institutions can no longer openly discriminate against minorities, lest they attract negative publicity or incite consumer resistance, institutional racism continues to exist. It can incorporate various discriminatory actions, from red-necked to polite, all of which combine to reward some and exclude others. The revelation that both Denny's Restaurant chain (U.S.) and Texaco went out of their way to discriminate against African-Americans provides proof that the more things change, the more they stay the same (see also Watkins 1997).

III. Systemic Racism

There is another type of institutional racism that appears to be impersonal and unconscious. Its unintentional and implicit character makes it that much more difficult to detect, much less to isolate and combat it. Systemic racism refers to the subtle yet powerful form of discrimination that is entrenched within institutional structures (rules, organization), functions (norms, goals), and processes (procedures) of social institutions. The standards and expectations inherent within these organizations may be universal and ostensibly colour-blind, yet they have the unintended but real effect of excluding those outside the mainstream while consolidating a racialized division of power and privilege.

With systemic racism, it is not the intent or motive that counts, but rather the context and the consequences. Policies, rules, priorities, and programs may not be inherently racist or deliberately discriminatory; that is, institutions do not go out of their way to exclude or deprive minorities. But institutional rules that are evenly and equally applied may have a discriminatory effect precisely because their universality may result in the exclusion of disadvantaged groups while conferring advantage to others. Systemic racism is defined by its consequences. It rests on the belief that institutional rules and procedures can be racist in practice, even if the actors are themselves free of prejudicial discrimination. Even explicitly non-racist policies and practices may be systemically racist if the relevance of difference is ignored as a basis for power-sharing (see also Simmons 1998). Institutions are systemically racist when they unintentionally ignore how organizational practices and structures reflect and reinforce white experiences as normal and necessary while glossing over minority realities as inferior or irrelevant. As such, systemic racism is rarely identified as being so by those who benefit from such arrangements. Embedded within institutional rules and procedures, systemic racism remains (a) beyond our everyday consciousness, (b) undetected and disguised by reference to universal standards, (c) taken for granted, and (d) powerful in reflecting an appearance of fairness and impartiality.

Several examples will demonstrate how the implicit bias of mainstream institutions can create unintended yet negative effects on minority women and men. For years, a number of occupations such as police, firefighters, and mass transit drivers retained minimum weight, height, and educational requirements for job applicants. Valid reasons may have been articulated to justify these restrictions; nevertheless, the imposition of these qualifications imposed a set of unfair entry restrictions, regardless of intent or rationale. No deliberate attempt is made to exclude anyone since these requirements or standards are uniformly applied. But such criteria have the net effect of excluding certain minorities who, as a group, tend to lack these requirements for entry or promotion. In short, enforcement of these criteria may be interpreted as systemically discriminatory because of their unintended but real effect in favouring males over females, white applicants over people of colour, rules and majority agendas over minority priorities. The logical consequences of these seemingly neutral actions are systemically discriminatory because they have the effect of further marginalizing minorities from full and equal participation.

IV. Subliminal Racism

Subliminal racism operates at the unconscious levels of individuals, often reflecting deeply held yet contradictory values (Dovidio 1986; Fleras and Elliott 1991, Henry et al. 1995). This new kind of racism reflects a compound of hostility, rejection, denial, and ambivalence towards minorities that unintentionally has the effect of otherizing minority actions that fall outside conventional ways of doing things (Croteau and Hoynes 2000). It entails a subtle kind of racism that normally goes beyond individual awareness yet exerts a negative impact on those victimized by this subliminality. Like its institutional counterpart, systemic racism, subliminal racism does not involve deliberate intent or conscious motive; nevertheless, its impact on minorities may have the effect of consolidating the very racialized order that is often criticized by seemingly progressive persons. Double standards are quickly apparent: Individuals may profess a commitment to equality as a matter of principle while opposing minority measures that would remedy the inequality. Government initiatives to protect and promote diversity are acceptable, but only if they don't cost money or impose burdens for those in positions of power and privilege. Employment equity programs for historically disadvantaged minorities may be endorsed in principle, yet disparaged as unfair to the majority. People of colour are chided for being too demanding or assertive, or, alternatively, for not taking advantage of the opportunities open to them. Diversity is endorsed as good for Canada yet minority espousal of cultural differences that go against the mainstream grain are repudiated if they are seen as interfering with the rights of individuals, violate the law of the land, or undermine core Canadian values or institutions.

To be sure, opposition is coded in muted language that politely skirts the issue or that rationalizes criticism of minorities on grounds of mainstream values, national interests, or appeals to a higher sense of fair play, equality, and justice. Aversive feelings rarely entail outright hostility or explicit hate, but usually connote discomfort or unease, often leading to patterns of avoidance rather than intentionally discriminatory behaviour. There is a commitment to judge people fairly and equally rather than discriminatorily, yet there is continued belief in white superiority. In a democratic society, persons are supposed to be judged as individuals, yet there is no criticism when mainstream individuals derive benefit from a system that privileges whiteness at the expense of minorityness (Ben Jelloun 1999, Ayers 1999, Mura 1999). In other words, subliminal racism is located among that class of persons who abhor openly discriminatory treatment of minorities. Yet, these same individuals are incapable of discarding the cultural blinkers that foster a dislike of others for who they are or what they do. Still, the net effect is the same, that is, minority groups are cast as troublemakers or "problem" people, whose interests are unacceptable in liberal-democratic societies and whose demands fall outside the orbit of acceptability.

Clearly, then, even those who profess egalitarian attitudes and a commitment to racial equality are unwilling—or incapable—of realizing the contradiction between the professed ideal and the preferred option. In acknowledging the mixed messages conveyed by this unease or criticism, the subliminality of this cultural racism appears to reflect an inescapable dichotomy in our core values (see Myrdal 1944). On the one hand, Canadians place a premium on the public good, with its emphasis on collective rights, special treatment, equality of outcomes, and fair play. On the other, there remains a powerful commitment to competitive individualism, with its focus on personal freedom, self-reliance, meritocracy, and competition. This dichotomous orientation enables individuals to maintain two apparently conflicting values: that people should be treated equally regardless of who they are and that people should be treated differently because of disadvantage. The *subliminality of racism* is animated by the dynamics of "Westocentrism." Westocentrism entails the automatic and routine tendency to interpret the world from a mainstream perspective on reality as normal and necessary, as well as universal and superior, and to assume that others are doing so as well (or would do so if given a chance), while dismissing others as inferior or irrelevant by evaluating them on the basis of mainstreams standards and values. Such Westocentrism invariably bolsters the existence of cultural values that reinforce the interests of the dominant sector at the expense of the subdominant. Consider the primacy of liberal pluralism in Canadian and American society. Liberal pluralist principles are based on a belief that our commonalities as morally autonomous individuals are much more important than differences because of membership in a group; that what we do and accomplish is more important than who we are; and the content of our character is more important than the colour of our skin. Differences are tolerated under a liberal pluralism, but only to the extent that everyone is different in the same kind of way. Compare this universalism with the particularism of ethnicity with its focus on taking differences seriously rather than a "pretend pluralism." This ambiguity within subliminal racism may be played out in the representational politics of media-minority relations.

Racist Media or Media Racism?

Canada is sometimes accused by its harshest critics as being a racist society (Alfred 1999; Backhouse 1999). Such an accusation can be only partially true, least in comparison to overtly racist regimes that once existed and continue to prevail. In the final analysis, the validity of this accusation varies with how racism is defined, which dimension of racism is invoked (as race, as culture, as power), and the different types of racism (polite, systematic, systemic, and subliminal). As a result, this accusation is more problematic than as it might appear to critics. Questions need to be asked: Are Canada's mainstream media racist in the conventional sense of the term? How valid is a distinction between media racism or racist media? On what grounds can such accusations be made? Can the representational basis of racism in the media be measured? Should assessments reflect the number of racial incidents per year or should the focus be on systemic biases that unobtrusively but systemically perpetuate racialized minority images? How is racism in the media expressed? Is racism in the media defined by what it is or is not? By what people do or don't do to others? By what is said or not said? Should media aspire to be anti-racist? What would a non-racist media look like? Answers to these questions are critical if only to illustrate the magnitude of the problem that confronts the challenge of multiculturalizing the mainstream media.

There is little doubt that racism informs the representational basis of Canada's mainstream media with respect to postion and process as well as outcomes. However accurate such an appraisal, this observation is not the same as defining the media as racist or equating media with racism. Some say that all the mainstream media are racist by virtue of their preferred placement within mainstream society. Others would say that pockets of bigoted decision-makers continue to hold sway within the mainstream media. Still others prefer to emphasize those institutional structures and media agendas that have effectively

denied or excluded minority women and men. What, then, can we conclude
about racism in the media? Is it a case of media racism or racist media? A sense
of perspective is critical: just as no one should ever underestimate the
pervasiveness of racism in sectors of society and exercise constant vigilance to
that effect, so too is a degree of caution required in exaggerating and advancing
the idea of a racist mainstream media. Most racist incidents may be instigated
by a relatively small number of protagonists. The actions of a few are hardly
representative of media at large and should not be manipulated as a measure by
which to cast blame on an entire industry. Nor can reference to racial incidents
account for racism in the media. The pervasiveness of structures and media
agendas have given rise to subliminal and systemic biases that have exerted a far
more powerful effect in eroding media inclusiveness.

I. Racist Media

A key distinction in determining racism in the media lies in distinguishing
between a racist media and media racism. Broadly speaking, a racist media is
one that officially encourages or condones racism, either by omission or
commission. Such racism is (a) institutionalized as normal functioning, (b)
supported by cultural values and expressed through widely accepted norms, (c)
tacitly approved by the state or government, (d) intrusive in many media outputs,
and (e) largely impervious to reform or eradication (Aguirre and Turner 1995).
A racist media also prevails when minority representations are systematically
(deliberately and wilfully) distorted through denial, exclusion, or exploitation
on the basis of race or ethnicity. Not only is prejudice towards others formally
institutionalized as a basis for recognition and reward, but there are no formal
mechanisms to prevent or deal with racist incidents at individual or institutional
levels.

Mindful of these criteria, it may be necessary to reassess this charge of
media as racist. Mainstream media can no longer be regarded as racist—as was
once the case in Canada's not-too-distant past—even if racism does exist in the
media. Canada officially prohibits racism and racial discrimination at
constitutional and statutory levels by way of human rights legislation, criminal
codes against racial hatred, and constitutional guarantees that make it unlawful
to discriminate against others because of race or ethnicity. With such safeguards
in place, the idea of a racist media in Canada cannot be accepted at face value,
despite the existence of racist personnel. Nevertheless, no one should
underestimate the possibility that mediacentric values may reinforce racism in
the media through the one-sidedness of media messages in perpetuating a race-
based status quo.

II. Media Racism

Rejecting the concept of a racist media is hardly cause to uncork the celebratory
champagne. Mainstream media may not be racist in the conventional sense of
close-minded but openly articulated bigotry that denies or excludes. While

incidents of systematic media racism may be diminishing, mainstream media continue to endorse structures and values that have the systemic consequence of denying or excluding minority women and men. Racism in the mainstream media is more likely to embody seemingly neutral acts of behaviour that have the unwitting but real effect of perpetuating an unequal social order. The unanticipated consequences of universally applied institutional rules and practices—largely created by the white "malestream" to normalize the preservation of power and privilege—may inadvertently have a controlling effect of privileging some and disprivileging others. When combined with the power to put these normative expectations into practice, inequities arise. Both tacit assumptions and arrangements prevail that privilege mainstream values and institutions as natural, superior, and inevitable rather than as "constructed" sets of principles and practices.

Consider, for example, mainstream news coverage of minority women and men. Mainstream media select those race-related incidents that are atypical but deemed newsworthy, frame them in a stereotypical fashion, and contrast them with the behaviour and standards of whites—in effect reinforcing a discourse of whiteness as normal or superior and minorityness as deviant or inferior. Such a controlling effect is accomplished in different ways, namely, through (a) negative stereotypes, (b) the racializing of certain activities such as crime, (c) the assertion of Eurocentric judgements that reinforce the normalness of whites while demonizing others as substandard or irrelevant, and (d) the imposition of double standards; for example, white crime is framed as individual aberration while a black offender is defined as typical of the community at large. Such a mediacentrism is neither an exception nor deliberately pursued, but systemic to how the mainstream media go about their business.

III. Racism in Media

What can we conclude? First, racism exists in Canada's mainstream media. Mainstream media provide a site in which racist individuals and racialized agendas continue to exert some degree of sway. Second, it would be an exaggeration to label Canada's mainstream media as racist if a racist media were defined by a systematic and deliberate attempt to racialize the representational basis of media-minority relations. Third, it would be accurate to describe the systemic bias in media minority representations as a case of media racism. Media racism is manifested in the articulation of policies and ideologies, reflected in the collective belief system of the dominant culture, and woven into the language, laws, rules and norms of the institution at large. Media racism acknowledges the pervasive influence of both structures and agendas that have an unintended yet negative effect—both systemic and subliminal—of misrepresenting minority women and men. Inasmuch as the structures, values, and institutions of the mainstream may inadvertently advantage some while minority experiences are dismissed as irrelevant or inferior, racism informs the representational products of the mainstream media. Media racism is also rooted in those foundational structures and operational principles that systemically define "how things are done around here," while remaining anchored in a mediacentric mindset that appears beyond challenge, and is secured by subliminal biases that inadvertently deny or exclude. The following case study on mainstream news and representations of Canada's people of colour provides an interesting slant in the debate on media racism.

CASE STUDY: Racializing Minorities in Print

Mainstream news media are widely regarded as a primary source of beliefs and values from which people develop a picture of the social world they occupy. In providing people with knowledge about the issues and events that are unfolding around them, mainstream news media play a critical role in constructing reality through media images and narratives that convey powerful but coded messages about what is socially desirable and publicly acceptable. But according to a study by Carol Tator and Frances Henry (2000), the mainstream media do not always objectively report facts or seek neutrality in shaping news narratives, despite a widespread commitment to reflect alternative perspectives, ensure equitable access for all Canadians, and secure balanced coverage. What appears as mainstream news is instead socially constructed by media personnel who make choices in contexts that reflect (a) professional and personal ideologies, (b) corporate and commercial priorities, (c) organizational cultures and discursive spaces, and (d) institutional norms, values, and biases that define a "business as usual" mindset.

Nowhere is the power of the news media more evident than in their ability to articulate and disseminate messages about minorities. On the basis of four cases studies that linked language and discourse with racism in Canada's English print media, Henry and Tator concluded that people of colour continue to be victimized by news media bias, often deliberately but also systemically. People of colour were frequently rendered invisible by the racist discourse of mainstream news media, either by ignoring stories about minority women and men or by silencing minority voices. On those occasions when they do appear, minority women and men are usually (a) misrepresented by being refracted through the prism of whiteness, (b) denounced as social problems and outsiders that are eroding Canada's social fabric, and (c) criticized as "others" in contrast with hardworking and law-abiding white Canadians. To be sure, the mainstream media do not necessarily openly oppose minorities or initiatives such as employment equity. Rather minority actions or actors are framed by news media as contrary to core Canadian values such as meritocracy or equality of opportunity. The end result is that racist assumptions and discourses not only erode any pretext towards balance or impartiality, but a racialized discursive framework also contributes to racism in Canada by articulating and transmitting powerful yet negative messages about minority women and men that unwittingly, perhaps, intensify their marginalization and denigration.

Consider the *Globe and Mail* coverage of the Jack Ramsay case. The central characters in the case were Jack Ramsay, a parliamentarian, and an aboriginal woman who accused Ramsey of sexual assault while he was a RCMP officer posted in Pelican Narrow, Saskatchewan, three decades prior. Usually, in such a case, attention would have been on the victim. However, this was not the case for all media coverage of this trial. The *Globe and Mail* devoted much space to describing the Native community in Pelican Narrow as poverty stricken and rife with violence and other social problems. Ramsay was depicted as the good RCMP constable who championed for Native rights, a loving father and husband, and a respected politician. Little attention was devoted to the victim. The article provided all the stereotypes of aboriginal peoples, generating sympathy for the accused. In contrast, *The Saskatoon Star Phoenix* and *The Regina Leader Post* approached the coverage from the court proceedings, which reflected the perspectives of both parties. Unlike the *Globe and Mail*, local coverage of the trial tended to steer away from the stereotyping of Native communities. The authors attributed these differences to the *Globe and Mail*'s traditional ideology that often emphasized the distance between the mainstream and the "other," mainly visible minorities and aboriginal peoples.

Compounding the problem of media miscasting is a general ignorance or indifference that borders on the racist. Racism in the news media is not about the conscious or unconscious actions of an editor or journalist, according to Tator and Henry. Rather, it is embedded within institutional structures and culture and unobtrusively expressed in the content and everyday discourses of print news. For example, there is a vocabulary that serves as a coded language with the result that policies intended to achieve workplace equality such as employment equity are described as quotas or preferential hiring. Immigrants are referred to as gate crashers or queue jumpers, while non-white Canadians are invariably labelled as ethnics or otherized as dangerous, unreasonable, or undesirable. Those who protest against the status quo are defined as troublemakers whose agenda is not to be trusted. Advocacy initiatives are dismissed as special interest groups, political correctness, or bleeding heart liberalism. Criminal activity is routinely racialized as "black crime," while geographical areas such as the Jane-Finch corridor or Regent Park areas of Toronto are criminalized as sites of racial chaos. Reference to the term *black* is no less demeaning in reinforcing negative stereotypes, as in black art (sorcery), black and blue (discoloured through bruising), blackball (to exclude), blackmail (extortion), black market (illicit trade), blackout (pass out), black day (disaster), and black hole (nothing good comes out of it) (Ayers 1999). By threading together loaded terms, inflammatory images, and negative texts, this racist discourse undermines the status of minorities in Canadian society. A racialized discourse also influences the formation of public policies with respect to organizational planning processes, everyday rules and practices, and decision making (Tator and Henry 2000).

To the extent that mainstream news media are complicit in otherizing Canada's minorities, Tator and Henry (2000) conclude, a profound contradiction is revealed. To one side, the mainstream media are valorized as a cornerstone of democratic society and the process by which democratic ideals are promulgated. Yet as purveyors of racialized discourses, the mainstream media have proven to be an all-too-complicit ally for sustaining racism in Canada while normalizing white privilege and power as natural and inevitable. To the other side, the highly valued standards of objectivity and neutrality are often compromised in favour of untested assumptions, unchallenged patterns of thought, subjective and cursory interpretations of complex issues, and heavy reliance on stereotypes that serve to reinforce negative images of minority women and men. Such a dereliction of responsibility has prompted Valeria Alia (2000), a former distinguished professor of Canadian Culture at Western Washington University, to issue a sharp rebuke over mainstream coverage of northern aboriginal issues:

> I look forward to the day when the North will be portrayed as a complex and important part of Canada, with newsworthy people, issues and events that require hard work for reporters to understand. I look forward to the day when the [N]orth will be reported, not romanticized, and paternalism will have died. The issue is not just one of higher purposes and commitments. It concerns values all journalists say they revere above all—accuracy in reporting.

***

There is little doubt that media-minority relations were historically tainted by the stain of blatant prejudice, open discrimination, and racialized discourses. Media miscasting of minorities reflected and reinforced this dislike of others, together with a belief that conformity rather than diversity should serve as the basis for reward, recognition, and relationships. But overt expressions of prejudice, discrimination, or racism are currently ill-advised. Covert or polite displays continue to persist, however, often manifested as *prejudice* (a set of pre+judgements both irrational and unfounded in light of existing evidence but "useful" in imposing a pattern of order and control on social realities), *ethnocentrism* (belief in cultural superiority), or *Eurocentrism* (tendency to filter reality through Western "gazes." Both ethnocentrism and Eurocentrism involve processes by which reality is routinely and automatically interpreted from a white (male) point of view as natural and normal as well as superior and universal, and others are assumed to have a similar perspective when offered a chance to do so, while whiteness is portrayed as the norm and standard by which others are judged and found inferior or irrelevant. Media "whitewashing" should come as no surprise. According to Paul Farli, a *Washington Post* columnist (1995), middle-aged white males comprise as much as 98 percent of the TV writers and producers in Hollywood, with the result that minority realities are refracted through the prism of whiteness. Such biases are not necessarily racist in their own right. But denying or excluding others because of a Eurocentric ethnocentrism may be racist in consequence because of its effects in reinforcing unequal relations.

CHAPTER 3

THE MAINSTREAM MEDIA: DISCOURSES IN DEFENCE OF IDEOLOGY

Framing the Issue

Is there any Canadian who has not capitulated to the lure of the mainstream media or succumbed to the persuasiveness of media messages? Probably not. For if there is a common denominator that underpins all Canadians, it is our absorption into a media culture, either as producers or consumers. Contemporary life is inseparable from mainstream media; their pervasiveness is such that media infiltrate into our lives without much awareness or resistance on our part. Incidents that matter become media events; media events are those that matter— almost by definition. Reality is not lived per se except through images and representations that shape people's lived experiences (Gray 1995). Personal identities and interpersonal relations are so inextricably saturated with media messages about normalcy and acceptability, writes media analyst Neal Gabler in *LIFE the Movie* (1998), that existence itself is inseparable from entertainment. A craving for media attention is inevitable among those whose realities are animated by celebrity coverage and gossip columns; after all, nothing in their lives is of sufficient import to offset the impact of television, movies, or video games as substitute parental authorities. As Nicole Kidman once quipped during the filming of *To Die For*, "You're not anybody in America unless you're on TV. Because what's the point of doing anything unless people are watching? And if people are watching, it makes you a better person." Not surprisingly, in an image-based world where life imitates art rather than vice versa, an ability to distinguish real from "reel" can no longer be taken for granted, especially since the very realities under observation are refracted through the prism of the mainstream media (Fiske 1994; Abercrombie 1995; Owen 1997).

Concern over the media and their impact on society continues to escalate. Mainstream media not only construct realities by shaping people's perceptions of the outside world, but they also constitute a constructed reality in their own right, with specific agendas and biases—both explicit or systemic—many of which clash with audience interests and societal needs. This agenda-setting function is secured around a specific cultural framework as a reference point for articulating what is important, normal, and acceptable in society. Such reality construction is doubly articulated: To one side, media values and priorities create a cultural context for framing our experiences of social reality. Dependence on the mainstream media for reality construction is further sharpened when, in the absence of first-hand experience, people rely on media texts as a preliminary and often only point of contact with the world "out there." To the other side, the mainstream media themselves are socially constructed by powerful forces in securing the status quo by "manufacturing consent" (Herman and Chomsky 1988). Mainstream media construct the images around which reality coalesces, then confer legitimacy on the constructed image through sustained exposure to a particular ideology. Mainstream media are ideological insofar as they reflect a constructed view of the world; they are also ideological in advancing the ideas and ideals of the dominant sector while dismissing alternative perspectives as inferior or irrelevant (Abel 1997). As a result, ruling-class interests rather than minority needs are promulgated by the mainstream media while minority concerns are compromised or dismissed. A pervasive mediacentrism prevails; that is, cultural differences are automatically and routinely slotted into a single perspective that privileges media-defined values as the standard by which others are judged for what they are not, rather than in terms of who they are (Shohat and Stam 1994). A set of questions captures this increasingly contested dynamic underlying the representational basis of media-minority relations.

1. The representational basis of media-minority relations are ultimately relations of control and resistance. How is this relationship of power and inequality constructed, expressed, maintained, challenged, and transformed?

2. Is this relationship direct or indirect? How do the mainstream media assist in codifying reality, organizing data, shaping experiences, and establishing agendas? Is it the content that shapes outcomes, or the mere act of participating in a particular media?

3. How do individuals read media "texts" (or products)? To what extent are consumers capable of going beyond the preferred readings implicit within media texts?

4. Are the mainstream media messages of benefit and/or of detriment to society? Does the answer lie somewhere in between, with the result that media outcomes are ambivalent and dialectical?

5. To what extent are the mainstream media a conservative or a progressive force in society? Do they reflect and reinforce prevailing socio-cultural patterns or do they constitute transforming forces in their own right?

6. What are the implications of media messages for minority women and men in terms of re-shaping social patterns, cultural values, and personal experiences?

Responses to these questions reveal how implicated the mainstream media are in the politics and processes of contemporary society building. In a strict sense, the media per se are not a problem. Problems arise from failing to situate the mainstream media within the broader social context of divergent and often contradictory public expectations. Criticism of media is inevitable, given the lack of consensus about what the mainstream media should do, that is, inform, entertain, persuade, challenge, or transform. Contrast these possibilities with what the media prefer to do, namely to (a) make profits, (b) attract audiences, (c) bolster advertising, and (d) secure consumer patterns that massage the message of more for the many. Problems also stem from underestimating the magnitude and scope of the mainstream media as socially constructed systems of communication in their own right. Mainstream media are not simply passive or neutral channels for delivery of content; more accurately, media are the message when reflecting, reinforcing, and advancing the interests of those who control media processes, agendas, and outcomes. To their credit, many Canadians generally seem cognizant of the media as a powerful social force, with the capacity to distort, conceal, or evade reality. Few, however, possess the critical skills necessary to dissect the logic and techniques behind the dynamics of media persuasion. Even fewer are equipped to put these media literacy skills into practice in a way that challenges and resists.

Clearly, then, we must go beyond the knee-jerk reaction of reducing all mainstream media to a social problem. The challenge lies in accepting the mainstream media as a normal and important component of contemporary life, without necessarily ignoring their powerful potential to harm, deny, or exclude. The pervasiveness of the mainstream media ensures that virtually no part of our society or culture is untouched as a point of reference, debate, or comparison (Davies 1996). Such potency reinforces the absurdity of conflating media with a mechanical transmission of standardized information on a massive and unidirectional scale. It also reminds us that power is most potent when least visible.

Mainstream media are powerful social forces with consequences as disturbing as they are revealing, and this chapter explores the logic and dynamics of media as a system of persuasion that reveals as much as it conceals, evades, denies, and distorts. Of particular concern throughout the chapter is de-constructing what the mainstream media are in terms of what they do or hope to do, and how this impacts on the representational basis of media-minority relations. This chapter argues that the mainstream media can be interpreted as discourses in defence of ideology that cumulatively have had the effect of securing thought control without alarming the populace. Mainstream media are framed as a contested site of competing agendas whose inner logic, institutional values, and commercial imperatives induce a reading of reality at odds with the aspirations of those outside a mainstream orbit. Also acknowledged in this chapter are shifts in how people think and talk about the media in light of technological advances, and this emergent discourse provides a useful counterpoint for re-thinking earlier approaches. Finally, the chapter looks at the indirect yet powerful effect that the mainstream media have on individuals and society. The ambiguous yet potent relationship between media and society is analyzed, together with how this contested relationship is defined and secured or challenged and transformed. To the extent that the mainstream media are not simply neutral conveyors of disinterested information, but are actively involved in shaping the content of information for securing certain interests while dismissing others, this chapter provides an analytical framework that casts light on a key dynamic in shaping the representational politics of media-minority relations in a multicultural society.

Deconstructing Mainstream Media

Defining the media is more enigmatic than should be the case for something so popular and pervasive. In general, the mainstream media are best conceptualized as systems of persuasion, although much revolves around the who, what, how, and where of this persuasion process. Mainstream media were once defined as the rapid transmission of largely standardized information to a large audience. A transaction transpired between sender and mass audience involving a technologically mediated exchange of information across time and space. Central to the concept of traditional media was the notion of "mass." "Mass" was applied to the different facets of the communication process, including standardized message, mechanized transmission, a large and undifferentiated target, impersonal contact, and linear, one-way flow of information. Of particular relevance was the application of "mass" to audiences. Audiences were defined as large and amorphous aggregates, of predominantly atomized individuals, both passive and disorganized, as well as widely dispersed, subject to manipulation, and susceptible to harmful persuasion (Gillespie 1996). Mass audiences were also perceived as uniform in their needs and wants; as a result, media messages could be pitched accordingly. To be sure, such a myopic mindset hardly reflected the reality of consumer audiences who were much more discerning—and differentiated—than they were credited with being. Nevertheless, this reductionism did simplify the process of moving goods off the shelf without unnecessary complications.

1. Taking the "Mass" out of the Mass Media

With advances in user-friendly technology, the concept of mass media underwent a change in structure, function, and process. The introduction of new possibilities for creating, storing, and transmitting large bundles of diverse information at dizzying speed has had the effect of inverting conventional meanings while bending orthodox rules (Katz 1997). At the core of this astonishing transformation are breakthroughs in what the media can do and how. Technology has taken the "mass" out of mass communication, in effect imparting a new dynamic to media-society relations, in addition to new ways of thinking about the mainstream media as a deceptively complex system of persuasion. Increasingly discredited is the idea of audiences as passive, undifferentiated ("homogeneous"), and uninvolved in processing media information. Interactive technologies, from the Internet to interactive television, from remote control to "Napster," have purged the perception of passivity from audience-media relations. Information is no longer the preserve of the linear and authoritative accounts from central authorities. Access to information consists instead of ideas that are readily accessible in digital form to be cut and pasted, interpreted, or dispersed at will in a non-linear and interactive fashion (Chambers 1997). Creative control has shifted from producers to consumers. Consumers can control what they see, have access to instantaneous feedback, and interact with others through networked connections. Interactive technologies have also dissolved the structures that once secured monopolies of knowledge for purposes of social control (Madger 1997). Finally, assumptions about the mass audiences have been discarded because of technologies that can pinpoint demographic segments on the basis of lifestyle, concerns, and buying patterns. Instead of comprising a single mass market, society is viewed as a kaleidoscope of diversity that fractures along the lines of race, class, gender, sexual orientation, and age (Rothenberg 1997). The advent of market niches and target marketing strategies has compelled a more customized view of an increasingly segmented audience, with particular attention to the emotionally connected needs and consumption patterns of individualized consumers.

Even the way people talk about the media ("discourses") reflects the impact of technological innovations and intellectual trends. Comprehensive models of media–society relations such as Marxism or mass society theory–are gradually losing their lustre because of a postmodernist turn in social science thinking (Curran and Gurevitch 1994). In place of foundational explanations are those newer approaches that privilege the primacy of text, intersubjectivity, textual analysis, and interpretation, rather than macro-models, causal relations, and totalizing explanations. A critical perspective is challenging behaviourist approaches to the study of media. Interest is growing in how people use the media rather than in how media use people, with a corresponding shift in focus from audience measurement through surveys or controlled experiments to a perspective on media as a socially constructed system of meanings that reflect, reinforce, and advance the cultural contours of contemporary society. Audiences are not depicted as passive dopes or all-knowing rationalists, but as being actively involved in creating or "negotiating" meanings and processing information (Sreberny-Mohammadi 1994). Meanings are neither fixed nor focused on predetermined readings according to this new line of thinking, but constructed and reconstructed through interaction between text and context (Ang and Hermes 1994; Fiske 1994; Thomas 1995). Not surprisingly, media are no longer portrayed as monolithic institutions with dictatorial powers to dominate. Rather, what is promoted is a view of the mainstream media as a "contested and contradictory site" in which opposing interests (from owners to audiences) engage in a competitive struggle for control or resistance. As sites of contestation, media are not impervious to criticisms by progressive journalists, activist community members, or ethnic presses. A dissenting dimension "opens" the way for re-thinking the social dimensions of media-minority relations, albeit within the parameters of the prevailing distributions of power and privilege.

II. Discourses in Defence of Ideology

Mainstream media have long been equated with the Althusserian notion of ideological state apparatus. That is, the mainstream media are the most important instrument for maintaining the ideological supremacy of contemporary capitalism—itself a dynamic system that leaves no stone unturned in its relentless quest for profit, even if individuals or social systems are sacrificed in the process (Hall 1981). Ideas and ideals are promulgated by media texts that have the intent or effect of influencing people to think and act in a manner consistent with the dominant ideology. This conditioning process is not necessarily deliberate or malevolent, nor are the media neutral or value-free in the construction and dissemination of ideas. Mainstream media embrace instead a hidden agenda of values and priorities that has had the effect of securing the prevailing distribution of power and privilege—even if claims to neutrality tend to conceal vested interests behind a smokescreen of national interests. Media are powerful in being able to encode particular values by pretending to be something they are not (see also Abercrombie 1995). Media ideologies are hegemonic in practice, inasmuch as the controlling processes have the effect of changing people's attitudes without any awareness that attitudes are changing. An unwitting consent to this domination and inequality rarely involves direct stimulation of thought or action. A preferred reading of reality as superior and universal is formulated instead around an ideological framework that influences without awareness of this influence. This passage from John Fiske (1996, 117) astutely captures the ideological hegemony at the core of media discourses:

> Social norms are realized in the day-to-day workings of the ideological state apparatuses. Each of these institutions is relatively autonomous ... yet they all perform similar ideological work. They are all patriarchal; they are concerned with the getting and keeping of wealth and possessions; and they all endorse the individualism and competition between individuals. But the most significant feature is that they all present themselves as socially neutral, as not favoring one particular class over any other. Each presents itself as a principled institutionalization of equality: the law, the media, and education all claim, loudly and often, to treat all individuals equally and fairly.

In short, the mainstream media may be interpreted as discourses in defence of ideology. Ideology for our purposes can be defined as a system of ideas and ideals that justify the prevailing distribution of power and privilege in society by way of representations that purport to "explain" reality. Mainstream media are ideological in two ways. First, as sites for the dissemination of ideas and ideals, the mainstream media are actively involved in bringing people around to a preferred way of thinking about the world that advances vested interests rather than the common good. Second, all media are loaded with ideological assumptions: media ideas and ideals reflect a dominant discourse by framing reality from a mainstream perspective as normal and superior, while oppositional values and counter-hegemonic views tend to be dismissed as inferior or irrelevant (Abel 1997). The constructed character of mainstream media texts are rarely conveyed to audiences, many of whom are often unaware of the production process behind the apparent "naturalness" of media products (Abercrombie 1995). Media construct realities by "naturalizing" our perception of the world as normal rather than conventional and constructed, while stereotyping other world views as invisible or problematic. Media messages combine to "naturalize" contemporary social arrangements as acceptable and inevitable rather than as self-serving social constructs by (a) representing dominant interests as universal and progressive rather than particular and parochial, (b) denying contradictions such as those related to capitalist production and distribution, and (c) naturalizing the present as "common sense" (Maracle 1996).

To be sure, the mainstream media are not monolithic structures with conspiratorial designs on the general population. Media texts may have preferred readings, but not everyone subscribes, preferring, instead, interpretations that challenge, resist, and transform. Mainstream media might be better interpreted as a contested site, a kind of ideological battleground where different interests struggle for control over media agendas (Wilcox 1996). Nevertheless, there is little question that the mainstream media are powerful agencies with the capacity to dominate, define, or dismiss. In some cases, the exercise of media power is blatant; in others, media power is sustained by an aura of impartiality, objectivity, and balance while establishing agendas in ways that bolster the status quo. Mainstream media do not exist to inform or to entertain or even to persuade. As a rule they are not interested in solving social problems or fostering progressive social change unless consumer goods are directly involved. Mainstream media are first and foremost business ventures whose devotion to the bottom line is geared towards bolstering advertising revenues by attracting audiences and securing ratings. At the same time, the ideological dimension of the media as a system of persuasion cannot be discounted.

III. Thought Control as Systemic Propaganda

The concept of propaganda may advance the idea of the mainstream media as discourses in defence of ideology for the pursuit of profit. A distinction between conventional and systemic propaganda is critical. Propaganda can be defined as a process of persuasion by which the few influence the many. Symbols are manipulated in an organized and one-sided fashion to modify attitudes or behaviour (Qualter 1991). In contrast, systemic propaganda dismisses the element of intent or consciousness as part of the persuasion process. Consequences are the defining characteristics of systemic propaganda. That is, the mainstream media do not set out to control or persuade; nevertheless, the cumulative effect of largely one-sided messages may have a controlling effect in shaping how people think and act. In taking this perspective, systemic propaganda is not equated with blatant brainwashing or crude displays of totalitarian censorship. Neither equivalent to deliberate lying nor something that is consciously inserted into the media, systemic propaganda is inherent in the rules and practices of media operations, in the same way that systemic discrimination reflects the negative but unintended effects of even-handed procedures or well-intentioned policies. The controlling effect is the same in both cases: a one-dimensional interpretation of reality is endorsed that normalizes as it marginalizes.

At the core of systemic propaganda is an unswerving Eurocentrism. Ethnocentrism (or mediacentrism when applied to the mainstream media) asserts the superiority of Westocentric values and practices in a manner that is pervasive yet unmarked so as to escape detection. Under mediacentrism, reality is routinely and automatically interpreted from a media point of view as natural and normal, while other perspectives are dismissed accordingly (Shohat and Stam 1994). According to this perspective on thought control, the collection, organization, and distribution of media information has had the effect (or consequence) of promoting one perspective to the exclusion of others. For example, what passes for news is defined as a social construction in which the attribute of "newsworthiness" is applied to something rather than reflecting anything that is natural or inherent about reality. The social construction of news is not random but embraces definitions that reflect organizational structures, commercial imperatives, and media values. The one-sidedness of the final product can be deemed as systemic propaganda.

The interpretation of media as systemic propaganda in consequence if not intent is gaining ground (Fleras 2001). According to Herman and Chomsky's propaganda model (1988) media objectives are directed towards the goals of "manufacturing consent" by "generating compliance." Their very unobtrusiveness in achieving these goals has the effect of transforming the media into a powerful agent of domination and control. Media images about what is desirable or acceptable are absorbed without much awareness of the indoctrination process. Mainstream media fix the premises of discourse by circumscribing the outer limits of acceptability for discussion. This agenda-setting process is accomplished by suppressing information at odds with powerful interests, by advancing prevailing patterns of acceptance as normal and necessary through the perpetuation of stereotypes and ethnocentric value judgements. Moreover, as Herman and Chomsky (1988) remind us, (a) powerful interests can fix the parameters of debate while excluding alternative points of view; (b) government and the corporate elite have monopolized access to what eventually is defined as news; (c) major advertisers can dictate the terms of newscasting; and (d) media owners can influence what will or will not appear, thus reducing dissension while bolstering consensus. Situations are defined by imposing "frames" of interpretation that "normalize" media priorities or corporate imperatives rather than consumer needs. This desired effect can be attained by the placement of articles and their tone, context, and fullness of treatment.

Admittedly, the media do not act in collusion when presenting a monolithic front. Nor are media biases driven by a cabal of conspirators. Media authorities are known to disagree with each other, criticize powerful interests for actions inimical to the best interests of society, expose government corruption and corporate greed, and rail against measures to restrict free speech and other rights. Yet disagreements in the mainstream media are more apparent than real (Herman and Chomsky 1988), often reflecting differences over the means rather than commonly agreed-upon goals. Thus, the illusion of diversity and debate is fostered. But the underlying agenda remains largely untouched, with the result that debates are limited to squabbles over details, not substance. Spirited discussion and lively dissension may be encouraged, but only within the framework of assumptions that constitute an elite consensus. The fundamental premises driving our society—the virtues of materialistic progress and competitive individualism—are generally off limits.

For example, the mainstream media provide a venue for debating the pros and cons of free trade or global competitiveness; conspicuously absent from these discussions are questions about the desirability of capitalism as a system that destroys as it enriches. Also unexamined are the tacit assumptions underlying the interpretation of reality from a predominantly white, male, middle-class, heterosexual, and able-bodied orientation. The universalizing discourses associated with liberal pluralism remain unshakeable as well: what is emphasized over and again is our commonalities rather than differences, our individuality rather than tribalness, our accomplishments rather than inheritance, and our character rather than colour. However unintentional the consequences, the effects of this systemic propaganda are anything but inconsequential. With mediacentrism, the messages are clear: (a) cultural diversity is forced into a single paradigm of acceptability; (b) the West is assumed to be the pinnacle of evolution and progress; (c) as a centre of civilization and rightness, the West has a right to do as it pleases; and (d) the West is sanitized of all wrongdoing while "others" are blamed.

In short, the mainstream media can be interpreted as a process of systemic propaganda that has the effect of securing majority interests without explicitly violating the practices of a free and open press. The singularity of media messages are indeed a case of system propaganda, by consequence if not necessarily intent. To the extent that social inequality is invariably cast by the mainstream media as a matter of individual choice rather than structured experience—not as social and constructed by way of power differences but natural and normal—the media may be interpreted as systemic propaganda. That every advertisement and all TV programming say that it is better to buy than not to buy if one wants to avoid the essential nightmare of a consumer society— namely, the fear of failure, and the envy of success—the media constitute systemic propaganda. That all newscasting defines consensus, order, and social stability as the norm while framing protest, rapid social change, and chaos as deviant and newsworthy, the mainstream media represent a case of systemic propaganda. The fact that minorities are invariably stereotyped as people who have problems or create problems at odds with Canada's national interests, the whiff of media as systemic propaganda is all too real. Insofar as social reality when refracted through the prism of "whiteness" and "maleness" is superior and universal, the mainstream media are inseparable from systemic propaganda. However indirect the manipulation, the cumulative effect of such one-sided persuasion should be obvious: people are exposed to a largely lop-sided view of the world in terms of what is normal, natural, acceptable, and desirable. Such a paucity of viewpoints imperils the principles and practice of diversity in a multicultural Canada.

Media Effects

What effect have the mainstream media on people's beliefs and behaviour? How "effective" (pervasive, important, durable, or debilitating) is the impact of media on society or individuals? How do we interpret the dynamics of this relationship? Is there a causal relationship? Will increased exposure to media increase the probability of antisocial behaviour, as many are prone to believe (Potter 1999)? If so, what precisely is the nature of this cause-effect relationship? How can this relationship be proven? Do media provide the cues, establish the models, serve as reinforcement, or stimulate the learning of behaviour patterns? Or does the causality work in reverse? Is it possible that certain individuals are drawn to media messages, with the result that exposure to negative media texts simply reinforces a pre-existing disposition? Do media exert a similar influence on everyone, or is the probability of negative effects dependent on (a) types of portrayals of violence, (b) types of viewers, and (c) types of environment? (Potter 1999). Even more intriguing is the possible absence of any direct relationship between media and behaviour. In a society saturated with many sources of socialization, from peers to parents, causal relations may be impossible to detect. In fact, the media-behaviour relationship may prove correlational rather than causal because of the difficulty in isolating causes from effects in a society where competition and aggression are the norm rather than the exception. To isolate media as the prime culprit and to blame the media for everything while ignoring other sources is, we believe, both sociologically irresponsible and socially dangerous.

Re-Thinking the Relationship

Sociologists are confronted by a host of questions when analyzing the link between media and behaviour. Foremost is the question of whether prolonged exposure contributes to attitudinal or behavioural modification. Consider the notion of the link between media and violence: most published results in this area—more than 3,500 since the 1940s—support a direct link between media violence and violent behaviour (Grossman and DeGaetano 1999). To be sure, differences in how violence is defined, narrowly (as in physical harm) or broadly (any antisocial behaviour, including psychological stress), make it difficult to synthesize the findings (Potter 1999). Nevertheless, prolonged exposure to TV violence is thought to generate several negative side-effects, including (a) learning about aggressive behaviour; (b) a callous indifference to the suffering of others, together with an inability to feel outraged or do something when exposed to even the most depraved atrocities; and (c) an exaggerated fear of becoming a victim of violence in a world that is increasingly perceived as mean and dangerous (Grossman and DeGaetano 1999). The harmful impact is further intensified when violence is associated with humour, glamorized as "cool" or acceptable for solving problems, associated with an attractive or exciting perpetrator, or sanitized by being stripped of sordid consequences such as pain or punishment.

Common sense would have us believe that such conclusions are reasonable. Not all sociologists would agree with them, however, and the basis for this disagreement may well reside in the different research strategies of different disciplines. Most experimental and survey research conclude that those who consume media messages tend to behave in antisocial ways. Yet this relationship is not as direct or as predictable as is frequently implied. While high on internal reliability, many of the these studies lack what researchers call external validity. That is, the studies were conducted in artificial contexts where social significance and sanctions did not apply, and for this reason, the individuals being tested lacked any incentive to act normally. In other words, these studies, which often involved university students or pre-school children, looked good on paper but bore little application to reality. To overcome this lack of external validity, investigation turned to natural environments and relatively undisturbed settings as a basis for study (Williams 1995). Naturalistic studies to date confirm the general pattern of evidence in the laboratory—at least in some contexts but not in others.

Prolonged exposure to media would appear to induce attitudinal change and behaviour modification, yet a causal relationship is not as often assumed. A number of variables must be taken into account, since the influence of television varies from person to person. For example, the amount of television that people watch varies by region (those in Atlantic Canada watch the most), by gender (women watch more than men), and by age (older people watch more than younger people). Other important variations pertain to socio-economic status and levels of education, in addition to race or ethnicity. Even more important is the reason for watching television. The elderly may watch it for entertainment and presumably are less affected by it. Younger people may turn to television as a source of information about how they should act; thus, they would be more impressionable. Put bluntly, people may only see what they want to see; they may absorb only what they are predisposed to accept. Too mechanical an interpretation of cause-effect relations is equally problematic. And while protracted exposure may influence people's attitudes or beliefs, the mainstream media may not directly determine behaviour. Fostered instead is a cultural climate in which aspects of reality are defined as acceptable and desirable, right or wrong, good or bad. Such exposure tends to de-sensitize people by decreasing their empathy towards others while enhancing their apathy and indifference. Yet negative attitudes do not lead to antisocial behaviour, and this disjuncture between beliefs and behaviour complicates any analysis of media impacts.

In sum, research conclusions on the causal relationship between media and its effects on society are tempting but inconclusive. A relationship may well exist, but a causal connection may be difficult to prove or disprove, suggesting a need to think in terms of probabilities. Despite advances in statistical analysis and qualitative research, Davies (1996) points out that there are difficulties in "isolating" media effects within the context of a complex environment. Consider the contradictions: On the one hand, media are accused of deliberately employing violence to shock or titillate—even when condemning violence in society or the media (Pevere 1998). On the other, violence strikes at the heart of all media story-telling. Conflict and confrontation are integral to the narrative structure of news and programming, often involving a tension between a stable social order ("good") and breaches to that order by protests or violence ("bad") (Abel 1997).

Just as media and violence are inseparable, so too is it difficult to separate media effects from the construction of reality. Perhaps the media only provide a range of options, with a corresponding cultural frame of reference that defines some things as acceptable and others as unacceptable. Whether a person chooses to accept one option rather than another depends on a complex array of factors. Too many factors are at play, and a misleading picture arises from efforts to isolate one at the expense of others. A re-phrasing of the original question may be in order. Instead of asking whether media determine thought or behaviour, it might be more advantageous to inquire, "Under what circumstances and for what group of people does prolonged media exposure prove a probable factor in influencing how individuals will think or act?"

This conclusion will have important repercussions when looking at the representational basis of media-minority relations. It will be acknowledged that the mainstream media have generally portrayed minority women and men in a negative light. Both newscasting and TV programming, as well as advertising and moviemaking, have proven derelict in engaging constructively with minorities, preferring, in most cases, images of minority women and men as problems, stereotypes, invisible, or adornments. And while many have deplored this unfortunate state of affairs, we have yet to determine the effects of such mis/ under/over representation of minority women and men. Does negative representation result in changes to mainstream perceptions, beliefs, or actions? Are changes direct or do media representations create a cultural frame of reference with variable impacts depending on persons and contexts? To what extent do negative images influence the self-esteem of minority women and men? How has this negativity compromised the achievement of an institutional media inclusiveness? In what ways does media minority miscasting detract from the attainment of Canada's multicultural commitments? Inasmuch as answers to these questions remain as contested and lacking in consensus as those pertaining to the enigmatic link between media violence and violent behaviour, debates over the problem and solution will reflect a dialectical interplay, best summed up by John Storey (1996, 4), albeit in a somewhat different context: "We make culture, and we are made by culture; there is agency and there is structure. It is not enough to celebrate agency; nor is it enough to detail the structure(s) of power—we must always keep in mind the dialectical play between resistance and incorporation."

Media Impacts: Transforming Society

The impact of the mainstream media on society is not insignificant. It is both powerful and contentious. It is powerful in that society is inextricably infused with media images about what is acceptable or superior; it is contested in that not everyone is pleased with this interconnection. To one side, media provide a window onto the world in terms of what is or should be; to the other, they serve as a mirror that reflects prevailing cultural values and priorities. Media constitute a primary source of information about the world we live in. Yet much of the information we consume is increasingly "morselized" into entertaining bits whose one-sidedness renders a public disservice (see Atkinson 1994). Distortions in this information undermines people's ability to act upon this knowledge in a productive and progressive manner.

It is obvious that the mainstream media have profoundly altered the world in which we live. The world we inhabit is a media world; our reality is a virtual reality in which media are society and life imitates art. People have become so immersed in media images in negotiating the realities of everyday life that distinguishing fact from fabrication is an increasingly pointless exercise. The influence of media is of such pervasiveness that only an analytical distinction between media and reality is worth pursuing. The gradual transformation of the world into a computer-mediated "electronic bulletin board" has further underscored the media's prowess as an agent of change. In advancing the shift to digital culture from the linearity of a print culture, computer-mediated technologies have cultivated the potential to (a) dismantle traditional hierarchies of status and power, (b) shatter shared perceptions and modes of thought rooted in reason and causation, (c) democratize knowledge by making it more accessible and interchangeable, and (d) re-define how society organizes that knowledge in promoting national interests (Chambers 1997; Gates 1998). Media are thus implicated in hastening the transformation of society, from a vertically structured hierarchy to a more horizontally layered system in which deference to convention and authority is challenged by commitments to the here and now of multiple identities (Friedman 1998). The magnitude of this transformation has had the effect of gutting traditional authority by re-defining the rules that govern human existence, interaction, and standards of behaviour.

Reaction to the ubiquitous presence of the mainstream media has been mixed. Media are endorsed as a positive force for the advancement of human progress; touted as indispensable in the construction of a multicultural and cosmopolitan society; and seen as critical to the principles of free enterprise and liberal democracy. The mainstream media, and especially popular music (from Pete Seger to Bob Dylan to Live Aid to Jubilee 2000 Third World Debt Reduction), still has the power as one of the more potent forces for social and political change to inflame public opinion or to challenge the status quo (Quill 2000). Others are less sanguine about media impacts. Media are deplored as an insult to the human spirit, an instrument for promoting mediocrity or stifling creativity while encouraging antisocial behaviour, reinforcing racism and sexism at a time when people should know better, a cultural frame of reference at odds with social goals, and a discourse in defence of privilege and power. In Canada's multicultural society, where diversity is endorsed as integral to society building, the mainstream media have come under additional criticism for not reflecting, reinforcing, or advancing the goals of a pluralistic society (Fleras 1995). In between these extremes are those who are inclined to dismiss such debates as puerile and unproductive. Rather than being framed around good or evil, the mainstream media are portrayed as a complex social construction of contradictory roles, ambiguous messages, multifaceted functions, and diverse impacts (see Stone 1993). As "contested sites" of varying struggles, the mainstream media are conceptually neither good nor bad, but simultaneously both—depending on the criteria, context, and consequences.

Mainstream media processes and their outcomes are of sufficient complexity to blur often any distinction between positive and negative. To one side, the media are known to embrace a largely conservative and commercial agenda; to the other side, a combination of investigative journalism and ethnic and/or alternative presses wield the power to criticize those in power, raise awareness, mobilize the masses, and spark social change. Media have shown the potential to empower or enlighten as well as to alienate or disempower, and this interpenetration of "good" and/or "bad" raises a raft of issues.

This ambiguity is expressed in the love–hate relationship people have with the media; that is, people will buy, consume, and condone even as they curtail, block, and condemn (Katz 1997). Moreover, as the media continue to be rebuked for short-changing society, developments in communications technology have enlarged their capacity to control or contain. To be sure, the media do not necessarily set out to control; nevertheless, the manipulation of images has had a controlling effect on those who are subjected to unflattering portrayals. Mainstream media play an influential role in defining what is socially desirable or normal. This is accomplished in large part by defining a specific cultural framework that provides a reference point for acceptance or validity. As a primary channel of communication, the media have the potential to articulate a powerful statement about the legitimacy of diversity in our society. Yet they are likely to send out mixed messages about a commitment to engage with diversity. As Kamala Jean Gopie, former chair of Toronto's Urban Alliance on Race Relations, states in her article "Partnerships" (Gopie 1998, 12),

The media perhaps is the last of our public institutions which still has a significant influence on the lives of all members of society. It is everywhere, all the time, in many forms—print or electronic. The message it chooses to spread affects how we see the world—who is worthy of getting air time, under what set of circumstances, who are the messengers, the language used to convey the message, what is included and what is omitted. The assumptions which underlie the kind of programming provided, the voices which are heard or silenced as well as the perpetuation of stereotyping feed into notions of power and privilege for some and disadvantage and exclusion for others.

Such double-edged potency would suggest the media will continue to be a contested site, with advocates of the economic, political, and social status quo in competition with the forces of change for control of the agenda. At the core of this re-definition process is power. Until the issue of power is resolved—in terms of who owns it, who has access to it, and whose values will dominate—media-minority relations will remain riddled with ambiguity and fraught with frustration.

SECTION II

MISCASTING MINORITIES

It is one thing to acknowledge the existence of multiculturalism in Canada. It is quite another to explain the placement of the mainstream media within the framework of official multiculturalism and to concede the impact of both systemic and subliminal racism in undermining the shift towards an inclusive and multicultural media. To the sure, gradual improvements in media minority representations can no longer be ignored, thanks to the realities of a booming ethnic market and shifts in the social and intellectual climate. Nevertheless, mixed messages about the status and role of minority women and men in Canada continue to prevail. Recent trends in media minority representations provide ample grounds for optimism, indicating progress in this area. Yet there is a still a long way to go before an appropriate level of inclusiveness is achieved, and the challenge of multiculturalizing the mainstream media remains as enigmatic and elusive as ever.

This section explores the miscasting of minorities by looking at the representational dynamics of media-minority relations at institutional levels. Emphasis is directed at (a) how minorities are portrayed in key mainstream media processes related to newscasting, TV programming, advertising, and moviemaking; (b) how such depictions have evolved over time, from an explicitly racist past to increasingly positive portrayals; (c) how such evolving depictions tend to convey mixed messages (see also Croteau and Hoynes 2000); and (d) how deliberate are these constructions (Jakubowicz et al. 1994).

Mainstream media processes are analyzed and assessed with respect to (a) their underlying logic and organizational rationale, (b) verbal and visual (mis)treatment of minority women and men, (c) successes and failures in constructively engaging diversity, and (d) potential for improved inclusiveness. Improvements to date appears promising, especially in comparison with the past when media processes invariably maligned minorities as inferior and irrelevant. Despite signs of improvement, however, not all media processes have proven equal to the task of inclusiveness, and it is precisely the paradoxicality of "continuity within change" that secures the intellectual moorings for this section.

Four media processes are emphasized in this section: newscasting, TV programming, advertising, and moviemaking. Each of these media processes stands in a negative relationship to minority women and men: newscasts tend to problematize minorities, TV programming is thought to perpetuate stereotypes, advertising commidifies diversity, and films are guilty of otherizing. Chapter 4 approaches news media as a discourse in defence of ideology whose predilection for conflict and deviance confirms its status as a medium of negativity. Mainstream newscasting is shown to be socially constructed around "framing" minority women and men as people with problems that challenge core Canadian values or who create problems in need of costly solutions. In Chapter 5, TV programming is revealed to be equally culpable in reneging on its multicultural commitments. Reliance on stereotyping as a formula for framing TV reality has the effect of "boxing in" minorities in a way that sabotages minority concerns while bolstering dominant interests.

Of all media processes, advertising has demonstrated the most promise in promoting positive images of minority women and men. Yet as Chapter 6 argues, advertising retains an equally ambivalent relationship to minority women and men since improvements reflect a crisis in representation within mainstream advertising. Finally, Chapter 7 points out how moviemaking is situated to endorse a wide expanse of minority images. Despite its relative freedom to soar creatively, however, the representational basis of movie-minority relations continues to reflect a reliance on conflict narratives and one-dimensional protagonists for character development. The cumulative effect of these media processes in compromising the representational basis of media-minority relations cannot be underestimated. In securing a powerful if ambivalent force in advancing Canada's multicultural project, the mainstream media have proven to be riddled with ambiguity and contradiction in engaging diversity, to the detriment of living together with our differences. Minority interests are compromised by a media refusal to "take differences seriously" in favour of a "pretend pluralism."

CHAPTER 4

NEWSCASTING: "PROBLEMATIZING" MINORITIES

Framing the Issues

Much of what we know about the world is the result of information conveyed by the news media. In the absence of first-hand experience as an alternative source of information, mainstream news media often constitute the preliminary and often only point of contact with reality "out there." As a result, people's understanding of social reality is shaped by the definition of normality and acceptability put forth in newscasts. Such an assessment is particularly apt when applied to mainstream news coverage of minority women and men. Minorities have long served as "fodder" for coverage because of media preoccupation with negativity as a criteria for newsworthiness. Yet the framing of minority women and men as problem people in situations of conflict has proven profoundly unmulticultural. Even more dismaying is the tendency to interpret whiteness as the norm while maligning minorities as inferior or irrelevant.

Not surprisingly, Canada's newscasting system has rankled many people of colour, at least according to a survey conducted by the Canadian Daily Newspaper Association (van Rijn 1995). Those who participated in the survey and focus groups were critical of daily newspapers for depicting minorities as "foreigners" with un-Canadian habits. Many were also upset by coverage that linked crime suspects with a particular race or religion (Tator and Henry 2000). Minorities in Canada and abroad have long criticized news portrayals of them as belligerent, ruthless, or callously indifferent towards human life. No less flattering is their depiction as victims, vulnerable to social decay and societal disorder, enmeshed in graft and corruption, and without much capacity for co-operative or productive activity. Such miscasting of minority women and men is not necessarily the result of bad people doing their job poorly, despite a tendency to personalize blame or invoke conspiratorial theories. Rather, news media minority depictions tend to be embedded within the very logic and process of newscasting. Put bluntly, newscasting as a medium of negativity has a tendency to malign everyone in its relentless quest for angles, jolts, and "dirt." However, not everyone is equally effected by such media negativity, particularly in a society where specific vulnerabilities prevail (Elmasry 1999; Brazier 2000). Such an assessment casts light on the magnitude of the challenges in multiculturalizing the news media, even with improvements in the quantity and quality of minority depictions.

News coverage of minority women and men remains couched in compromise, and this chapter addresses the politics of inclusiveness in the placement of minorities in Canada's mainstream news media. This chapter argues that the miscasting of minorities is not something out of the ordinary but intrinsic to the very process of what is called "newscasting." It also argues that what passes for news does not reflect something normal or necessary about the world. What comes to be defined as news represents a convention constructed by individuals who make decisions in contexts not necessarily of their own making. This chapter also argues that newscasting continues to frame minorities as people who are a problem, who create problems, or who pose a threat to Canadian values. This negative framing of minorities is not necessarily the result of individual acts of omission or commission. Root causes may be attributed to the structures and processes inherent within mainstream news media, with its growing tendency to tabloidize news around visuals, the cult of celebrities, reliance on a conflict paradigm and crime stories, and unsigned gossip columns. The socially constructed nature of newscasting not only contributes to the miscasting of minority women and men. This social constructedness also suggests that media representations of minorities may say more about mainstream values and concerns than about minority lives or realities. In short, Canada's news media have fumbled the inclusiveness test, despite the prerequisites of a multicultural society, and the resulting disparities reflect the representational politics of newscasting in a profit-driven system.

The chapter begins by conceptualizing news as a socially constructed discourse in defence of dominant ideology. The news media are ideological by virtue of their constructed nature, in addition to their conveyance of ideological messages that bolster mainstream realities at the expense of minority women and men. Focus is brought to bear on the specific ways in which both verbal and visual images within newscasting have had the effect of miniaturizing minorities as perils or peripheral. Of particular concern is how news media tend to "frame" minorities as people who have problems (the "Indian Problem") or who create problems (criminalizing race and racializing crime). The chapter concludes by delving more deeply into news media coverage of aboriginal peoples in Canada. The failure of mainstream news media to capture the logic behind aboriginal issues and demands is shown to be systemic rather than personal, and such a structural bias may account for the persistence of negative coverage despite a growing chorus of criticism and concerns.

First, however, a case study sets the tone for the chapter. While the case study examines news media representations of developing world minorities, the analysis is applicable to Canada. News media coverage of Canada's minority women and men is arguably comparable to coverage of minorities overseas insofar as both are framed as people who create problems or have problems. This conclusion is not altogether surprising, given how the news media are a medium that thrives on the motto: "The only good news is bad news."

CASE STUDY: Miscasting Developing World Minorities

The world we inhabit appears to be in disarray or at least this would seem to be the case, judging by media sensationalism and the howls of public anguish (much of this is based on Steward and Fleras, undated). Too many people exist, according to the headlines, many of whom live in the wrong places, with too many problems, and with insufficient resources to go around. In this portrayal, contradictions abound: people of the developing world are perceived as craving the material trappings of a modern society, with a standard of living comparable to the North, yet most appear incapable of paying the price for economic progress. Visual bites convey an image of the developing world slipping along a slope into tribalism or fundamentalism instead of pulling together for national unity and the common good (Fair and Astroff 1991). Human life is portrayed as cheap and disposable, subject only to the vicissitudes of interclan killings or natural disasters. Events in the developing world are often framed as threats to democracy or free enterprise, while developing world minorities (who, of course, are a global majority) are subject to stereotypes and put-downs, or relegated to decorative ornaments in the unfolding of global history. Substantive issues are preempted by a fixation with topics pertaining to coups and quakes without any sense of history or context, to the detriment of those portrayed in such de-stabilized contexts. The cumulative result of this demonization of developing world realities is unsettling. As cameras whirr around a teeming mass of bodies emaciated by famine or disease, it becomes increasingly difficult to escape the prospect of yet another overwhelmed primitive peoples at the mercy of enlightened Western intervention.

Portrayal of the developing world is often couched within a negative framework, with particular emphasis on the melodramatic and confrontational (including crisis, civil wars, and catastrophes). Consider media coverage in Africa with its unflinching images of boys with guns, armies that hack off people's limbs, aggressive ex-soldiers forcibly seizing land and killing white farmers, a rampaging AIDS epidemic in sub-Saharan countries, and devastating floods with people stranded or starving (Brazier 2000). Little consideration is extended to the consequences of such depictions for audience attitudes. On too many occasions, the only news about the developing world focuses on the violent acts of ostensibly deranged people, with little regard for human lives or international condemnation. This seeming callousness and indifference is rarely explained or explored within the wider context, thus robbing actions of any rationale or underlying logic. News media coverage is angled in ways that portray contact with the West as an agency of modernization and improvement. The infusion of Western culture is seen as a welcome antidote to the regressive ideas and barbaric practices that mire the developing world in a morass of its own making. To be sure, news media coverage of mainstream women and men is also driven by negativity and the aberrational. However, Canadian stories are balanced by references to culture, sport, success, and humour within the context of ordinary life as experienced by most Canadians—that is, a routine and conventional life that is normally free of danger and violence (Brazier 2000).

The "bus plunge" story is typical of developing world news items. A bus or train veers off the road and over a cliff, killing dozens of passengers. The coverage is brief but intense, uncomplicated, and marketable—reflecting a commitment to coverage that is episodic, cursory, Western-driven, politically fixated, and focused on the non-West only when it impacts on Canada. The cause of the plunge is dismissed as individual fault, natural calamity, or act of God; rarely, however, are these disasters situated within a political or economic context that precipitated the crisis. The headline is usually sufficient to convey the entirety of the crisis (consider, for example, a very typical headline: "Monsoons Devastate South Asia" [*National Post*, August 10, 2000, A10]). The tragedy may be faraway yet resonate with familiarity because it dovetails with recurrent images of the developing world as replete with poor roads, lax standards, faulty equipment, and crazed drivers. Such coverage has the effect of not only reinforcing stereotypes and prejudices of the developing world, but the reporting of more important issues is displaced as well. The impact of such portrayals goes beyond inconvenience: developing world people are demonized as outside the pale of humanity and undeserving of sympathy or foreign aid.

How valid are these perceptions of developing world minorities? Is the developing world hopelessly mired in an endless cycle of crisis, conflict, corruption, or catastrophe, for which it alone must bear the brunt of responsibility and endure the costs of solution? Of course, disasters, violence, and danger exist. Yet network coverage of Africa as a site of war or famine conveys the impression of a continent that is uninhabitable, according to a CBC annual foreign correspondence town hall meeting on June 7, 2000, and in the process ignores the good things that happen that are seldom seen through the lens of the Western media. In other words, too much of our understanding of the developing world as "nasty, brutish, and short" reflects a media preoccupation with "triggers," such as India (religious conflicts), Bangladesh (natural catastrophes), Sri Lanka (killings in the name of nationalism), Peru (terrorism), Somalia (clan killings), Zimbabwe (land seizures), Botswana (AIDs epidemic), and Fiji (ethnic conflict). But not all developing world countries are patterned after these media "hot spots." Many are relatively peaceful; they are also reasonably well adjusted to their surrounding environment with co-operation and consensus being the rule rather than the exception. Let's put it into perspective: just as news media coverage of Innu suicides in Labrador or gangland slayings in Toronto or Vancouver are hardly typical of Canada or Canadians, so too is it incorrect to epitomize an entire people or country because of one sensational story (Brazier 2000). Moreover, a compulsiveness with the graphic tends to overlook the co-operative routines at the heart of everyday life for the vast majority.

Why such negative coverage? These largely pejorative perceptions are not necessarily the result of racist personnel but of news media reliance on the flamboyant and telegenic. News information is gathered and distributed according to free market principles without much regard for its impact on traditional societies. Priority is accorded to Western media values, including open access, freedom of expression, dictates of the marketplace, and commitment to the bottom line. After all, stories about co-operation and consensus rarely sell copy except as "relief" from relentless mayhem; nor do they provide compelling visuals for the six o'clock news. This selectivity reinforces a predominantly singular view of the developing world as a basket case of destruction and depression. Any sense of context vanishes because of a "shallows and rapids" mentality that snaps into action when crisis strikes and relaxes when the crisis subsides, only to be reactivated at the next appropriate crisis.

In recent years, coverage has been compromised by political expediencies following the Cold War meltdown, together with a rash of economic restraints, from the internationalization of capital to the globalization of markets and investment, with organizational downsizing in between. Mainstream media appear unwilling or unable to delve into causes or contexts, in part because of laziness or inertia, in part because of the economics of investigative journalism, and in part because of political circumstances. Additional constraints have been prompted by the combination of financial constraints with a perceived public disinterest in foreign affairs, resulting in cutbacks of foreign bureaus and international news. Those news media that insist on a high international profile are likely to pay for such a commitment by being unable to generate a single page of advertising. International developments have also altered the amount of foreign and Third World coverage. Cold War coverage meant uncovering who had won the latest global skirmish between Washington and Moscow (Hadar 1994). Good and evil were easily identified, while developing world countries were identified primarily as pawns in the global struggle for supremacy. The framing of issues into an East-West conflict proved invaluable to foreign reportage, with the Cold War imposing a coherent global road map in terms of what to cover and how to cover it. But the global news paradigm crashed with the fall of the Berlin Wall and the demise of the Soviet Union. The familiar terrains of Cold War politics have vanished as a basis for making sense of international events: editors and journalists must now confront relatively unknown and potentially sensitive conflicts pertaining to tribalism, identity politics, ethnic nationalism, and indigenous self-determination. Without an angle for framing what to say or how to say it, the quantity and quality of developing world coverage has plummeted.

Canadians need to be concerned with and aware of what is happening in developing countries. Yet many Canadians appear woefully ignorant of what is going on outside of Canada. What little information Canadians acquire is rarely derived from independent or first-hand sources of information. For better or worse, mainstream news media provide the bulk of our knowledge about the developing world, with uneven results at best. The otherizing of developing world minorities serves to secure a distorted and polarized vision of the "out there": to one side is the West, rational, democratic, virtuous and moral; to the other is the developing world, irrational, authoritarian, depraved, and morally evil. The effect of this systemic bias is to objectify developing world peoples as marginal and violent, and those of the West as peaceful, ordered, ethical, and humanitarian (Fair and Ashrof 1991). Without a balanced view of developing world successes and crises, stereotypes of backwardness and hopelessness are conveyed, which are neither conducive to finding solutions to problems nor appreciative of the diversity that envelops the world "out there" (Brazier 2000).

***

Conceptualizing Newscasting

Quickly now: define news. Isn't it astonishing that something so simple and routine can pose such difficulties in definition? News can be defined in terms of function (the role that news is expected to play in society), structure (its nature and properties), or at the level of processes (that is, whatever it is the news media do). However defined, what normally passes for news is associated with a property called newsworthiness (Osler 1993; Abel 1997). Generally speaking, news in North America is consistent with one or more of the following characteristics, often intuited rather than reflective of objective social significance: (a) news must be important (what the public should know); (b) immediate (focus on events at present); (c) interesting (it should pique audience interest); (d) be proximate (events further away are less likely to be reported); (e) feature prominent individuals or flamboyant personalities; (f) employ direct quotes and authoritative (although often unnamed) sources; (g) involve magnitude in terms of cost or loss of life; (h) embrace the unusual, graphic, or disruptive; (i) be obsessed with conflict, anguish, the shocking, and tragedy; (j) involve superlatives; and (k) be easily labelled and condensed for quick reference and recall (Fuller 1996). Or as caustically phrased by James Curran of London University, news in a market-oriented society is "simplified, condensed, personalized, decontextualized, with a stress on action rather than process, visualisation rather than abstraction, stereotype rather than human complexity" (see also Atkinson 1994).

News values tend to embrace those events and personalities that constitute a departure from social norms or the routines of daily life—thus reinforcing a notion of mainstream newscasting as a medium of negativity (Croteau and Hoynes 2000). Not surprisingly, coups and earthquakes get top billing, as do crimes, clashes, and crises (McGregor 1996). Yet a sliding scale applies: Situational factors such as time or budgetary constraints may account for why one item takes priority over another (Abel 1997). An item of local interest may take precedence over a global issue in a regional paper; conversely, a large urban daily may ignore regional interests unless news is especially "slow." On balance, however, conflicts involving Hollywood celebrities are more newsworthy than mass killings in Africa. The inclusion of items also depends on their "presentability," and this is determined by the media's access to visuals, easily identifiable protagonists, the availability of quotable reactions, and the novelty of the sound bites. Adversity and adversarial situations are preferred over the co-operative; so too are angles that play up the unusual or the perverse. The danger of seeing only the negative or conflict is nicely captured by Gwynne Dyer, a London-based journalist and historian whose 3,300 articles have been published in 45 countries. According to Dyer (1998), the world is not nearly as "stupid" or as "nasty" as the news would have us believe, despite the heavy predominance of bad news, but a far more "rational, less violent, and even kinder place than it used to be."

I. Newscasting: A Social Construction

People's understanding of social reality is derived from and shaped by the news industry. This is not surprising, since our knowledge of the world is not based on first-hand experience but on what is conveyed by news media. News and current affairs coverage provide elaborately packaged information about society and people's place in the world. This information may be crafted by a largely white malestream culture; nevertheless, people are seduced into believing that the news media represent a medium of impartiality, balance, and objectivity. Such a perception raises a host of issues. Although media speak from a position of authority, the question is, whose authority? From what position are they speaking? Whom do they represent? What social values influence the selection and interpretation of stories (Jakubowicz et al. 1994)?

Answers to these questions may be varied, but sociological consensus rejects the notion of news as a objective reflection of reality. Rather than representing something that is natural or normal about the world, newscasting constitutes a human accomplishment constructed around and negotiated by those with vested interests in preserving or promoting a particular point of view. In reflecting information that is anything but impartial but reflective of dominant values, news is created through a complex array of professional and aesthetic judgement, involving a process in which some events are ignored while others are angled—thus reinforcing the existing social and moral order. Values are encoded into this process in ways that reproduce dominant interests while other perspectives are whittled down to size as irrelevant or inferior. Central to the social construction of news is the transformation of "raw events" into "frames" that are intense, unambiguous, familiar, and marketable (Czerny et al. 1994). This process applies equally to local or international news. For an audience accustomed to a relentless barrage of media jolts, intensity in news is key. Editors choose events for their dramatic effect or focus selectively on the negative or disruptive within a sequence of events. Another criteria in establishing newsworthiness is the need for information to be cut and dried, without any ambiguity and allowing for quick recall. With protagonists in clearly established but polarized camps, the news industry is positioned to present a "balanced" or "objective" point of view by playing one side off against the other.

No less important is the need for events to be culturally familiar, a process that entails framing most issues in a manner to which audiences can relate. Finally, the news story must be marketable; that is, geared towards attracting the largest audience, often by emphasizing sizzle over substance. This assessment of newscasting as constructed and contested has important implications, no more so than in references to newscasting as ideological in reflecting, reinforcing, and advancing prevailing patterns of power and privilege behind a facade of impartiality and neutrality.

Yet news is not simply a formulaic process, both rigid and deterministic. Rather it consists of a series of judgement calls within the framework of organizational values and commercial commitments. As discourses in defence of ideology, news media texts are ideological because they serve as sites for the dissemination of ideas consistent with the status quo. The pervasiveness of this ideological slant subjects newscasting to charges of bias, both personal and deliberate as well as systemic and impersonal. Collectively, these constraints blunt the media's capacity for balanced and accurate coverage, particularly with minorities, with the result that news becomes a social problem when it is called upon to reflect and reinforce Canada's multicultural commitments. News is also defined as a problem for minority women and men when it (a) provides a largely one-sided point of view rather than even-handed coverage, (b) is driven exclusively by commercial interests rather than the interests of service, (c) is framed exclusively as entertainment rather than as a source of information and knowledge, (d) relies exclusively on conflict and violence as a catalyst for story-telling and narrative structure, and (e) privileges the interests and perceptions of the affluent and powerful as normal or natural.

II. Bias in Newscasting

The news media tend to see themselves as relatively unbiased. In purporting to present only the facts, the mainstream media have long endorsed the goals of objectivity with respect to fairness, accuracy, balance, and impartiality. However admirable such objectives may be, there is a tendency to gloss over barriers that obstruct the attainment of objectivity. Objectivity itself is a human impossibility since no one is so utterly disinterested as to be transparent (Fuller 1997). Put bluntly, then, news is not something out there waiting to be chosen as newsworthy. More to the point, news is a constructed reality by those with the power to make choices albeit in contexts not of their own making. Admittedly, news industries acknowledge bias in the newscasting process, but believe this bias is neutralized by soliciting different opinions on the same topic. Sociologists tend to disagree, however, arguing instead that bias is intrinsic to the very process of constructing news. Many of these biases arise from the corporatization of the news media, the selectivity inherent in the news collection and coverage, and the politics of news presentation. Each of these biases— rationale, coverage, collection, and packaging—undermines the potential of having an informed citizenry at the core of a functioning democracy.

A. Corporatization

Contemporary news (both print and broadcast) originates from several large corporate sources (Winter 1994). This is certainly the case in Canada, where independent news sources are a vanishing breed. In lieu of independents are chains such as Hollinger, CanWest Global, or Thomson. Often transnational in scope, these corporations approach the news sector as predominantly a profit-making business venture. Even publicly owned networks such as the CBC (at least until recently) appear to be increasingly market-driven. A commercial imperative exerts a considerable strain on the integrity of the news media. It sharpens the potential for a conflict of interest between corporate needs and consumer concerns. A preoccupation with profit can lead to erratic (or non-existent) coverage of diversity issues that require exhaustive investigative journalism. As Robert Lichter, president of the Centre for Media and Public Affairs says, "Networks now have higher priorities than diversity. The same competitive pressures that altered the definition of news [towards crime coverage] may have halted their commitment to diversity" (cited in Johnson 1999). This "bottom line" mentality ensures a version of the news that is anything but impartial or detached. More to the point, news becomes whatever the industry defines as news, especially when playing into the hands of the affluent and conservative. This implicit "collusion" between news and big business (and the government) is not necessarily conspiratorial in intent, but is rather a disquieting convergence of interests that has had the effect of bolstering vested perspectives while diminishing alternative points of view.

Is news media monopoly a problem? Canada's 1970 Special Senate Committee on Mass Media lamented that control over mainstream media was becoming increasingly monopolized, with a corresponding conflict of interest. Thirty years later this observation appears extremely astute. Corporate groups account for about 93 percent of all copies of daily newspapers sold in Canada, up from 77 percent in 1970. Canada's three largest dailies in 1958 controlled around 25 percent of the daily newspaper total; in 1996 the figure had risen to 66 percent (Winter 1997). While 41.5 percent of the daily newspapers in Canada were independently owned in 1970, the figure had fallen to 17 percent by the mid-1990s. Of Ontario's 42 dailies, only the Brockville's *Recorder and Times* is independent. As recently as late 1995, Hollinger Inc., a Vancouver-based mining consortium owned by Conrad Black, was a relatively minor player in the newspaper business. By 1996, Hollinger Inc. had emerged as a major player in Canada's newspaper sweepstakes with ownership or control of 58 papers from a total of 106 nationwide, 37 percent of the total daily circulation, and 42 percent of this country's readership.

Not surprisingly, corporate concentration has reached the point where four provinces are without English-language daily newspaper competition, three of which are under the control of a single owner. The Irving estate continues to control the English-speaking dailies in New Brunswick, while Conrad Black's Hollinger Inc. owns both of the dailies in Newfoundland and Prince Edward

Island in addition to the four dailies in Saskatchewan. Such concentration of circulation poses the potential for a conflict of interest. CanWest's buyout of much of Hollinger's print- and web-based holdings in July 2000 has intensified concerns over media concentration.

B. Coverage

There is a lot going on in the world at any particular point in time. How do the news media decide what is worthy of being reported? The mainstream news industry is nominally committed to the principle of reporting only what is newsworthy. In reality, the industry is equally bound to making a profit by "selling" as much copy as possible through advertising and subscription rates. This dual commitment puts a premium on bolstering audience size and network ratings by appealing to the broadest possible audience. The news collection process is driven by a flair for the dramatic and spectacular, with particular emphasis on conflict, calamity, and confrontation. Newsworthiness is enhanced by the presence of flamboyant, preferably corrupt personalities with a knack for the outrageous or titillating. The non-controversial and co-operative are often ignored because they lack intrinsic appeal for an audience that is "short" on attention but "long" on titillation. In other words, reporters and editors must continually select newsworthy items among a host of events according to their importance to viewers, in effect confirming what many have long suspected: that the news we see or read are events that mainstream news media perceive to be important to us.

The "jolts" and "jiggles" mentality inherent in the news process has been widely criticized. Tabloid-style journalism is taken to task for fixating on the spectacular, such as the Clinton-Lewinsky fiasco or the murdered prepubescent beauty Jon Benet Ramsay. Mundane but important topics are pushed aside, denying the realities of the everyday world in the process. The lack of context is especially disturbing. A sheen of superficiality is imparted to news that robs events and developments of any meaningful reality. A preoccupation with conflict is no less problematic. A relentless barrage of conflict, atrocities, and suffering may have the effect of diminishing people's capacity for genuine outrage, compassion, or committed activism. Nowhere is this more evident than in references to "compassion fatigue" (Moeller 1998). Advances in computer technology enable viewers for the first time in history to witness slaughter in the more remote corners of the world—from Bosnia to Rwanda to East Timor. But rather than fostering a response that reinforces the primacy of a moral order of co-operation and compassion, the proliferation of images of suffering and death have tended to numb and dull sensibilities. Instead of educating or informing by analyzing contexts, causes, and consequences, the press appears content with pandering to the lowest common commercial denominator through repetitive and sensationalized chronologies of conflict or calamity (Rieff 1999). The collective response to this package of war, genocide, and misery is one of confusion, cynicism, disengagement, and callousness. And this collective inability to experience compassion may induce despair or indifference without eliciting any humanitarian response. Even higher thresholds of violence may be demanded to attract the attention of jaded palates.

C. Collection

Another source of bias is in the news collection process itself. The investigative journalist with a nose for news may also be an unwitting agent in relaying bias. Social and professional assumptions create particular frames of reference that do not reflect a neutral view of reality (Abel 1997). Even a fierce commitment to objectivity and neutrality does not preclude the possibility of bias in news collection and packaging. All human beings, including those in the news industry, are embedded in social contexts that shape perceptions and interpretations. Neutrality can be difficult to achieve, according to Roger Landry, publisher of *La Presse* (*Globe and Mail*, March 4, 1997), especially since journalists are invariably influenced by personal interests or aversions. Words may be manipulated (unconsciously in many cases) when drawing attention to certain aspects of reality and away from other dimensions that are deemed less significant. The camera lens or tape recorder may not "lie" in the conventional sense of the term; however, each instrument only records a minute portion of what occurs around us. The ubiquity and pervasiveness of this bias undermines any pretext of objectivity and value-neutrality. For that reason alone, members of the public must cautiously approach what they are told, see, hear, or read— especially if they lack first-hand knowledge of the situation in question.

Bias also arises from news sources. Reporters are heavily dependent for their livelihood on official sources in the government, bureaucracies, police forces, and corporate sectors. Collectively these sources are difficult to access and prone to secrecy. Yet they are highly sought after because they lend credibility to stories and sometimes offer the promise of a "scoop." Not surprisingly, many organizations employ professional public relations and media consultants whose job description rarely includes telling the truth. They appear more interested in impression management than in providing the facts (Peart and Macnamara 1996). What emerge from these news "scrums" are highly selective morsels of information that make the organization look good at the expense of balance and accuracy. Even unofficial sources of information can be suspect. On-site reporting seeks to conjure up an image of painstaking and meticulous objectivity. Reality is reported as it unfolds before our eyes without the filter of interpretation. In fact, however, what passes for reality may be as contrived and manufactured as official reports. Demonstrations and protest marches may be staged and managed for the benefit of the evening news slot. The rhetoric produced by these telegenic displays is concerned with manipulating sympathy or extorting public funds, not with accurate reflections of the facts.

D. Packaging and Presentation

Bias in newscasting is compounded by problems in presentation. Distortions can be attributed to a variety of reasons. Problems arise from the very act of packaging a complex and fluid reality into the straitjacket of visual images and sound bites, with a beginning and an end, separated by a climax. In a society where the cult of celebrity flourishes, every story must be inflated into an morality play involving good and evil, where good triumphs and evil is punished (Rich 1997). An adversarial format is frequently superimposed to convey some edge to the presentation. Isolated and intermittent events may be spliced together in a story, accentuating a magnitude of crisis or urgency where none actually existed. The impact of "serious" news is blunted by the tabloidization of news into packages of "morselized" bits (Orwin 1999). The presentation can be twisted in other ways. How a story is framed for presentation, particularly through headlines or positioning, can dramatically affect its interpretation (Abel 1997). According to David Taras (1991), for each edition of the CBC's *The National*, up to one million words and 40 hours of videotape are collected. This volume needs to be distilled into 20 minutes of news and enough verbiage to fill about one-third of a newspaper page. This example shows why it is so important that we understand the grounds for editorial decisions regarding what is kept and what is discarded. Who decides and why?

In short, what finally appears as news hinges on decisions by editorial "gatekeepers." Editors are influenced by personal bias and political considerations. Editors are likely to identify with, and editorial decisions are likely to reflect, corporate goals or media industry values. The increased commercialization of the mainstream media places a premium on revenues and ratings, reinforcing the shared outlook of editors and owners. A highly conservative agenda is not explicitly spelled out. It may reflect instead a convergence of assumptions over what should appear as news. As a result of this indoctrination process, editors are prone to winnowing out the subversive or irritating, leaving behind the filtered residue they call news.

III. Constructing Reality

It should be clear by now that mainstream news is not an objective exercise in information processing or reality transmission. What eventually is defined as news is not something intrinsic to reality, with clearly marked and widely agreed-upon labels. Neither an impartial slice of reality reported by trained professionals nor a random reaction to disparate events, news as "invented" reality is shaped by organizational values and commercial concerns (Parenti 1992). According to a study by Frances Henry and Carol Tator (2000), the mainstream media do not always objectively or neutrally report their facts or stories despite a widespread commitment to reflect alternative perspectives, ensure equitable access for all Canadians, and secure balanced coverage. What appears instead as mainstream news is socially constructed by media personnel who make choices in contexts that reflect (a) professional and personal ideologies, (b) corporate and commercial priorities, (c) organizational cultures and discursive spaces, and (d) institutional norms, values, and biases that define how "things are done around here."

To define news as socially constructed is not to imply that news is fiction or a fabrication. Nor is it meant to imply a degree of capriciousness in newscasting. The intent is to draw attention to news, not as a thing, but as an attribute that is applied to something after the fact by those with the power to make this application stick. This constructed character is especially evident during election campaigns (Taras 1991; Levine 1997). A preference for image and angles rather than editorial analysis of party platforms exposes weakness in journalism—namely, biased reporting, quick judgements, fascination with the trivial, obsession with the horse race (who's winning), lack of historical perspective, and deep cynicism (McKie 1997). The necessity of competing for advertising dollars ensures a news package that not only sugar-coats reality with a dollop of entertainment but also reinforces media priorities, if necessary, at the expense of minority realities.

Contrary to popular opinion, TV news is just as biased as print news. The cliché "seeing is believing" is widely endorsed in our visually driven society. Yet there is ample proof that the camera lens is equally prone to personal bias. The "flash and dash" nature of TV reporting is no less vulnerable to selective coverage than newspapers because of biases related to ownership, collection, coverage, and packaging. After all, the camera-toting journalist with a penchant for news can capture only a minuscule portion of the world "out there." Cameras and camcorders can be manoeuvered to enhance the impact of a particular story. Playing up to the audience is also a factor. Lighting can be reduced or enhanced, close-ups may be manipulated with often unflattering consequences (for men, "a five-o'clock shadow" does not compute with a wholesome image), camera angles can be used to good (or bad) effect, and techniques of splicing can convey impressions that have no basis in reality. The vaunted claims of TV news need to be reconsidered, in other words, especially when combined with other tricks of the trade such as musical passages for accentuating tension, drama, or intrigue. In the final analysis, both broadcast and print news are subject to similar constraints. Each is vulnerable to similar organizational demands. Both are market-driven to attract audiences for commercial (advertising) purposes. For newspapers the challenge is to attract a wide readership; for television, the immediate goal is to deter channel switching. Any attempt to declare either print or broadcast news as superior to the other for newscasting excellence is as pointless an exercise as can be sociologically imaginable.

In sum, what eventually is "distilled" as news is expected to run a "reality" gauntlet in which the truth is the victim. Both print and broadcast news are subject to numerous biases and hidden agendas. They are formatted to attract audiences and secure advertisers, then filtered through selective mechanisms that serve only to enlarge the reality gap. In place of objectivity, there is an "invented" reality that embraces media priorities rather than any commitment to consumer needs or an honest appraisal of what actually exists. Reality is beamed or delivered into our homes, not in the sense of an exact replica, but as a form of realism purged of its sordid and messy elements lest it rattle nervous advertisers. This ambivalence has turned the news into an electronic equivalent of Orwellian doublespeak, a process whereby two opposing thoughts (entertainment and information) are accepted simultaneously without the experience of contradiction. There is nothing wrong with having news packaged in an entertaining fashion. Yet when all subject matter is presented as entertainment, as Neil Postman (1985) writes in his biting commentary on television, it is increasingly difficult to separate fact from fantasy.

Newscasting Minorities

Mainstream news media are widely regarded as a primary source of information from which people develop a picture of the social world they occupy. In providing people with knowledge about the issues and events that are unfolding around them, mainstream news media play a critical role in constructing reality through media images and narratives that convey powerful but coded messages about what is socially desirable and publicly acceptable. This process of social construction has proven to be double-edged for minority women and men, with potential for positive or negative effect. For the most part, however, news media minority representations have left much to be desired, particularly in terms of rendering minority women and men invisible, framing minorities as problem people by playing the race (or aboriginal) card, and subjecting both minorities and aboriginal peoples to negative treatment by racializing crime while criminalizing race—in effect damning them if they do and damning them if they don't. And news media depictions of developing world minorities are no less ambivalent in casting light on the representational politics of news media-minority relations. These ambiguities are reflected in three ways: (a) shallows and rapids, (b) framing minorities, and (c) mediacentrism and double standards.

I.   Shallows and Rapids

There is little question that mainstream news media tend to ignore minority women and men. In a society that reveres both power and celebrity status, neither of which exist in abundance in most minority communities, news media coverage of minorities is erratic at best, non-existent at worst. Visible minorities are reduced to an invisible status through "underrepresentation," newsworthy only as entertainers, athletes, or villains and subject to treatment as problems. Minority concerns and contributions to Canadian society are rarely addressed by the mainstream media, in effect further invisibilizing those most visible in our society.

Yet it would be inaccurate to say that the news media entirely ignore minorities. What the mainstream media do to minority women and men is best described in terms of a "shallows and rapids" treatment. That is, under normal circumstances, minorities are ignored or rendered irrelevant by the mainstream press ("shallows"). Coverage, however, is situated within the context of crisis or calamity, involving natural catastrophes, civil wars, and colourful insurgents ("rapids"). When the crisis subsides, mainstream news media interest diminishes accordingly until the next crisis comes along. This "shallows and rapids" perspective has the effect of framing minority women and men as the "other"— as people who fall outside the orbit of a civil society because of the threat they pose to a civilized social order. Or, minorities are otherized by the news media as people with a callous and careless disregard for human life or social values.

To be sure, conflicts and calamities occur in minority communities. However, the absence of balanced coverage results in a distorted perception of minority contributions, needs, concerns, or aspirations. This distortion may not be deliberately engineered; rather, the misrepresentation reflects media preoccupation with readership and advertising revenues. The flamboyant and sensational are highlighted to satisfy audience needs and sell copy, without much regard for the effects of sensationalism on the lives of those sensationalized. Mainstream news media may shun responsibility for their discriminatory impact, arguing that they are reporting only what is news. Nevertheless, such an exclusive focus has the effect of portraying minorities as undeserving of public sympathy or assistance.

II. Framing Minorities

Newscasting does not depict the world the way it "really" is. Just as people in everyday life must "frame" reality in order to define, organize, negotiate, and choose appropriate strategies of thought and action, so too must news media employ frames and framing techniques to enable both journalists and audiences to process large of amounts of information in a way that can be recognized as newsworthy (Skea 1993-1994). News items need to be "framed" if information is to be conveyed to audiences in digestible bites (Campbell 1995). Yet the selection of frames is neither an arbitrary exercise nor an exact science. Proposed instead is a "preferred interpretation" that reflects and reinforces the interests of those who control the news process. The framing of issues becomes even more critical when coverage encompasses realities that are beyond people's first-hand experience. When news media framing provides the first and often only point of contact with the world "out there," the mainstream media's agenda-setting capacities cannot be lightly brushed off.

Nowhere is the framing power of news media more evident than in media messages about minorities. The often subtly racist discourse of mainstream news media renders people of colour invisible, either by ignoring stories about them or by silencing minority voices. On those occasions when they do appear, minority women and men are usually (a) misrepresented by being refracted through a white malestream gaze, (b) denounced as social problems and outsiders that are eroding Canada's social fabric, and (c) criticized as freeloading "others" in contrast with hardworking and law-abiding white Canadians. Aboriginal peoples in particular are often framed in ways that do not reflect aboriginal priorities, realities, or experiences, and the following case study addresses how mainstream coverage of incidents around aboriginal peoples performs a disservice to all Canadians (see also Bannerjee and Osuri 2000).

CASE STUDY: Playing the Aboriginal Card

It is widely acknowledged that mainstream coverage of aboriginal issues is a monocultural blot on a multicultural society (Meadows 1993). Newscasting media are accused of perpetuating errors of omission or commission pertaining to the under-representation or misrepresentation of aboriginal peoples who claim to be fundamentally autonomous political communities that are sovereign in their own right, yet sharing in the sovereignty of Canada at large (Maaka and Fleras 1997). When not ignored because of media indifference or subliminal racism, most coverage is organized around the framing of aboriginal peoples as pathetic victims, noble environmentalists, or angry warriors (RCAP 1996). This stereotyping is compounded by reference to aboriginal actions in the context of conflict, disruption, or crime (Singer 1983). Few stories are situated within a historical context; fewer still incorporate cultural insights that reflect aboriginal concerns from aboriginal perspectives. Coverage is instead conveyed from an outsider's point of view, without much direct access to original sources because of fear or inexperience in dealing with aboriginal issues (RCAP 1996). Predictably, then, aboriginal issues are "too subtle, sensory, complex, spiritual, and emphermal" (Mander 1992, quoted in Meadows 1993) for the gross guidelines of contemporary news media.

Of particular note is the proclivity of mainstream news media to frame aboriginal peoples as problem people. The framing of aboriginal peoples as those who have problems or who create problems taps into a cultural and historical reservoir that has long taken exception to the so-called "Indian Problem." The concept of the "Indian Problem" reflects a belief that aboriginal inequities are largely their responsibility, with the result that any solution must be internally generated. Media depictions of aboriginal initiatives that seek to challenge these inequities both within and outside the system tend to focus on the confrontational aspects of any ensuing conflict rather than on the historical and social context underlying the issues involved. Not surprisingly, media coverage of aboriginal issues has been described as racist. However, mainstream news media are not overtly racist in the conventional sense. Racism is conveyed systemically rather than intentionally. This bias arises from coverage of aboriginal peoples that conforms with Eurocentric definitions of news but violates aboriginal realities. Racism may be manifested in the racist premises of unquestioned assumptions pertaining to what is included in news. Frames may be imposed that, despite a lack of malevolent intent, lead to interpretations that disparage or diminish aboriginal people. In other words, mainstream news coverage of aboriginal peoples is likely to perpetuate images and messages that are more likely to inflame rather than enlighten.

Consider the coverage of the crisis in the Atlantic lobster fishery. In late 1999, Canada's Supreme Court ruled that some aboriginal groups in Atlantic Canada (including the Mi'kmaq and Maliseet) were entitled by virtue of indigenous rights to hunt and fish without a license and out of season for subsistence purposes or as the basis for a modest livelihood. This exercise of aboriginal rights was centred in the lobster fishing industry, where a licence to fish for lobster was virtually tantamount to a licence to print money. Predictably, lobster fishing licences had proven difficult to come by, thus excluding aboriginal access to this lucrative industry, while access to lobster beds was jealously guarded to ensure some degree of sustainability. The situation between the aboriginal peoples and the lobster fishers deteriorated quickly when non-Natives smashed hundreds of aboriginal lobster traps as a result of the Supreme Court ruling that aboriginal people had the right to fish out of season and without a license, based on the contention that aboriginal people had never relinquished control of the land or resources. Eventually the Supreme Court acknowledged the right of federal authorities to regulate the fishery on behalf of national and environmental interests, but not before aboriginal fishing fleets were looted and burned, 4,000 aboriginal lobster traps destroyed, and three nights of violence that saw trucks burned, a man beaten with a baseball bat, and two structures torched (Toughill 2000). Eventually calm was restored by way of compromise with most but not all aboriginal groups, only to be shattered again by violence at Burnt Church, including the pelting of federal fishing officers with fish guts, the ramming of federal boats by Mi'kmaq fishermen, the handcuffing of aboriginal fishers and their subsequent appearance at local court houses to face charges.

Mainstream news coverage of the issue proved to be remarkably predictable, judging by the spate of provocative headlines along the lines of "N.B. Braces for Confrontations over Lobster Traps" (*KW Record*, August 8, 2000). A decade earlier the crisis at Oka had also attracted both national and international media attention. How did the news media respond to that defining moment in Canadian history? The overall thrust of the Oka coverage was framed around the theme of criminality and conflict (Meadows 1993). Simply put, aboriginal protestors were labelled by the news media as criminals engaged in conflict with Canadian law and authorities. Newspaper headlines clearly emphasized the salience of confrontation as the preferred slant, while the issue itself was framed around a struggle between the forces of order and those of disorder, involving the police, the government, the military, the Mohawk factions, and the Oka community. Articles invariably reduced the Oka crisis to an issue of law and order rather than a struggle over land or aboriginal rights. The Mohawk were vilified as terrorists or as hot-blooded radicals; the dispute, in turn, was criminalized as a blatant disregard of core Canadian values and national interests. This focus on criminality may not only have prolonged the dispute, but it also distracted the public's attention from the more substantial issues pertaining to aboriginal rights. To be sure, insightful articles were published that emphasized the social and historical context behind the controversy, but most were buried inside the paper, playing second fiddle to the catchy headline or photogenic visuals. The decision to frame the discourse about Oka as an armed confrontation involving criminal elements, rather than as a plea for justice involving aboriginal and treaty rights, established a powerful ideological framework that did little to advance the aboriginal cause.

Similarly, news media coverage of the crisis at Burnt Church proved to be one-sided in its preoccupation with conflict and confrontation. Mainstream media uncritically accepted a federal communications strategy that portrayed the Mi'kmaq as renegades, illegally plundering depleted resources without much thought for laws or conservation. Yet in its hurry to frame the conflict as a law-and-order issue, the same media generally failed to address the broader context that had led to the confrontation, and ignored the overfishing and illegal poaching by non-aboriginal fishers. References to Burnt Church conjured up images of an armed conflict involving a rump of white fishers against a perceived rabble of lawless aboriginal peoples. Coverage emphasized the breaking of the law, including the recourse to road blocks to step up the fishery fight (*National Post*, August 15, 2000, A1) while hiding behind the smokescreen of aboriginal rights to justify a host of criminal activities at odds with Canada's laws or of inconvenience to Canadians. A subtext implied that aboriginal fishers deserved what they got from white vigilantes for openly breaking the law by fishing without a licence and out of season. And press releases from the Department of Fisheries and Oceans routinely portrayed aboriginal peoples as irrational or greedy. Media coverage tended to reflect the position of the federal Department, as revealed in the following excerpts:

- The Supreme Court of Canada upheld Ottawa's absolute right to regulate fisheries
- Provide aboriginal peoples with larger role in fishery management
- Provide aboriginal peoples with a total of 17 commercial lobster licences, with a total of 5000 traps
- Recognize only one commercial lobster season (from spring to early summer), but allow aboriginal peoples access for ceremonial purposes in late summer
- Offer money to improve wharves, purchase new equipment, increase training in equipment up-keep

The mainstream media rarely included an aboriginal perspective:

- Canada's Supreme Court upheld an aboriginal and treaty right to make living from fishing, with the result that it's up to the government to prove the need for imposing any limits
- A right to self-regulated and self-managed commercial lobster fishery rather than just a say in management, including own tagging system and fishery patrol officers
- Two seasons, including a commercial season in the summer and autumn (cited in *Kitchener-Waterloo Record*, August 28, 2000).

In other words, the mainstream media missed the key issue of jurisdiction: how to balance aboriginal and treaty rights to hunt and fish for subsistence and livelihood purposes with the rights of federal authorities to regulate on behalf of all Canadians and for conservation purposes.

Admittedly, news coverage did not shy away from emphasizing conflict by non-aboriginal fishers. Even in these instances, however, the emphasis was directed at the righteous anger of non-aboriginal fishers, many of whom were portrayed as wanting to uphold the law or common sense, as outraged that aboriginal people were receiving an unfair advantage in a strictly controlled industry, and as guardians of dangerously depleted stocks. In other words, the confrontational aspects monopolized media attention. To one side were the aboriginal peoples, who were portrayed as recklessly defending an indefensible position articulated by the Supreme Court. To the other side were the non-aboriginal fishers, who were also defending their interests, violently at times and by taking the law into their hands, but protecting their livelihood from environmental ruin. The framing of aboriginal fishers as environmental predators could not be more ironic, given the long-standing stereotype of aboriginal peoples as custodians of the environment.

**

III. Mediacentrism: Double Standards

It is increasingly accepted that the mainstream news media do not hold a mirror up to society. Rather than presenting an accurate reflection of the world "out there," certain aspects of society are selected by the news media that reflect and reinforce the values of the institutions for which they work. News media tend to interpret the world of news through largely unconscious "frames" that impose conventional meanings by routinely and automatically interpreting reality from a majority perspective as natural and normal while other perspectives are accordingly dismissed. This selectivity is especially evident with respect to news coverage of minority women and men. A host of double standards can be discerned that undermine the contributions of minorities to Canadian society (see also Braden 1996). These double standards are not necessarily the fault of mean-spirited news editors, are but often implicit within and central to the organizational dynamic of the newscasting process. The most common double standards include the following:

1. News media are known to ask questions of minorities that are not asked of the mainstream. Focusing on the origins of minority Canadians ("So, where are YOU from?") may have the effect of otherizing minorities as people who are not real Canadians and who can never hope to make a contribution to Canada.

2. News media tend to minoritize people of colour in ways and wording that extol the traditional roles or stereotypical images of minority women and men. Coverage of minority women and men tends to emphasize their status as athletes, entertainers, or criminals, while the occasional fawning reference to minorities in positions of political or economic power represents an exception that simply proves the rule. Minorities are extremely visible and the most dramatized of news subjects, yet they are undervalued or rendered invisible by exclusion from the centre.

3. News media invariably judge minorities on the basis of style or appearance. Yet when minorities demonstrate concern with style or appearances, this preoccupation may be trivialized as shallow or as a sign of weakness. This is often seen in the criticism of minorities when they act too different or not different enough. Minorities are constantly reminded of their differences, but they must conduct themselves as if these differences didn't matter.

4. News media often hold entire communities accountable for the actions of individuals; by contrast, mainstream actions are regarded as the actions of individuals who have fallen outside the orbit of normalcy. A robbery gone bad, such as the one at Just Desserts where the accused killer was black and the victim was a white female, is framed as a hate crime by playing on the race card. By contrast, white criminal violence (such as Paul Bernardo) is a matter of individual responsibility in media reports, since the race card stays in the deck regardless of how horrific the crime (Carter 1999).

5. News media may criticize minorities for behaviour that is regarded as acceptable for the mainstream. For example, assertiveness in white males is deemed acceptable, even necessary, to get ahead; in contrast, assertiveness in minorities is seen as pushy, domineering, or unteam-like. Constant scrutiny inevitably takes it toll on those handpicked by the media as standard-bearers for their "kind." This imposed status as ambassadors and role models practically guarantees that any mis-step on their part will confirm the worst, thus reinforcing their sense that the future of others is dependant on them.

6. News media expect minority communities to speak as a unified voice on controversial issues such as youth violence. Mainstream communities are expected to have a variety of diverse viewpoints, and news media make an attempt to get at least two sides to every story. Moreover, individual minority women and men tend to be portrayed as represen-tative of their race when they fail, yet are often deemed to be an exception when they succeed—in effect exaggerating their differences yet minimizing their commonalities.

News media mistreatment of minorities appears to reflect a pervasive double standard that has the effect of misrepresenting minority women and men in three ways: (1) minorities are expected to uphold mainstream standards of behaviour as acceptable while minority actions are dismissed for their failure to conform to public expectations, (2) minorities are taken to task regardless of what they do or don't do, and (3) minorities are criticized for behaviour that is excused within the white malestream. In many ways, this double standard is achieved by effect rather than intent. Consider how the media take pride in announcing that they are equal opportunity maligners (we malign everyone) (see Siddiqui 1999). Yet the miscasting of minorities according to the media law of negativity has an entirely different and disproportionate impact on minorities: minority women and men are packaged as troublemakers rather than as normal members of Canadian society with the same human needs and a similar willingness to contribute to Canadian society.

One area in which double standards are commonly invoked is in coverage of race and crime. Several studies indicate that mainstream presses in Toronto routinely practice subliminal racism by using one standard of coverage for white criminals and another for people of colour, especially Asian (particularly Vietnamese) and African-Canadians (particularly Jamaicans and Haitians) (cited in Siddiqui 1999a, b). In one study by Frances Henry involving newspaper articles from 1994 to 1997 in the *Toronto Star*, *Toronto Sun* and the *Globe and Mail,* nearly half of the 2,622 articles that alluded to Jamaica or Jamaicans fell into the sport and entertainment category, while 39 percent dealt with social issues such as crime, justice, and immigration (cited in Infantry 1999). The image of Jamaicans constructed by the media did not flatter but vilified them as "a people who come from a crime ridden poverty stricken, and problematic country who are good at sports and entertainment but who consistently present Canadian society with myriad social problems." Vietnamese too have been labelled as criminals by the news media, with nearly 75 percent of news stories related to crime and justice issues or to social problems.

How do double standards apply? News media coverage rarely draws attention to anomalies in the data regarding minority crime. Minorities such as Vietnamese or Jamaicans may not be committing more crimes, but their visibility and poverty make them much easier to arrest, charge, and convict, thus distorting the figures on criminal behaviour. The overpolicing of minority communities on the basis of racial profiling leads inevitably to more arrests and charges, in effect making the racialization of crime and the criminalization of race a self-fulfilling prophecy. In other words, the police, in partnership with the news media, may be making minority crime seem worse than it is. Nor does the news media remind viewers that crime has more to do with background and circumstances and nothing to do with race or biology—at least no more so than white-collar crime is a function of race or even ethnicity. No one is suggesting that the media are racist, although the police may be motivated by negative coverage of minorities to ensure budget increases. However, the logical consequences of actions that reflect media priorities are more likely to hinder rather than help minorities. And finally, the willingness of the police to release generic-looking composites of black males, even as witnesses sought for information rather than as suspects (as in the case involving the so-called Scarborough bedroom rapist), makes all black males even greater targets for the police and intensifies public attention until a suspect is found (Infantry 1999). The fact that no one, including the victims or the police, had the slightest inkling of whether the suspect was black or white, together with the vagueness of the police sketch, put all black males under suspicion. In the final analysis, then, the racialization of crime and the criminalization of race has the effect of inviting convictions on the basis of the skin colour of the accused rather than on the evidence (Carter 1999).

Newscasting or Miscasting?

It is assumed that a colour-blind news media is the preferred goal of Canadian newscasting. Yet Canadian mainstream news have proven to be colour-conscious in their coverage of minority and aboriginal issues. Mainstream news media are known to ignore minorities unless something happens, to frame minorities as problem people who pose a threat to society, and to subject them to double standards that criticize minority women and men regardless of what they do. To be sure, mainstream news media do not necessarily openly oppose minorities or initiatives such as employment equity. Rather, minority actions or actors are prone to misinterpretation by their being framed within the context of defending core Canadian values such as meritocracy as preferred or superior. Compounding the problem of media miscasting is a general lack of awareness or concern on the part of the mainstream media. Racist assumptions and discourses not only influence media standards and practices, but a racialized discursive framework also contributes to racism in Canada by articulating and transmitting powerful yet negative messages about minority women and men that unwittingly, perhaps, intensifies their marginalization and denigration.

News media have undeniably born the brunt for stereotyping or misrepresenting racial minorities in Canadian society. Admittedly, some news media have made efforts to improve their reportage on racial minorities. Their efforts have not gone unnoticed. In March 2000, the *Toronto Star* received an award from the Joint Centre of Excellence for Research on Immigration and Settlement in Toronto (CERIS) for its "Beyond 2000" series. The series consisted of articles documenting the lives of selected immigrant and/or ethnic communities in the Greater Toronto Area. Using polled data as well as personal interviews, "Beyond 2000" covered a wide range of issues on immigration and diversity, including access to employment, housing, and policing. CERIS lauded "Beyond 2000" as a "shining exception" to the norm. Unlike most reports on immigrant communities, the reportage was even-handed and insightful. On the series' piece on refugees, CERIS directors noted:

> It took sober vision to analyse the country's relative failure to use the talents of immigrants we select with such care. It was an act of bravery to present an even-handed discussion of Canada's refugee determination system during a time of mounting hysteria about strangers invading our unprotected shores. It was important to shine a lamp into our supposedly tolerant house and expose the discrimination against immigrants and minority groups which continues to lurk in our closets and dark corners (Beiser and Truelove 2000, 10).

Nevertheless, while the reportage on diversity may have improved over time, column articles on immigration, ethnicity, and racial discrimination remain uneven. This type of discourse serves to "promote, support and communicate a particular ideology, that is, the maintenance of power by White able-bodied males" (Henry and Tator 2000, 70). The complicity of mainstream news media in otherizing Canada's minorities reveals a profound contradiction. Mainstream media are enlisted as a cornerstone of democratic society and the process by which democratic ideals are promulgated. Yet as purveyors of racialized discourses, the mainstream media have proven to be an all-too-complicit ally for sustaining racism in Canada while normalizing white privilege and power as natural and inevitable.

CHAPTER 5

"Who's On?": Programming Minorities

Framing the Issue

Television is arguably the most powerful yet enigmatic of contemporary social forces (Andersen 1996), with the power to enlighten and persuade as well as diminish and dehumanize. From a piece of furniture stuck in the corner of a room to the single most influential medium in the world, television has infiltrated the lives of all Canadians while capturing the largest slice of advertising revenue (Jenkinson 1995). Once a marketing gimmick (a kind of radio with pictures) for moving a glut of post-war goods off the shelf while massaging the glamorizing of consumption as an acceptable lifestyle, television continues to extol the virtues of a consumer society. Television is bound up with capitalism both as a set of economic activities as well as a cultural force that is constituted by and constitutive of a global world-marketing strategy of capitalist modernity. The agenda-setting properties of television are also openly acknowledged. They range in scope from creating awareness and attitude formation, to establishing priorities by fixing the outer parameters of what is acceptable and what is not. Television as a cultural product and cultural producer does more than entertain. As a medium of cultural power in which identities are modelled after celebrities and peers in the absence of credible alternatives, television has consolidated its status as a primary and preferred source of social information. Yet this very information is programmed in a manner that trivializes and simultaneously magnifies, with the banal juxtaposed with the significant in a way that erodes the important while celebrating the trivial.

The very popularity of television invariably fosters a backlash. For some it is a "revolution in a box," for others, a "tyranny of the trivial" with few redeeming qualities. Criticism of TV programming spans the spectrum from fears of individual dwarfism and cultural "rot" to charges of global decay, with accusations of racism and sexism in between. Such criticism tends to gloss over the profoundly contradictory aspects of television (Dow 1996). To one side, television continues to marginalize or stymie minority attempts at self-definition or self-determination; to the other side, an unrelenting focus on television as a social problem blinds us to the complexities of TV programming as being, concurrently, a commodity, a marketing tool for delivering audiences to advertisers, an art form, a textual system anchored in history and culture, and an important ideological forum for public discourse involving social issues and social changes. What critics have also failed to recognize in their zeal to denigrate television is the magnitude and intensity of viewer enjoyment. As implied by Neil Postman in his widely acclaimed book *Amusing Ourselves to Death* (1985), Canadians are into the third generation of children for whom TV programming represents their first and most accessible teacher, companion, and guidepost. Such a dependency may explain why watching television confers more pleasure and satisfaction than any other activity, according to a 1986 survey of 1,550 American adults by *TV Guide* (Kottak 1990, 7), including being with friends, reading, vacationing, food, or having sex. A ringing endorsement may be indicative of a fundamental love-hate relationship that many of us have with television (Real 1989).

Criticism of television may be unfounded since much depends on what people expect from TV programs (entertainment, information, challenge, or transformation), what television as a commercially driven enterprise can possibly deliver, and how TV programming should relate to a particular vision of society. Television in its own right is neither good nor bad, as noted by John Pungente, director of the Jesuit Communication Project in Toronto (1996). It just exists, with goodness or badness contingent on its usage. In other words, if television is defined as a problem, who says so and why? And what if anything should be done about it? Curiously, critics appear unfazed by the juxtaposition of seemingly contradictory impacts: media pundits blather on just as readily about the hyperactivity associated with TV violence as they do about the passivity engendered by its unremitting monotony (McKibbon 1992). In short, the major area of concern should not be with "what's on," but with what's underneath, and this distinction provides an entry for understanding the representational basis of minority-TV programming relations.

Like other forms of media, TV programming has not had a happy relationship with minority women and men. TV programming initially included minorities only as objects of contempt or of derision by playing them for laughs. Over the years, however, improvements in the quantity and quality of representations of minority women and men have expanded beyond the original constrictiveness of black and white television. Programs aimed at younger audiences have become more "diversity-friendly" than those geared towards older and more culturally homogenous audiences. As a result it would appear that minority women and men are generously represented in certain types of TV programming, such as sitcoms or reality-based shows, but rarely as lead actors in dramas—with several exceptions, including the series *North of 60* and *ER*. Yet appearances can be deceiving. First, the quantity of representations has improved, but quality representations that situate minorities within an ethnocultural context are still lacking. Thus, while the inclusion of minority women and men is widely applauded, attempts to include minority ethnicity as part of the programming mix have faltered. Second, prime time programming remains as segregated as ever: there is little integration of minority women and men in TV programming that occurs outside the workplace, and audiences continue to be segregated in terms of their likes and dislikes, in effect complicating efforts at multicultural programming. Third, stereotyping continues to define the representational basis of TV programming. One set of stereotypes has been replaced by another set that collectively have "miniaturized" minorities while de-politicizing their contributions to society. To the extent that these stereotypes are structural and systemic rather than personal and malevolent, the challenge in improving minority images must go beyond attitudinal change to focus on the underlying logic and operational dynamic of TV programming.

Television is an extremely complex and contradictory medium because of its commercial imperatives, cultural texts, organizational structures and values, and relationship to everyday life (Gray 1995). For television to do its "work" in terms of a discourse in defence of profit and ideology, it has to draw upon and operate on the basis of a generalized common sense about society and the social location of people within it. It is the contention of this chapter that television representations of minority women and men operate primarily within the boundaries of a racialized discourse about the unmarked superiority of whiteness as natural and normal. This dominant discourse establishes a normative universe in which minority representations and the marginalization of diversity in commercial network television are positioned within the existing institutional hierarchies of power and privilege. Hence, television representations of minority women and men have had the effect of securing and legitimating the terms of the existing social and cultural order (Gray 1995).

This chapter is concerned with how minority women and men, including aboriginal peoples, have fared as objects of representation across a broad range of TV programming. The chapter argues that minority women and men continue to be misrepresented by TV programming despite gradual improvements in the representational basis of minority-TV programming relations. It also contends that this misrepresentation is neither accidental nor attitudinal but intrinsic to the nature of programming in a medium that is designed to connect consumers with advertisers by way of hefty ratings. To be sure, television as a medium thrives on the stereotyping of everyone as a basis for plot lines and character development. What else could be expected given the constraints of a 22-minute, boxed-in reality? Nevertheless, the impact of systemic stereotyping is substantially different when applied to unequal situations, and it is precisely this distinction that raises the question of how to portray minorities and their ethnicity in TV programming. That is, are numbers enough or inclusiveness based on including ethnicity in a meaningful fashion? Is it best to ignore differences as a means of achieving equality between races or should ethnicity be taken into account as a basis for equitable treatment? That these questions have yet to be satisfactorily answered is a reflection of the complexity of the issues and the diversity of the viewing public. The chapter begins by exploring the animating logic behind TV programming, with particular emphasis on the commercial dimensions and institutional values. This is followed by an examination of how TV programming (mis)treats minority women and men, both formerly and currently. The chapter concludes by pointing out that continued misrepresentation of minorities is not an egregious error that can be rationally rectified. Its embeddedness within the very structure of programming will make it difficult to solve, especially as debates escalate over the merits of colour-blind or colour-conscious programming.

"Send in the Clones": Decoding TV Programming

> Television is just like any other business.... It's a toaster with pictures (Mark Fowler, Commissioner, FCC under the Reagan Administration, quoted in Angus and Jhally 1989, 3).

> TV stations are gigantic advertising machines there to be filled with product[s] (Izzy Asper, president of CanWest Global, cited in *Wente*, August 1, 2000).

Television programs have come and gone in the last half century. To the casual observer, television appears blessed with a bevy of plots and personalities. Despite the illusion of creative diversity, television programming is locked into a remarkably formulaic process. Network TV offers a semblance of diversity but only through endless variations of the same prototype, whether sitcom genres, reality-based police dramas, quiz shows, reality programming, or scandal-driven, talk-and-peep exposés (McAllister 1995). Cloning is key: Faces may change as photogenic stars come and go; props, in turn, are adjusted accordingly to reflect changing trends and fashions. Programming continues to be both slick and shallow, as well as stupefying and glib, because of a perpetual quest for the younger demographic. Tele-voyeurism remains popular, with TV shows that provide "real" life situations where we can savour people admitting to affairs, revealing they are of a different gender, and disowning their parents and/or offspring. But the essential themes and underlying messages are circulated over and over. Little that departs from the norm is offered outside of the derivative and formulaic since innovative and controversial material contradicts the demands of a commercially driven medium that prefers to pander rather than to provoke.

This uniformity reflects the presence of implicit codes and tacit assumptions that govern program clones. These codes or conventions are hidden from viewers but still infuse both audiences and programming with ideas and ideals about what is and what should be. Foremost among these programming codes is the injunction to keep it *safe*, *simple*, and *familiar*. By recycling the formula over and again, the terminally adolescent world of television is sanitized and bleached, purging it of anything offensive that might alienate audiences or advertisers. In striving for popularity, television relies on the least objectionable programming for the lowest common denominator by avoiding controversial positions or by pushing them to the margins (Croteau and Hoynes 2000). Television characters are narrowcast in roles that cater to audience expectations by tapping into dormant fears and craven desires. Complex and sensitive issues are superficially addressed or scrubbed clean lest they interfere with the undisturbed balm of advertising messages. Plots and characters are organized around simplistic morality tales where good triumphs over evil, virtue over vice, honesty over urban slickness. This "dumbing-down" formula for the bland and the innocuous is so routinely applied that exceptions only confirm the rule. Defiance against this conventionality is the rarest of all qualities in a medium devoted to the derivative and formulaic: that may help to explain the popularity of shows such as *The Simpsons* or *Sex in the City* or *Seinfeld*, with their spoofing of well-worn clichés and pre-programmed mentality.

The unwritten rules that comprise television's "holy codes" should come as little surprise. The persistence of the family (both real and fictive) has proven to be a central motif, as are values of secularism over religion, a belief in individualism rather than collective enterprise, a fascination with conflict and confrontation, and adherence to traditional virtues. These codes impose frames of interpretation that audiences can relate to without fear of disorientation. The end result of this programming conformity is nothing less than the perpetuation of a boxed-in reality. TV programming is "boxed-in" to conform with the rectangular constraints of a 26-inch screen, a 22-minute time slot for plot resolution, followed by a story line filled with unblemished characters of implausible virtue and free-spending habits. Nothing of substance changes from one year to the next; only the actors and predicaments are re-packaged to cash in on the "flavour of the month." To be sure, the ground beneath television is shifting, with experimentation in TV styles that depart from convention. Role reversals, disjointed plot lines, open-ended conclusions, and quick cutaways are just a few of the Seinfeldization innovations in play at present. Still, the primacy of entertainment as the basis for TV programming remains unchallenged. Television wants to embrace as many consumers as possible, with the result that any extremism is generally sacrificed for fear of alienating audiences or repelling advertisers. Issues pertaining to diversity or change may be compromised or excluded in the rush for some common middle ground.

How do we account for this remarkable conformity in an industry with such potential creativity? An imperative to pander to mainstream audiences is one reason. As Jane Feuer (1987, 119) notes in commenting on television's inherent conservatism, "television takes to an extreme the film industry's reliance upon formulas to predict audience responses" (cited in Dines and Humez 1995). TV producers subscribe to a host of working rules that guide production practices and decision making from line-up to plot lines (Clarke 1996). The most important production values include: (1) the need to access and sustain a market, (2) the availability of program material, and (3) the practical economics of program production. Of particular relevance is television's reliance on advertising as a primary source of revenue. Most revenue is generated by big advertising and when advertisers are willing to pay $2.2 million for a 30-second slot during the Super Bowl, what other choice does TV programming have except to bow to commercial imperatives? Not surprisingly, the content of TV programming is driven by commercial imperatives rather than audience concerns. Programming is created to please advertisers who prefer programs that create the right atmosphere for product amplification. To the extent that audiences are important to programmers, they are seen as products (or commodities) for sale to advertisers. The bigger the audience, so says the cliché, the merrier the profits (Tehranian 1996).

If this line of argument is true, and evidence supports these assertions (Andersen 1996), the relationship between advertising and programming needs to be re-thought by way of inversion. Programming is not the normal function of television, with advertising as an interruption to the norm. Rather programming may be interpreted as an interruption to television's normal function as a medium of advertising. If programming is the filler between commercials, then television itself is one long commercial for connecting advertisers with the right kind of audience by way of programming breaks. Yet another inversion might to help us think "outside the box." We normally think that audiences watch television; more to the point, however, television watches people to monitor our interests, habits, and concerns. This monitored information is then used to create programs that target those audiences of special interest to advertisers. Even the distinction between programming and advertising has blurred ("commercialtainment") with the proliferation of placement ads, programming environments (certain products will advertise only on certain types of programs), MTV (music videos are ads), and tie-ins (especially on children's shows). As a result, TV programming has become more like advertising in its drive to glamorize consumption, while advertising becomes more program-like as a basis for breaking free of the commercial clutter. In short, the quality of programming is aimed at pleasing advertisers rather than audiences. Such a conclusion may have potentially unsettling implications for the representational basis of TV programming-minority relations.

Programming Diversity: The Good, the Bad, and the Really Ugly

Television has been widely criticized as being contrary to minority interests. Criticism has ranged from charges of discrimination to attacks on the media as a propaganda machine for white supremacy (hooks 1995). From the beginning, television has not known what to do with black characters (Wilkerson 1993). Just as society has struggled in the post-civil rights era, so too has television equivocated in its search for a role or status for Blacks that is acceptable to white Americans. On balance, TV programming appears to have cast minorities in the mould of marginal, problematic, stereotyped, decorative, or the "other." However useful such an assertion is for analysis, this framework cannot possibly address the dynamic aspects of TV programming, as images and symbols have evolved over time in response to shifting social and political circumstances (Gray 1995). As a result, TV representations of minority women and men are neither static nor consistent. What prevails instead are somewhat confusing hybrids that reflect and reinforce evolving representations about the status and role of minority women and men in society.

Consider a positive dimension. As Todd Gitlin (1996) notes in the journal *Dissent*, television has served as an instrument for advancing tolerance in a society that historically has thrived on intolerance beneath a veneer of self-righteous excuses. In the early years of network domination, when Americans watched the same shows, television helped to erode ethnocentrism while advancing the cause of tolerance and civil rights. Early television did not always foster conformity and stability: inadvertently, perhaps, a social climate for change was encouraged by eroding the parochialness of local experience and by enhancing cultural awareness about women and minorities (Meyrowitz and Maguire 1993). Television's greatest impact was on those whose physical location in society had restricted their social experiences. Prior to television, people's sense of belonging and positioning in time and space were narrowly bound by historical or geographical knowledge (Real 1989). With television, boundaries that once isolated the experiential world of majorities from minorities was challenged and transformed (Meyrowitz and Maguire 1993). Images of brutality towards Blacks were beamed into the living rooms of white America, with as much impact on the collective conscience as the videotaping of Rodney King's beating by the Los Angeles Police Department. Distinctions between black and white were further blurred with the portrayal of professional-class Blacks who were identical to their white counterparts in terms of outlook and values.

Four levels of discourse can be discerned with respect to TV images of diversity over time whose discursive framework can be compared and contrasted; namely, *denial, tolerance, acceptance*, and *contested*. This typology, in turn, appears to reflect comparable developments in Canadian and American society, with their evolutionary shift in the perception of diversity from assimilation and separation to integration and multiculturalism. Generally speaking, this typology reveals how television's depiction of minority women and men has evolved from one of denial of diversity to its tolerance and eventual acceptance, culminating in recent years in a focus on challenging conventionality in an age of defiance. To be sure, this typology itself is typically ideal in that categories can be interpreted as mutually exclusive, even if overlap and contradictory coexistence prevail in reality. Moreover, this typology reflects the work of Herman Gray (1995) in black ethnicity in American television, but has been adapted and broadened to include TV depictions of minority women and men in general.

I. Denial

A commitment to denying race by way of caricature characterized the core of TV programming from its inception. This seemingly contradictory objective reflected an intent to offer sponsors the least jarring entertainment to secure the largest possible audience. It ensured a medium that was largely exclusionary, and every effort was made to ignore subject matter or characterizations that might strike a discordant note with both sponsors and audiences. This denial took place on two fronts. First, the earliest TV shows, such as *Amos 'n Andy*, simply ignored diversity as relevant except as a basis for bad jokes and plot twists. These shows caricaturized minorities as stereotypes in conformity with white interests and the perpetuation of a racist and white supremacist social order. Then as now, Blacks were portrayed as lusty lotharios or ticking time bombs "straightjacketed as nitroglycerin explosive, fat-cat lazy, make daddy randy, or some combination of the three" (cited in Darling 2000, B3). The "latino-ness" of Lucy's husband, Ricky Ricardo, rarely intruded in the plot lines of *I Love Lucy*, except to make fun of his accent and mannerisms. In short, both minority women and men could be ignored except as objects of derision while being excluded on the grounds of their irrelevance or inferiority.

Second, later TV shows tended to eliminate or subordinate diversity in exchange for shared similarities and a commitment to formal equality. Denial accompanied this assimilationist mindset: minority women and men were shown to have been absorbed into society without much so much as a hint of racism or discriminatory barriers in the process. Yet the privileging of the hegemonic gaze of whiteness could hardly be ignored in the assimilationist rush to silence cultural and racial differences. In short, a dual invisibility was at play. Not only were minorities as minorities rendered invisible, but also ignored were the realities (both structural barriers and cultural inequities) that pervaded the lives and life-chances of minority women and men.

II. Tolerance

The very earliest TV shows espoused an image of diversity that denied as it assimilated or segregated. But the civil rights movement brought about a general shift in attitude, culminating in the first interracial kiss when Captain Kirk embraced Lieutenant Uhuru in the November 1968 airing of *Star Trek*. An assimilationist orientation endorsed a more tolerant attitude towards diversity as a basis for cultural difference in society. Variation existed to be sure, but minorities and majorities were fundamentally alike except for superficial differences that could be played for laughs or provide a plot twist without undermining a commitment to equality.

Casting minority characters as essentially white clones ensured the acceptance of TV programs such as *The Nat "King" Cole Show* or *The Lone Ranger* as well as the 1960s hits *I Spy*, *Julia*, or *Room 222*. Differences were deemed as incidental or irrelevant except to add a "dash of colour" to the program. Nor was there much opportunity for minorities to articulate their minorityness even if they had they wanted to. TV treatment of minority women and men was firmly planted within the framework of a dominant cultural discourse that defined racism and social problems as an individual problem in need of personal solution. Intergroup breakdowns were couched in the discourse of prejudice for narrative purposes. Once identified, prejudice was resolvable within the framework of a 22-minute plot sequence. Issues pertaining to history, social structure, racial conflict, and power sharing were generally ignored in keeping with television's superficial emphasis on character, dramatic action, and narrative.

In this discourse of tolerance, minorities were situated in circumstances that paralleled those of white mainstream society. Assimilation in this sense differs from pre-civil rights segregation in that TV shows and representations were anchored in the normative ideal of individual equality and social inclusion. Yet contradictions were easily exposed: black characters remained "tethered to a white middle class hegemonic universe" (Gray 1995, 88). Black representations were constructed from the perspective of a privileged white gaze whose angle of vision was defined by that normative order. As with the assimilationist perspective, the social and historical context of minority lives and life-chances were ignored. Shows that reflect this line of thinking include the 1970s and 1980s sitcoms *The Jeffersons* or *Fresh Prince of Bel Air*.

III. Acceptance

A commitment to multiculturalism reflects a shift in public discourse from tolerance to acceptance of diversity. Many black shows acknowledge this multicultural turn. The 1970s and 1980s witnessed the efflorescence of black shows that responded to activist demands for programs that were authentic and relevant to black experiences. Shows such as *Good Times* and *Sanford and Son* attempted to valorize the poor urban black experience without abandoning a commitment to middle-class values. The 1980s saw a displacement of the urban poor in a trend towards representations about upward mobility and middle-class affluence. Both *The Cosby Show* and *Different Strokes* fell into this category with their contradictory readings (for example, criticism of *The Cosby Show* as a middle-class family that happens to be black). Blackness may have been explicitly marked as preferred; yet these discourses and representations were generally (but not always) adjusted to conform with the privileged but unmarked gaze of whiteness.

At the core of this shift towards acceptance is an attempt to explore black lives from the perspective of black realities, experiences, and sensibilities. *The Cosby Show* proved pivotal in exploring what it meant to be an American from an African-American point of view. *Cosby*'s legacy is measured in the proliferation of black shows whose content, aesthetics, and narrative capitalized on black experiences. African-centricity was central in reconstructing black lives. Blackness was positioned at the centre of their social and cultural universe, not in the sense of privileging, but for the purpose of examining reality from a host of diverse perspectives (including class, gender, sexuality) and across a range of diverse issues (sexism, classism, homophobia).

IV. Contestation

There are signs of a new aesthetic best exemplified by shows such as *In Living Color*. *Frank's Place* and *Roc* are also good examples of this shift in the representational basis of TV programming. Representations of blackness differ from previous images in ways that challenge the status quo. Much of this boom in minority television programming and images can be attributed to the increasing fragmentation of the marketplace and the profitability of programming aimed at minority women and men (Cuff 1996). This shift in programming content allows greater exposure to both the political views and the social and cultural experiences of minority women and men. Yet there was some question as to whether minority perspectives that differed radically from the culture of consensus would be allowed in a medium so entrenched in conventional assumptions of acceptability that only safe minority entertainers with cross-over appeal (from Oprah and Whitney to Ricky and Jennifer) could hope for exposure. First, images of blackness tend to be multilayered and multiperspectival, even to the point of being contradictory. There is a willingness to play with and play off ambiguity, while engaging in a cultural critique of those versions of blackness that are rigid or unresponsive. Second, these images are not inherently resistant or explicitly oppositional but implicitly impart an alternative reading to dominant representation. This resistance is conveyed by a variety of techniques, including role reversals, reverse stereotyping, and satire and parody of whiteness. Third, there is no effort to conceal issues pertaining to race and racism as they apply to black representation. Instead of being hidden or silenced, they are openly interrogated and challenged—at least to the extent that is allowed by commercial network television.

Multicultural patterns of representation pose a challenge to the conventional aesthetic. Foremost is the possibility of offering new ways of representing blackness, apart from the hegemonic strategies of containment. Yet the failure of shows such as *In Living Color* or *Roc* is indicative of the barriers that need to be surmounted. Such unconventionality in programming may demand too much effort on the part of the audience. These disruptions to the hegemonic representation of minority women and men are not eagerly embraced by a commercial media whose natural inclination is to keep minority representation safe, simple, familiar, and non-threatening. That in turn created its own set of problems in which minorities were not minority enough. In the words of Sandra Oh, Korean-Canadian actor, as quoted in the *Globe and Mail* (Dec 28, 1996, C3), "Its tough being marginalized because of what you look like. There were a lot of times when I couldn't get an audition because [I didn't have] the right Asian features." The table below provides a brief comparison and contrast of these discourses.

Table 5.1:   Television's Images of Diversity

SOCIETAL ATTITUDES	SEGREGATION	ASSIMILATION	INTEGRATION	MULTICULTURALISM
STATUS OF DIVERSITY	denial	tolerance	acceptance	challenge
SOURCE OF SOLUTION	individualism	cultural differences	structure	hegemony
POLITICS OF DIVERSITY	absorption	fundamentally the same & equal	different but equal	identity politics/ politics of recognition
PERSPECTIVES ON DIVERSITY	melting pot	different in the same way	minorityness	radical differences
WHOSE GAZE?	white gaze	white/minority gaze	minority gaze	oppositional gaze
OUTCOME	whiteness	residual diversity	celebrating differences	resistance

How do we assess these changes in the representations of minority women and men? Herman Gray has argued that structural changes to television best account for this shift in network programming. A host of political, economic, and institutional conditions have accelerated changes in media representation of minorities since the mid-1980s. The appearance of Fox network and the proliferation of cable TV has eroded the audience base that networks would like to deliver to advertisers. That in return has altered the kind of advertising rates that networks can charge. The network's share of the viewing audience plummeted from 76 percent in 1983 to only 60 percent in 1990. Yet minority viewers continued to remain constant, with estimates of 40 percent more black network viewers than white. Those kinds of numbers prompted a re-thinking of minority audiences as potentially lucrative markets.

As competition intensified in TV land, the stakes became higher. Niche marketing and narrowcasting emerged as strategies for negotiating complex and competitive environments. Programming aimed at black audiences was perceived as a low-risk and highly exploitative market niche. The presence of high-profile media stars from the Michaels to Oprah helped to translate blackness into a saleable commodity. Conversely, the popularity of shows such as *Roseanne* and *Cosby* revealed that audiences would accept departures from the norm of middle-class whiteness. No longer constrained by the principle of the least objectionable programming with the fragmentation of the market, networks found themselves in a position to translate blackness into a commodity for packaging and marketing. Images of blackness were incorporated into a strategy that would allow the media to do what do they best: "generate profits by identifying and packaging dominant social and cultural moods" (Gray 1995, 69).

CASE STUDY: Between the Lines: *The Cosby Show*

The pernicious effects of negative media racial stereotyping are widely known (Cowen 1991). Stereotyping can lead to the scapegoating or dehumanizing of minorities while minority women and men may experience a sense of inferiority and marginality. What happens, however, when minorities are portrayed in non-stereotypical fashion? A host of questions arise: Is it possible to eliminate stereotyping in the media or do new stereotypes replace the old? Should such a portrayal be endorsed as enlightened and progressive or shunned as duplicitous and degrading? Is positive stereotyping conducive to improving public attitudes, or does racist thought reappear in a different format to justify privilege or rationalize (away) inferiority in a market-driven society? What does the acceptance of positive minority images say about society at large? The popularity and universal appeal of the long-running situation comedy *The Cosby Show* provides a valuable case study for answering these questions. Was Cosby a straightforward sitcom about an affluent middle-class black family, or was it really a cynical attempt by corporate America to employ a racist subtext to pretend that hard work can overcome racism and those who fail only have themselves to blame? (Ross 1996).

The Cosby Show needs little in the way of introduction, even for those who restrict their television viewing to "channel surfing." The program, which aired between 1984 and 1992 and ranked near the top of the yearly Neilson's ratings, involved a black middle-class family. The parents were professionals, namely, Cliff Huxtable, a gynecologist, and his partner, Clair, a lawyer. Both parents coped cheerfully and successfully with a host of middle-class problems involving their children Theo, Sondra, Denise, Vanesa, and Rudi as each grew into young adulthood. The show dealt with numerous issues of relevance to middle-class families, but few incidents involved the grittiness of everyday black reality, which would have marred the Huxtable's idyllic existence. This progressive image contrasted sharply with the dysfunctionality that confronts some black families in the real world as a result of racism, drugs, unemployment, single parenting, and violence.

Critics and the general public reacted variably to this enlightened image of black family life. Historically, according to John Fiske (1994), Americans have had little difficulty in accepting African-American males as long as their power was confined to sports or entertainment. Cosby (along with O.J. Simpson) emerged as one of the few African-American males who typified the tamed and successful black man. This benign image contrasts sharply with public perceptions of uncontrolled black males who pose a sexual threat to the social and cultural order (Fiske 1994). For some, the Cosby family imparted a badly needed positive "spin" to the largely negative portrayal of Blacks on television. Others were not so sure about its alleged benefits. They saw a sinister underside that not only glossed over black reality in a white-dominated society, but also fostered unrealistic expectations. *The Cosby Show* "proved" that Blacks could make it in a white society; those who failed had only themselves to blame (rather than class or race)—a philosophy consistent with the Reagonomics of the 1980s. The following criticisms were most common:

- Black reality is airbrushed by being scrubbed clean of a world with guns, drugs, dysfunctional families, and violence.
- The Cosby characters are accused of being "Afro-Saxons" or "oreos"— white middle class on the inside, black outside.
- The show reflects a "mammy-syndrome" — white actors put on black faces to mimic Eurocentric conventions while entertaining white audiences.
- While presenting a functioning black family in a positive light, the show revels in their "middle-classness" rather than in their "blackness," in effect denying or rejecting the value of the "Other" as the "other."
- Blacks and whites may coexist in harmony only as long as there is no infringement on white supremacy in the racial hierarchy (hooks, 1995).

In short, a negative spin could easily be applied to *The Cosby Show*. Blacks were being set up for failure, while whites basked in the munificence of the status quo. Rather than diminishing the importance of race, in other words, the show reinforced more subtle and sophisticated patterns of racial thought.

It is obvious that *The Cosby Show* can be interpreted positively or negatively: positive, in dashing conventional ("negative") stereotypes; negative, in inventing new stereotypes consistent with a belief in the (a) American dream and the essential fairness of the American way, (b) decline of poverty as a pervasive problem, (c) elimination of racism with the entrenchment of equal opportunity and government intervention, (d) sanctity of self-sufficiency and a conventional family, and (e) acceptability of others as long as they conform and obey. Its two-edged quality is demonstrated in audience reactions. Some rejected *Cosby* as just another put-down of Blacks, albeit in a circuitous manner; others endorsed the show as a progressive step forward in reversing debilitating stereotypes. Still others saw its popularity as a vindication of the American way as well as a sign of diminishing racial barriers because of civil rights laws and affirmative action. In short, the enlightened racism in *The Cosby Show* is about power and privilege. It reflects the ability of those with power to define what is acceptable and what is not. Blacks must deny ("whitewash") their blackness if they hope to avoid exclusion. Issues related to race and racism are sanitized of any disruptive properties. Black families such as the Huxtables are "bleached" of their blackness in accordance with the principles and practices of a fantasy world.

***

Programming outside the Box

How then does the medium handle diversity without eroding its centre or erasing differences? Nearly a decade after the appearance of *The Cosby Show*, the report card on television and race is as uncertain as ever. Is the emphasis on minority males as inherently aggressive evidence of a brave new realism, or a more sophisticated form of stereotyping that focuses on demeaning and one-sided portrayals rather than the whole picture, where the exception *is* the rule, where mainstream audiences can project their phobias and fears onto scapegoated groups, and where stereotyped programming is easier to execute because of less consumer resistance? (Wilkerson 1993). However, the appearance of diversity is one thing, the implementation of meaningful diversity is another, especially when the vast majority of minority characters appeared on screen for less than one minute (Weintraub 2000). Furthermore, most of the characters were concentrated on Monday and Friday nights, and on the UPN and WB networks, rather than the major networks. The study concluded by pointing out that the politics of the inclusion or exclusion reflect, in strikingly visual terms, unresolved questions about power imbalances in our society" (cited Reuters/ Variety 2000).

Nor is there evidence of blacks and whites coming together. Current programming provides a mirror reflection of the social cleavages that continue to segregate white Americans and African-Americans (Storm 1996). The sitcom world remains as rigidly segregated as it did in *The Cosby Show*. The few series that show minorities in a household setting are generally restricted to sitcoms or air on networks that command only a small fraction of viewers (Weintraub 2000). Of the 64 sitcoms that aired between September and March of 1995-96 on the six American networks, only 12 had racially mixed casts. The remaining 52 sitcoms were segregated, with 40 having all-white casts, 12 with all-black casts, and the rest featuring minorities as peripheral to the lives of the main characters. This prompted Anne-Marie Johnson of the Minority Employment Committee of SAG to comment, "We're furniture. We're isolated from the main action and dependent on white characters. We really could be rented and moved around" (cited in Weintraub 2000, D5). The situation is a bit better in dramas, most of which occur in workplaces such as hospitals or law offices. Of the 41 dramas that aired in 1996, 21 were racially mixed in having at least one featured black and one regular white character (Storm 1996). Even tastes differ, with prime time segregation alive and well in terms of white preferences and black preferences (Croteau and Hoynes 2000). Not one of the 10 most popular sitcoms in black households made the list of the top 10 favourites in white households. In 1998 *The Steve Harvey Show* was ranked as "number one" in black households but 98th in white households (and 127th in 1999). By contrast, *Friends* remains the number one show in white households but only 91st in black households (88th in 1999) (Huff 2000). Such segmentation appears to reflect a growing tendency to narrowcast audiences for pitching products appropriately.

How do we account for this disparity in popularity? Why do black and white viewers share the same preferences in drama but divide along racial lines when tuning in to sitcoms? The politics of humour and comedy are critical. In the workplaces where most TV dramas occur, Blacks and whites must learn to interact and get along by speaking a similar language, according to Jonathan Storm (1996). In the homes and neighbourhoods of sitcoms, Blacks and whites live in different worlds. As well, there are greater risks associated with comedy and humour. Sitcoms must rely on humour to comment on cultural differences or to expose prejudice. Yet making minorities the object of humour may backfire if it fails to take into account unequal contexts and differential consequences. After all, African-Americans have historically figured in the culture as objects of humour, as Herman Gray (in Storm 1996) notes. This in turn makes them more susceptible to derision, stereotype, and scorn through humour.

At the core of the crisis in the representational politics of TV programming is the politically loaded issue of diversity. What exactly is meant by engaging diversity, and how much institutional inclusiveness is sufficient to please everyone? Two separate issues are at play: first, the inclusion of minority women and men and, second, the inclusion of ethnicity as different, real, and legitimate. The inclusion of minorities in TV programming is beyond dispute, even to the point where minority representations on television are disproportional to their numbers in the population. According to a Screen Actors Guild study of 295 prime time programming hours on six broadcast networks, African-Americans are overrepresented, accounting for 16 percent of all characters. Yet physical presence is one thing, representation by ethnicity, another. Inclusion of ethnicity as different yet equal requires a much sharper and sustained commitment towards inclusiveness. It also means that the television industry must be prepared to endure criticism regardless of what it does. For some, the point of equality is to ensure that differences are irrelevant in determining who gets what. For others, true equality and commitment to diversity occurs when differences are taken into account. For still others, ignoring diversity in TV programming leads to charges of racism by default, yet playing up the racial angle is viewed as condoning stereotypes and essentializing the ethnicity of minorities to the exclusion of other attributes. To date, television appears to have fumbled the opportunity to engage ethnicity, and this disparity continues to play politics with the representational basis of minority relationship in TV programming.

TV programming occupies an awkward position in constructively engaging diversity. This ambivalence may be inevitable in those kinds of reality programming that crave conflict and resolution, and both heroes and villains, thus making it easy to fall back on recognizable stereotypes. For TV programming it might be easier to retreat into deeply embedded cultural codes given the realities of a multichannel universe controlled by roving fingers on the remote control (Darling 2000). And when diversity issues are addressed in a thoughtful manner, they are damned if they do, and damned if they don't. Doing nothing invites accusations of racism and Eurocentrism; doing something can invoke charges of tokenism or pandering to "political correctness." Other initiatives are perceived as little more than political expediency in complying with government dictates or staying one step ahead of the law. Positive portrayals are accused of airbrushing reality; negative depictions are denounced for peddling stereotypes. Attempts at more realistic portrayals are doomed, not because of inferior quality, but because of constraints from TV formulas to boxed-in realities. Programming that deals with complex issues or painful experiences is thought to be inconsistent with the happy-face subliminalities conveyed by advertising. TV programming is intent on offering sponsors the least jarring entertainment by ignoring references to minority women and men that might strike a discordant chord. By its very nature, TV programming must collapse, distil, and distort "reality" because of time constraints, dramatic expediency, and the perpetual motion imagery and sound expected by a speeded-up audience. The nature of humour is particularly problematic. Sitcoms must rely on humour in milking a situation for all its angles. Yet humour does not always carry well across social and cultural boundaries. Accordingly, a "playing them for laughs" angle has the effect of de-politicizing minority contributions to society while neutering differences to minimize their political potency.

Nor is there any consensus as to how to depict diversity. Should differences be highlighted to draw attention to disadvantages or is it best to ignore differences in hopes of conveying a message of commonality "under the skin"? Responses vary. To one side are those who believe race should not be an issue if everyone is the same and is treated accordingly. To the other side are those who believe that ignoring race is irresponsible because differences matter in real life, whether we like it or not. Paradoxically, the problem may not lie in applying different standards, but in casting everyone as the same, since the consequences of a one-size-fits-all casting has a different impact when the starting blocks are different and the playing field is uneven. The stereotyping of a minority is different than the stereotyping of a majority; after all, minorities carry a cultural weight in society that renders them more vulnerable to typecasting (Elmasry 1999). This inconsistency crosses racial boundaries. Just as the mainstream divides into different publics, so too are minorities divided over proposals for improving media representation. Some minorities prefer to be depicted in high-status images, thus providing role models; others want to be portrayed as an ordinary part of the mainstream, thus reflecting the realities of ordinary minority women and men. An endorsement of cultural separateness as a preferred representational basis is counteracted by the principle of integration as the preferred route. J. Fred MacDonald (1994) expresses the conundrum at the heart of media minority representations:

> Should blacks be shown only as middle class and assimilated, as are most whites, or is this a denial of racial authenticity? Should blacks be portrayed in terms of the urban underclass, especially when such imagery might appear crude or unaccomplished? Should the folk images of rural blacks ... be propagated now as authentic, or should they be buried as anachronistic and self-defeating?

Even programs that break down racial stereotypes are subject to scrutiny and criticism. Good intentions are insufficient—sometimes counterproductive—if the producers fail to appreciate the social context and cultural consequences. That ambiguity alone may account for media reluctance in moving upwards and forwards in taking differences seriously.

CHAPTER 6

ADVERTISING AND MINORITIES

Framing the Problem

In our consumer-oriented society, a complex system of advertising and marketing has evolved that conflates popularity and self-esteem with conspicuous consumerism. Advertising is the catalyst behind the consumerism of a capitalist society, and the financial footing that drives the mainstream media. That is, the mainstream media, as powerful marketing tools, are little more than an excuse for the promotion of advertising. In the words of a former publisher of the *Globe and Mail*, "By 1990, publishers of mass circulation daily newspapers will finally stop kidding themselves that they are in the newspaper business and admit they are primarily in the business of carrying advertised messages" (cited in Czerny et al. 1994, 124). A reciprocal relation is thought to exist: Mainstream media arguably exist to provide an outlet for advertising by attracting as wide an audience as possible. Pressure to secure high audience ratings, in turn, shapes the media's form and functions. Yet the relationship is lop-sided. As Matthew P. McAllister (1995, 29) says with respect to the pivotal role of advertising to the mainstream media, "The rule of thumb in modern television is what advertising wants, advertising gets." As well, advertising represents a powerful social force in its own right, with the capacity to shape and to mould while unmasking insights into the cultural dimensions of society (Goldman 1992; Barr 1994; Singer 1995). As process or outcome, advertising connects consumer products with what is socially acceptable by capitalizing on our insecurities and dormant desires. Its power and pervasiveness ensures that many of us harbour a love-hate relationship with advertising. We enjoy being massaged by the message of "more," but nevertheless deplore the banality of capitulating to the superficiality of a material world. Much of this ambiguity is the result of the sheer volume of advertising to which we are exposed. Most of us will see millions of ads that cumulatively "squander" nearly three years of our lives (Jacobson and Mazur 1995). This kind of exposure can be a blessing or a curse depending on what is expected of the mainstream media and where we stand on the socio-political spectrum.

Public reaction to advertising is mixed. Media pundits drone on about the pros and cons without taking into account the broader context in which advertising derives its meaning, legitimacy, and punch. Advertising is interpreted by some as a highly sophisticated system of twentieth-century art whose aesthetic dimensions must be valued and appreciated (Rutherford 1995). Others endorse advertising as a necessary cost of doing business in a consumer society. Still others equate advertising with capitalist propaganda whose duplicitous messages from mouthwash to toilet cleanser are just about as accurate and as equally corrosive (*The Ecologist* 1989). Put bluntly, advertising is blamed for everything from the collapse of contemporary society to intellectual dwarfism. Advertising not only exploits our obsession with appearance-based self-esteem; it also creates unhealthy dependencies because relief is promised to be only a purchasable fantasy away. Worse still, advertising encourages waste, contributes to the disfigurement of the environment, distorts human values by massaging the message of more to the many, and bolsters the prevailing distribution of power and resources in a capitalist society. Even "green" advertising is suspect since the underlying message is the same, that is: use more, not less. After all, an environmentally friendly car is still a gas-guzzling, steel-bending commodity at odds with clean air and public transit. Not surprisingly, even the widely acclaimed slogan to reduce, recycle, and reuse has been co-opted by big business for corporate enhancement or market penetration (*The Ecologist* 1989).

No less controversial is the relationship between minorities and advertising. A degree of ambiguity in the representational basis of advertising-minority relations can be expected of a process whose dynamic is organized around the principle of image-based persuasion. Much of this ambivalence reflects the power of advertising to define what is acceptable and normal by emphasizing certain aspects of reality while dismissing others as irrelevant or inferior. Until recently, neither ethnicity nor minority women or men were regarded as central to mainstream advertising, given a widespread belief that only "white sells." Minorities rarely appeared in ads for fear of alienating a white consumer base. When they did appear, albeit briefly, minority women and men were often cast as problems, in stereotypical terms, in the decorative sense of adding a splash of colour to mainstream products, ghettoized into serving the minority market, or positioned around goods consumed by minority women and men. In recent years, however, advertising has embraced the symbols of diversity as a key component for massaging the message of more to both mainstream and minority markets. Minority women and men are routinely porated into all types of advertising and marketing strategies, with the result that inclusiveness initiatives would appear to be setting the pace for other media. But while the inclusion of minorities in advertising is to be applauded, appearances may be deceiving, with progress in some areas neutralized by stagnation in others. Increases in the quantity of minority women and men may be offset by the quality of representations that continue to stereotype, deny the legitimacy of ethnicity for branding or marketing, or run the risk of commodifying diversity for ulterior purposes. And, as always, the inclusion of diversity in stereotypical or superficial terms may aggravate the very problem that inclusiveness in advertising sought to circumvent.

To the extent that representational images of minority women and men continue to be couched in compromise by mainstream advertising, this chapter explores the improving yet contested politics of minority-advertising relations. It acknowledges the inclusion of minorities into mainstream advertising in response to several factors, including expansion of a minority market, strategic shifts because of a crisis in advertising, and changes in social attitudes towards diversity as a basis for recognition and reward. This chapter also contends that "diversity sells"; nevertheless, inclusion runs the risk of commodifying minorities by appropriating only the symbols of diversity as a basis for connecting with mainstream audiences. Until advertising is taken to the next level and stops playing "pretend pluralism," its commitment to diversity will be subject to criticism as token or superficial. The chapter begins by examining the logic behind the goals and functions of advertising as a medium and sales tool. This is followed by a look at the crisis in advertising that has prompted a re-thinking of the strategies for connecting with increasingly diverse and demanding audiences. The next section looks at how minorities have fared under advertising, both in the past and at present. The final section explores some of the dilemmas associated with improving the representational basis of minority-advertising relations. The likelihood of resolving these challenges is uncertain, insofar as mainstream advertising is experiencing dual pressures, namely, to cater to emergent minority groups as well to convey positive minority images to mainstream audiences, without losing sight of the bottom line.

The Dynamics of Advertising

The ubiquity of mainstream advertising would suggest the impossibility of deriving patterns from its varied forms. Yet advertising as a system of persuasion appears to follow certain patterns that transcend particularities associated with print or electronic media. Many of these patterns may be attributed to the commercial imperatives associated with connecting audiences to commodities by way of verbal and visual images. Foremost is the need to generate profits by selling products, to generate brand name recognition, and to foster corporate legitimacy (Williamson 1978). Central to all advertising is a simple message: for every so-called need, there is a product solution (Andersen 1996). Widely regarded strategies for manufacturing discontent while glamorizing consumption are employed to ensure product amplification, namely, targeting a market, capturing attention, arousing interest, fostering images, neutralizing doubts, and creating conviction.

Acknowledging a distinction between manifest (articulated) and latent (unintended) functions yields insights into the logic behind advertising. A manifest function is to sell a product by symbolically linking consumers with a commodity or service. A social value component is conferred on the product beyond its material need through images and messages that purportedly strike a responsive chord with the right kind of crowd. The latent function entails the selling of fantasies by manufacturing a discontent with the present while glamorizing consumption as a solution to the problem of "keeping up with the

Joneses." Strategies have evolved to perpetuate this latent message: As recently as the mid-twentieth century, ads sold a product by touting its virtues and practical applications. However, contemporary advertising sells fantasies by employing images that massage the message of more to the many. Buying into fantasies by way of images transports people into a world of popularity and a lifestyle anchored around the pursuit of conspicuous consumption. Consumer advertising exploits audiences by preying on gaps in their self-esteem by way of seductive images and fantasies (popularity, sex appeal, intelligence) whose cumulative effects remind us that we are never good enough. This association makes it difficult to separate advertising from discourses embedded in capitalist ideology (McAllister 1995). Equating advertising with dominant ideology reinforces its hegemonic properties on behalf of capitalism. The normalizing consumption within the framework of a capitalist society ensures that audiences become more actively involved in perpetuating patterns of control by consent rather than coercion.

In short, advertising is much more than a process of moving goods off a shelf. It goes beyond a fact sheet about the product in question. In the final analysis, advertising constitutes a discourse in defence of dominant ideology. Advertising is ideological in being loaded with ideas and ideals that extol the existing and unequal social order while excluding perspectives at odds with the message of "buy, buy, buy." It also upholds a philosophy of life commensurate with core societal values about the good life in a capitalistic society by spinning seductive images and fantasies (popularity, sex appeal, intelligence) that define who we would like to be and how we would like others to see us. Advertising promotes a lifestyle dedicated to the pursuit of consumerism, with its cultural correlates of greed and envy and environmental destruction through waste and materialism (see Linden 1997). As a system of persuasion, advertising is akin to systemic propaganda: To the extent that every ad says it's better to buy than not to buy, advertising is propaganda; in that every ad reinforces the social ideal of consumerism as inevitable, advertising is propaganda; in that advertising masquerades as a secular religion that declares, "buy and you will be saved," advertising is said to be propaganda; insofar as advertising teaches us to stroke our self-esteem from taking pride in our external appearance and material possessions, it is propaganda; and by equating consumerism as a matter of individual choice rather than a socially structured process, advertising is propaganda (see also Jhally 1989). The cumulative effect of advertising as propaganda is formidable. Singly, and taken out of context, each ad may not make much difference. Collectively, however, their impact cannot be discounted since advertising instils the essential cultural nightmare in our society: the fear of failure and envy of success. And in a society where conformity and consumption have been perceived as the solution to this paradox of fitting in while standing apart, the notion of minorityness is likely to receive a frosty reception in terms of what is acceptable and what is undesirable.

I. Deconstructing Advertising: "Manufacturing Discontent"

The content of advertising is highly diverse because of print and electronic media. Language, symbols, and imagery vary over time in response to evolving trends and across space with respect to prevailing norms. Yet all advertising must conform to certain codes if it is to communicate successfully as a system of persuasion. These codes (or rules) apply to all advertising, from print to electronic, from conventional ads to the new advertisements. The fact that these rules are violated on occasion tends to reinforce their pervasiveness, as was the case with Volkswagen Beetles or with Benetton clothing. Even the "new" anti-ad advertising reaffirms the rules for connecting audiences with the message of more, despite utilizing a different tact for pitching products to an increasingly jaded public. The essential components of successful advertising are six-fold: target a market, attract attention, arouse interest, construct images, neutralize doubts, and create conviction.

A. Targeting Markets

In contrast to the days of mass marketing, advertising strategies are based on targeting groups who are identifiable, accessible, measurable, and profitable. Advertisers prefer to link a specific product with a particular target group by designing a campaign around the needs, fantasies, anxieties, and values of the desired segment. Complex tests are employed to determine what kind of advertising and marketing strategy best responds to the likes and dislikes of a particular market. Those between the ages of 13 and 25 are a widely sought commodity because they are perceived to have money to burn, be free of financial responsibilities such as mortgages, and be susceptible to influence regarding brand preferences (Klein 1999). The middle-aged and senior citizen tend to be ignored by advertising. Their high per capita incomes are offset by perceptions of fixed brand preferences or by age-specific products such as dental adhesives and anti-continence shields (Singer 1995). Minority women and men have been ignored for these and other reasons, although a booming ethnic market is exerting pressure for more visibility.

B. Attracting Attention

Before something can be purchased, it must first be noticed. Because the world is inundated with ads, each vying for our attention and commitment, it is doubly important to catch people's attention. This commercial clutter exerts pressure on advertising to stand out from the crowd by way of attention-seeking devices, such as the use of humour, shock value, noise, juxtaposition and oppositions, or bold splashes of colour. The use of minority women and men as attention-grabbers has been effectively exploited by the branding tactics of Benetton (see case study, this chapter).

C. Arousing Interest

Interest is created by playing on audience emotion or stimulating new needs—
in the main, by tapping into people's fears, insecurities, and emotions. In that
disenchantment with the present is not necessarily a "natural" state of affairs,
advertising must generate an interest in new needs that go beyond basic
functions. At the heart of this arousal process is the manufacturing of discontent
by exploiting our fears of being unattractive, unpopular, and uncool. For
example, underarm deodorants exist, not because we perspire, but because
unwanted perspiration has been defined and marketed as an anxiety-laden
situation that threatens our self-image as cool under pressure. In others words,
the underlying message of each and every ad is all too familiar: "Hey, you. Pay
attention. Have I got something for you that you can't refuse, especially now that
I've drawn your attention to those shortcomings that you didn't even know
existed before."

D. Fostering Images

At one time advertising sold products by pitching information and attributes.
This style of advertising has been replaced by ads that sell by image-association.
Since the 1980s, advertising has again shifted its focus, from the promoting of
actual products to selling a lifestyle based on images surrounding a particular
brand such as Nike or Tommy Hilfiger (Klein 1999). Why images? An image
can condense messages by relying on symbols or metaphors that elicit an
appropriate emotional response by associating a product with a particular market
segment that is receptive to these messages. For example, many have de-cried
beer ads as sexist, with their emphasis on blondes, partying, and rock and roll.
Yet the primary consumers of beer remain young white males whose interests are
animated by lust, sex, and good times (Salter 1989; see Insider Report on
Marketing Beer). In short, advertising signifies a connection between the
meaning of products and the corresponding images associated with their
consumption.

This linkage suggests that ad effectiveness rests with appropriating
meaningful elements of our lived world, then grafting these cultural meanings
onto the world of consumers by tapping into fantasies or fears related to
popularity and power. It also suggests that ads bestow commodities with special
meaning and socially added value by creating pleasing images that transform
anxieties into satisfactions (Rutherford 1995). This focus on images suggests
that advertising is really about buying customers (rather than selling products)
by linking commodities with what is defined as socially desirable. In this sense
advertising represents a discourse, not about things, but about how advertising
images are connected to important domains in our lives and definitions of the
good life. And it is precisely this imaging process that has proven to be both a
benefit and cost to minority women and men, depending on prevailing images
of diversity in society.

E. Neutralizing Doubts

It is important to neutralize any doubts an audience may have about a certain product. Consumers are understandably sceptical about ads, with their exaggerated claims for the good life. Doubts about the product must be erased; appeals to reason, tradition, or science are often employed to convey a positive image. The use of celebrities and sports figures to endorse a product is an effective way of neutralizing doubts. Reliance on minority women and men has proven somewhat controversial, given public ambivalence about diversity as a problem or a solution.

F. Securing Conviction

People need to be convinced that they are making the right choice—that the product under consideration will make them feel smarter, bigger (or thinner), more popular, or healthier. Conviction needs to be created through positive reinforcement. To reinforce decision making, the advertising media rely on reassuring images (puppies and babies), evocative symbols (natural world or opulence), and positive associations (sex, science, celebrities, or tradition). The degree to which minority women and men will foster confidence in a product will vary with the product in question, the intended audience, and the prevailing social climate.

These six stages (or components) lie at the heart of all successful forms of persuasion, including advertising and marketing. Yet too mechanical an endorsement of these rules can prove problematic, especially when audiences become bored or see through the charade of massaging the message of more for the many.

II. Crisis in Advertising

In the early 1980s the advertising industry confronted a crisis of identity. The combination of advertising clutter and remote control technology sent the industry scurrying to devise new means for overcoming these obstacles. Even more worrying was the industry perception that conventional ads had become emotionally bankrupt because of viewer cynicism and attitude. Consumers exhibited a pattern of resistance at being manipulated and positioned by overstructured ads and preferred readings. Traditional images lost their lustre as well-worn formulas began to exhaust themselves. Recurrent frames elicited yawns of "seen that, done that" among disaffected and media-savvy viewers, many of whom bristled at the duplicity behind the process and withdrew their support. Feminist and minority critics became increasingly edgy over media misrepresentations of women and people of colour. Not surprisingly, the advertising industry had little option except to cast about for more innovative aesthetic structures and salient images if viewer interest was to be recaptured (Goldman 1992). Of those developments that contributed to the criticism, these proved most challenging:

1. Audiences are swamped by the sheer volume of advertising. Of the hundreds that people "see" each day, only a small number even register in our consciousness, let alone strike a responsive chord. The combination of ad saturation and clutter, together with viewer alienation and zapping technologies, creates the potential for consumer resistance (Goldman 1992).

2. Many are openly hostile to advertising. Ads are castigated as visually polluting and deceitfully insulting to a person's intelligence. The fact that advertising must create a demand for things we don't need or necessarily want does not bolster its credibility.

3. Surveys indicate that the things that make us "happy" are not material but social (from personal autonomy to self-esteem to friendships). Advertising by contrast is guided by the principle that satisfaction can only be derived from the marketplace. If things are not the locus of perceived happiness, Jhally (1995) contends, then this puts pressure on advertising to link commodities or brands with what is defined as the good life.

4. Brand name recognition is increasingly problematic. We are under pressure to consume commodities that are virtually indistinguishable from others in that category (think commercial beers). Without product variation, ads must focus instead on creating images that cater to specific markets. Yet this strategy subjects advertising to charges of phoniness, shallowness, and manipulation.

5. Advertising must produce commercial messages that do not offend anyone. In an era of identity politics and political correctness, charges of racism or sexism or homophobia can quickly erode a cultivated product image or corporate credibility. Regulatory agencies also need to be placated. That puts the onus on advertising to be creative without being offensive.

The industry responded with a raft of different strategies. Most seemingly violated the golden rules of advertising (see Goldman 1992 for full discussion). Some ad campaigns sought to camouflage the content and strategies of conventional advertising behind a haze of black and white photography, grainy images, ambiguous messages, jerky camera movements, a blasé and indifferent prevailing mood, non-conventional editing, and greater transparency of the persuasion process. Unorthodox images proved appealing precisely because of their difference from conventional images and clichéd strategies. Other strategies aimed at "outing" ads. Advertisers incorporated a criticism of ads by adopting positions of mocking self-awareness with respect to the advertising process itself. Strategies used by advertisers included incorporating consumer resistance into the promotional strategy, foregrounding those conventional codes that once organized advertising design, and mocking the ads of competitors or the use of advertisements in general. By co-opting attitudes of defiance and indifference into the ad, advertisers hoped that the resultant parody would counter viewer alienation and resentment at being blatantly exploited. Goldman (1992, 182) comments on the message in Levi's "thinking wink" campaign of the mid-1980s:

We know that you're fed up with phony bullshit about owning commodities and being all you can be. We know you're fed up with mindless conformist consumerism so.... It also says I recognize I'm in a commercial, and that what came before me was only a commercial, a fantasy. And you (the viewer) recognize that too. But that's okay, because I (like you) can appreciate and enjoy that.

Put bluntly, the new advertising was designed with viewer resistance in mind. Advertising was aimed at the disaffected young with ads that captured the detachment and resentment of a generation weaned on commercial media. Attention-grabbing devices prevailed; grittiness replaced glamour as a key image; ambiguities took precedence over clarity as overt statements that revel in resistance rather than compliance. Resistance could be neutralized by incorporating images of resentment that extolled ironic detachment and laconic indifference (the "knowing wink"). Viewers sought reassurance that they were too media "hip" to be duped by the phoniness of advertising. Coolness was the ultimate goal, either the street-cool of inner-city kids or the white male cool of indifference.

Yet appearances can be deceiving. The messages remain the same: buy, buy, buy. Even the codes remain the same, since all advertising must target a market, attract attention, foster interest, create images, neutralize resistance, and create conviction. Only the content has changed with an array of images that inverts convention by standing orthodoxy on its head (Goldman 1992). Nevertheless, the relationship between advertising and its representations of minorities has shifted accordingly because of this postmodernist inversion with respect to definitions of acceptability and desirability. The next case study will explore the increasingly contested relationship between diversity and the new advertising.

CASE STUDY: Benetton—Ads of Colour

How would you respond to an advertising campaign whose *images* revolved around newborn babies covered in blood and connected by an umbilical cord? Around a black women breastfeeding a white baby, a nun and priest kissing, the bloodstained T-shirt and pants of a freedom fighter, a black horse mounting a white horse, or a lower torso with HIV Positive tattooed on it? Many will recognize this reference to ads for Benetton, the enormously successful Italian clothing giant with sales of $2 billion (U.S.) and 7,000 retail outlets on six continents. In spite of (or because of) the controversy generated by these ads, Benetton has become an international household name primarily on the strength of an issue-oriented advertising campaign based on selling the image of social consciousness (Hume 1994).

Benetton has relied on minority women and men—often in juxtaposition with whiteness—as a basis for advertising. By invoking what are often startling contrasts between blackness and whiteness, the use of visually arresting images of diversity has rescued Benetton ads from the commercial clutter while forging brand loyalty with media-savvy and socially consciousness young people. Reliance on minorities has helped to target an audience, attract attention, arouse interest, construct appropriate image, neutralize resistance, and create conviction. To be sure, these images rarely entail references to ethnicity beyond the physical aspect. Nor are these images situated within the context of power and privilege except perhaps in an oblique way. Nevertheless, the high-profile use of minority images puts Benetton at the front of the postmodern shift that celebrates differences as something to be endorsed rather than rejected. There is no question that the jarring images associated with Benetton violate the fundamental rules of conventional advertising, most of which seek to lull the audience through promulgation of "feel good" content into acceptance of a fantasy-filled status quo. Most ads operate on the principle of creating needs that can be satisfied only with the purchase of product x (Hume 1994). Advertising claims for product x have nothing to do with the truth but everything to do with deception, in the same way that cavorting about in a crystal-clear stream has nothing to do with the purity of cigarettes but everything to do with positive associations. By contrast, Benetton specializes in pricking people's conscience through the use of images that startle or provoke. Except for their eye-catching appeal, these ads appear to violate every rule in the book about seducing the masses. However, these Benetton ads are not intended for everyone: they are aimed at the relatively affluent segment of the population between the ages of 18 and 45, who have ample amounts of disposable income with which to put their principles into spending. As "badge goods," in other words, they say something about the users above and beyond the functionality of the product.

Reactions to this unique strategy for selling a product have varied. Some applaud Benetton's boldness; they welcome the idea of making the masses more aware of contemporary issues through the medium of advertising. Placing images within an altered context invests advertising imagery with a formidable range of power that has yet to be fully appreciated or explored. Others recognize that Benetton is selling an image based on attitude rather than anything to do with the product. The ads may convey a message of concern and willingness to be connected with the world at large, yet Benetton's ads, like others, pitch colourful images to attract the interest of a specific market. Still others are critical of Benetton for capitalizing on the diversity or misfortunes of others as a basis for generating profit. Benetton exists to make money, and the radical assumption that corporate awareness and risk taking could be selling points in their own right (Hume 1994) is simply a marketing ploy of ethically dubious value.

Benetton fully understands that many are repulsed by these hard-hitting images; that is precisely the point. Benetton has written off that part of the market that is unlikely to buy into these images or what they stand for. These ads prefer to zero in on that segment of the market that responds to unorthodox pitches. For young people who are tired of "fake" ads, Benetton provides an image and product association that encourages sceptical individuals to feel clever through the creation of their own messages about social consciousness. It also provides eager consumers with the go-ahead to make purchases without forsaking their principles. And as every leading-edge company recognizes, jumping aboard the youthful bandwagon is likely to pay dividends by appealing to those markets that are still at an impressionable age, not locked into name brands, and still formulating ideas about future buying habits (Strauss 1995). This focus on customer needs rather than product specifications confirms how advertising is not about selling products but for buying specifically targeted consumers by associating a product with socially relevant images. Such a mercenary approach suggests that the colour that still appeals to the United Colours of Benetton campaign is green.

***

III. Advertising through the Prism of Whiteness

Mainstream media and advertising are mutually dependent. Each of them in turn depend on consumers (viewers or readers) for their existence. Advertising revenue is critical for the survival of newspapers, magazines, and TV programs. Without mass advertising through the mainstream media, business would have to rely solely on direct marketing, which would be very costly. Apart from their inseparable relation, advertisers do have more leeway in presenting their products or services, for two reasons. First, unlike news reporting, an ad is not expected to be completely true to life. For example, few would believe that a certain skin care lotion or potion will magically reduce the fine lines on their face within a short period of time. Viewers, however, expect more accountability from news reporters. Second, unlike other media outlets, advertising is not regulated under the same set of rules that govern news reporting and TV programming.

Advertising is "a discourse through and about objects" (Jhally 1995). It is in the realm of advertising that the "politics of diversity and its concomitant insistence on representation" have the most impact (hooks 1992, 28). Through advertising, consumers are presented with a product or service that connects us with a lifestyle and a set of values with which we are familiar. Advertising is based on stereotypes, that is, a set of images or assumptions about the people and the world around us. These images are then reinforced in our subconscious through advertising and become the norm. They are also variable. As our experiences changes, so do our images of the world around us. For this reason, stereotypes are not simply misperceptions. Rather, they reflect the social order because of their role in justifying the prevailing distribution of power and resources.

A primary goal of advertising is to increase sales. Understanding the product and the values of its potential consumers are key to a successful campaign (Ogilvy 1983). If, for example, the depiction of visible minority women as decorative or primitive results in fewer vacation bookings, then advertisers will take note. Given that visible minority consumers do not want to be seen as subservient or on the fringe of the society, why then do racial stereotypes still exist in beauty and tourism ads? Can we assume that these ads are intended for the so-called "mainstream"? If so, is it justifiable to say that we have been socialized into the ideology of white supremacy and are unconsciously accepting the white standard of beauty and the image of the "lost world"? (hooks, 1992). Perhaps the persistence of these images reflects the thinking of mainstream consumers.

Over the past few decades, advertising has been criticized for reinforcing the existing social order through the use of stereotypes. No group in society is spared from being typecast, although some are cast in a more positive light than others. Gender-role stereotyping is one example. The roles portrayed by men and women in advertising are often representations of "ideal" relations between men and women. White males were often portrayed as strong and noble, as providers of peace and security. White females came across as fragile, domestic, or as objects of desire. Visible minorities continue to be depicted as convivial and docile, hardly roles to which we aspire. These images reinforce and justify the gender and racial hierarchy in society. Visible minority women are seldom spokespersons for beauty products. Rather, they are expected to emulate the white beauty standards on the age-old assumption that only "white sells." Such an attitude is currently being contested. With the changing cultural landscape of Canada's multicultural society, white no longer automatically sells. A consumer survey (1990) in Canada reveals that most people feel that advertising in Canada is still too white. Many of the respondents would prefer advertisements to reflect the cultural diversity in Canada. Visible minority respondents indicated that they made their purchase decisions based partly upon whether the ads included visible minorities in a positive way (CAF, National Consumer Survey 1992). Even non-racial minority consumers would not reject a product or service if it were promoted by a racial minority spokesperson. Instead, they would see this as a sign of a progressive organization. In other words, diversity sells.

The advertising media have taken steps to improve their relation with visible minority groups. Depictions that fail to incorporate diversity in a meaningful way run the risk of being labelled as staid and boring by consumers that count. At the forefront of this is an increased awareness of the racialization that complicates and compounds the sexual stereotyping of visible minority women. In many cases, inclusion of visible minorities has become the norm. However, adding a few more visible minority members in advertising does not automatically address the demand by ethnic groups for equitable representation.

How is diversity presented in advertising? Most ads are positioned within two broad spheres of life: work (such as banking, using a computer) and leisure (such as entertaining and vacationing). For example, commercials for alcoholic beverages are often centred around leisure settings (Kunz 1997), and resort vacation promotions are usually built around the concept of escape from the mundane routines of everyday life. If this is the case, perhaps we as consumers need to examine our perceptions about cultural diversity. For example, do we regard travel to non-European destinations as an encounter with the "uncivilized" world? Although colonialism is something of the past, hooks

(1992) found that the desire to "conquer" the "primitive" non-European cultures is still alive among many white people.

Even for non-white people, many may have unconsciously accepted the standard of beauty presented by the media. Instead of taking pride in their cultural heritage, visible minorities may want to downplay their ethnic features. For example, some may want to straighten or bleach their hair (hooks 1992) or lighten their skin tone. Perhaps a more important challenge is for us as consumers to "de-colonize" our thinking so that we can break away from the confines of white supremacy and truly celebrate our differences through self-love (hooks 1992, 9-20).

"Miniaturizing" Minority Women

Historically, of course, advertising rejected the inclusion of minority women and men in advertising except as stereotypes or embellishments. As hooks (1992, 21) once argued, "Within commodity culture, ethnicity becomes spice, seasoning that can liven up the dull dish that is mainstream white culture." Images of "exotic" visible minority women are therefore meant to "enrich" the daily life of white people. Such an observation cannot come as a surprise, given the nature of a system of persuasion based on linking products with positive images. When not openly ignored, minority women and men had to endure advertising images of diversity as inferior or irrelevant. And in an era when minorityness was generally perceived as a liability rather than an asset, the representational basis of advertising-minority relations suffered accordingly. Rarely were minorities portrayed in ads as "typical, normal, everyday Canadians, who go to work, have families, and live ordinary lives, just as whites are currently portrayed" or as Westernized Canadian consumers who fit comfortably into the Canadian lifestyle—wearing jeans and Reeboks, not turbans or saris" (CAF, 1992a, 10). Even though advertisers have taken notice of the demands from consumers, in many ads images of visible minorities are still filtered through the prism of whiteness (Wilson and Gutiérrez 1995, 114-117).

Consider the advertising of women. Women have long been the target of misrepresentation through stereotyped advertising (Graydon 1995). Images of women were defined and deflated through androcentric fantasies of what women ought to be. Women were sexualized in a way that equated existence with nurturing qualities and supportive roles to the exclusion of other attributes. More often than not, women were sexualized in areas that reduced their relevance or contributions to society to little more than pleasant props for stroking male egos (Gist 1993), or were depicted as frivolous commodities whose primary concerns revolved around appearances and relationships. They were also portrayed as being obsessed with grooming or appearance, as unfulfilled outside of a male-female relationship (with father, husband, or son), as domestic drudges in need of miracle products, as not terribly bright beyond the realms of dating and nurturing, and as invisible except as cheerleaders along the sidelines. This perceived preoccupation with appearances, both personal and domestic, made women vulnerable to an array of advertising pitches for keeping unwanted "dirt" at bay. Media were also known to infantilize women by casting them as silly or child-like or as mechanical cardboard figures devoid of intelligence. Women's bodies (and parts thereof) were paraded over and again for pitching images that reflected fairly rigid standards of beauty (white, slim, youthful, and flawless), in effect instilling in many women a sense of being uncomfortable in their skins. Even women of colour were not spared the irony of conforming with white standards of beauty, with its narrowcasted focus on thinness, blondeness, and Caucasianness (Bledsloe 1989).

Minority women confront a similar set of problems with advertising (hooks 1992; Creedon 1993; Graydon 1995; Kunz and Fleras 1998). However, visible minority women have also been subjected to additional media mistreatment because of race. If women in general confronted the spectre of sexualization through stereotyping, women of colour were racialized through stereotypes that simultaneously denied their difference (if different, then inferior) or criticized their sameness (if the same, then loss of authenticity). Media stereotypes derive their potency by tapping into a collective pool of popular but often unconscious racist attitudes (Shohat and Stam 1994). In the past, white women were blonde and beautiful; aboriginal women were depicted as "princesses" or "squaws" (but Métis women, as hot-blooded spitfires) (Harris, 1993); and Indo-Pakistani women were seen as manipulative and irrational. Asian-Canadian women were portrayed as "China dolls" (docile, submissive, and passive) or as "Dragon Ladies" (both scheming and backstabbing); Jewish women, as meddlesome nurturers; Polynesian women, as insatiable love goddesses; and Middle Eastern women, as hopelessly repressed. The portrayal of minority women as dangerous or evil, with the potential to destroy everything good about society or civilization, played into the race card (Jiwani 1992).

Whether by omission or commission, visible minority women were portrayed as fringe players who deserved to be ignored, insulted or caricaturized, and marginalized because their purchasing power did not justify any shift in presentation. They occupied domestic(ated) roles, a process that tends to consume their lives while reducing their life-chances to a singular process. Their bodies were gratuitously paraded to sell everything from esoteric fashions to sensuous fragrances, with a host of exotic vacation destinations in between (see Graydon 1995). When emphasis was placed on fantasy, white females represented the object of romantic desire, beautiful and fragile, whereas non-white females symbolized the "lost world," primitive and docile. When the emphasis was on escape, white females could usually relax on a tropical island or enjoy the high culture of Europe. Visible minority women, however, were seen working to make this escape possible. These ads dichotomized individuals into the "visible" (coloured) and the "invisible" (white). When it came to tourism, visible minorities were not expected to explore the "white" European culture, whereas white tourists automatically had the nostalgia to experience the "primitive" world. These tourism ads reflected the white supremacy that originated from the colonial era and that continues to undergird the foundational nature of contemporary society and its institutional correlate (hooks 1992).

Stereotyping of such magnitude has exerted a powerful influence. Visible minority women were type-cast with certain products or services, presumably on the basis of market-driven research that reinforced a "natural" propinquity with products or services. Visible minority women were rarely employed in beauty and/or personal hygiene ads, so deeply entrenched was the image of whiteness as the preferred standard of attractiveness (Bledsloe 1989). The image of feminine beauty is still white, slim and youthful. In current beauty ads, therefore, black women are usually shown to have a lighter skin tone and straighter hair than in reality. Cosmetic products are often placed on the dressing-room counter of a white woman, although visible minority women are just as likely to use make-up. In so doing, visible minorities are relegated as the inferior "other." Cosmetic products are meant to make women, white or non-white, conform to mainstream beauty standards. For visible minority women, it is often difficult to find products that fall outside the stereotypes. Minorities were rarely associated with luxury items in an industry that glamorized consumption through positive associations. Yet, who better to hype foreign airlines, quality chamber-maid service in hotels, tropical destinations, or sexual experiences? (O'Barr 1994). Through stereotypes, in other words, minorities are put down, put in their place, put up with, or put out of mind. That kind of dormant hostility makes it difficult for people of colour to break free. Ellen Holly (1979) explains the dangers of perceiving style over substance:

> The way we are perceived by this society affects the most basic areas of our lives. When you apply for a job the interviewer in personnel reacts to you not only in terms of who you are but also in terms of who he *thinks* you are. There are countless images floating around in his head and many of them are traceable to the media. You may sit in front of him as a neatly dressed, intelligent female who would do an efficient job, but if he has been fed one stereotype too many he may look and see not you but Flip Wilson's "Geraldine" goofing on the job, painting her fingernails, and calling up her boyfriend to chat on company time. If so, for all your qualifications, you're not the one who is going to get the job...

This "stereotyping" also has the effect of disempowering minorities by de-politicizing their status and contributions to society (see Farli 1995). To be sure, stereotyping facilitates the advertising process by codifying patterns of persuasion by tapping into widely shared and deeply embedded cultural codes. Yet stereotyping may alienate those markets eagerly pursued by advertisers, especially when such unwarranted generalizations are perceived as an accurate appraisal of social existence with universal applications, rather than as a static and specific slice of reality. The cumulative effect of such stereotyping not only demeans and debilitates by silencing or distorting; as a double standard, it resonates with a patriarchy that fuels the growing estrangement between women and men.

Skimming the Surface

In recent years, images of minority women and men in advertising have improved to the point where criticism may be inappropriate. Put bluntly, the slogan "white sells" is being contested by a belief that "diversity sells." Much of this shift can be attributed to (a) the crisis in advertising (b) changes in social climate pertaining to minorities and (c) the growth of the ethnic market. With the multicultural shift in both Canada and the United States, diversity has acquired a trendy cachet as something that is authentic and chic. Images of diversity no longer conjure up associations with negativity. To the contrary, those ads that persist in whiteness are increasingly criticized as staid and boring, and lacking in appeal to younger target groups. Increased reliance on diversity images was also enlisted to address the crisis in advertising—a crisis that reflected concerns over clutter, conventionality, and boredom. Images of minority women and men could be marketed as something that was different and could stand out from the crowd. Not only would diversity allow a product to escape the commercial clutter of whiteness, it would also tap into the disaffected youth by eroding their resistance to advertising. The Benetton ads of the 1980s and 1990s provide an example of this shift in advertising and its relationship to minority women and men.

This assessment, however, needs to be tempered as well. Consider, for example, the portrayal of minorities in Canadian television advertising. An informal survey by Henry Mietkiewicz (1999), the *Toronto Star* media critic, confirms the cliché that the more things change... Based on 1,787 television commercials over 114 hours of programming on Canadian and American channels in February 1999, 30.8 percent of the 1,314 commercials aired employed minority actors, however briefly, while only 10.4 percent of the ads provided more than a token appearance of at least 3 seconds of screen time. Whether these figures are consistent with Canada's evolving demographic depends on a particular point of reference. Visible minorities comprised 11.2 percent of Canada's population in 1996, but constitute 15.8 percent of the population of Ontario and 31.6 percent of Toronto's population. However, the conclusion seems inescapable insofar as Canadian advertisers are reluctant to cast minorities in prominent roles in TV commercials. Why? According to Elizabeth Reade, co-chair of a council on diversity for the Canadian advertising industry, it is not a case of racism; rather, it is a case of racial "uncomfortableness." Advertisers do not want to risk offending a white customer base or stumble across a cultural landmine. Hence the goal is not to reform bigots but to find a way to remove discomfort about race (cited in Mietkiewicz 1999).

Consider how inclusive advertising is coping with the shifting cultural and demographic fabric of Canada. The economic clout of visible minorities in Canada is growing, with assets estimated to be in the vicinity of $300 billion or about 20 percent of Canada's GNP (Samuel 1998). Nevertheless, steps to address this booming minority market appear to be tentative. For example, TV ads about specific products may be targeted at specific minorities in their ethnic language. Yet advertising seems hesitant about breaking through to the next level by attempting to forge an emotional bond with minority consumers through the use of culturally relevant brand image advertising (Allossery 1999). In failing to provide the kind of advertising that secures a compelling reason to choose one product or brand over competitors, the industry is missing the mark by failing to build brand relationships. Why? Part of the reason is that those who work in advertising and marketing feel unqualified to create or authorize expensive targeting programs towards ethnic communities that they know little about in terms of language or culture. There is also considerable unease because the data base of how minorities use the media is non-existent (Allossery 1999). The relative lack of reliable research makes it particularly difficult for advertisers to implement image-based advertising that targets minority groups that is, by definition, designed to be effective only over the long run.

Not surprisingly, interactions between whites and non-whites still remain rare in print advertising. White and non-white models can be promoting the same product in two separate ads. While acknowledging the changing face of Canadian society, some advertisers still seem to insist on targeting two markets, the "ethnic" (non-white) and the mainstream (white). This insistence on the mainstream versus the "ethnic" completely ignores the reality of the Canadian mosaic in which the "ethnic" is the mainstream (Lynn 1995). In other words, ethnic minorities are no longer fringe players stuck in their ethnic enclaves. Rather, they are becoming major forces in Canadian society. And until this shift in power is acknowledged as normal and legitimate, advertising is likely to only skim the surface rather than take differences seriously.

CHAPTER 7

FILMING THE "OTHER"

Framing the Issue

Movies (the terms *movies*, *film*, *cinema*, and *motion pictures* are used interchangeably) remain the most seductive and powerful of mainstream media, thanks to their ability to manipulate audiences with a potent combination of sound and image (Hagedorn 1994). The proliferation of video games, computers, and television notwithstanding, films continue to have a riveting effect on people that is more intense than any other medium—at least judging so by the millions of patrons who paid billions of dollars to sit in the darkened cocoon of a movie house with nothing to interrupt this singular experience (Vivian and Maurin 1999). Such continued popularity has consolidated filmmaking as the world's foremost expression of cultural entertainment in its first century of existence. The emergence of new creative artists, aggressive marketing, innovative techniques, and film-marketing strategies virtually assures the continued prominence of the film industry (Puttnam 1996). To be sure, there are worrying signs. The overhyped publicity surrounding movie celebrities and blockbuster bonanzas cannot disguise a basic and fundamental fact: the movie industry ranks last of all major media in their share of income (Biggio and McKie 1999). Moreover, the film industry (a) has yet to match the audience numbers of 50 years ago, (b) is about one-half the size of the video games empire, (c) remains heavily dependent on cable and television for its profitability, (d) earns more from video sales and merchandising linkages than from paying customers, and (e) increasingly relies on formulaic and derivative products as the backbone of the industry. Still, despite continued reliance on an almost primitive technology (a film is a series of still photographs in tiny frames run at high speeds through a projected light [Groen 1999]), movies seem as poised as ever to consolidate their lofty status as the silverest of screens.

There are many ways of approaching a study of film. A sociological perspective emphasizes the social dimension of film by focusing on how the relationship between film and society is created, expressed, sustained, challenged, and transformed. This social dimension transforms films into an important chronicle of who we think we are, who we were and are, how we think others see us, and who we would like to be. Films reflect and reinforce the values and aspirations that pervade our current world, as well as its uncertainties and fears. Films also constitute works of art that engage the senses, are inseparable from the imperatives of a profit-oriented society, and serve as an instrument of persuasion, both deliberate and inadvertent. Within a sociological perspective, different dimensions of films are apparent: as art, with its embrace of the aesthetic at a particular time and place; as a business whose obsession with returns on investment has transformed the art of moviemaking; as a kind of propaganda in defence of national interests; and as a chronicle that informs as it entertains. Each of these perspectives illuminates a different dimension of filmmaking. The often oppositional interplay of these dimensions also complicates yet enriches our understanding of the representational basis of minority-movie relations.

Minorities have for the most part received a cool reception from the motion picture industry (Omi 1989; Wilson and Gutierrez 1995; Hanamoto 1995). In the past, screen portrayals reflected popular beliefs about minority women and men and their place in society, spanning the spectrum from acceptance to hostility, with ambivalence in between for comic relief or dramatic foils. Audiences pounced on disparaging and stereotypical images as one way of putting minorities in their place while accentuating white prowess, civilization, or intelligence. Early films such as *The Nigger* (1905) or *The Wooing and Wedding of a Coon* (1905) bolstered the themes of white superiority by reinforcing the intellectual and moral inferiority of non-whites. Even critically acclaimed motion pictures such as *Birth of a Nation* (1915) openly demeaned Blacks as dupes, dopes, or deranged. Minority moral qualities were no less suspect: people of colour were perceived to have a low regard for human life. They also possessed a proclivity towards criminal tendencies, hot-blooded temperament, sexual promiscuity, submissive personalities, and dishonest personalities. This inferiority played into the hands and minds of white supremacists who were not averse to juxtaposing white humanity (civilization) with the treachery and brutality of the "other" for maximum impact. Aboriginal peoples, in particular, were routinely portrayed as obstacles that had to be domesticated (or broken) as part of the westward expansion (Churchill 1994). And despite gradual improvements in quantity and quality (consider for example, the films by Spike Lee or critically acclaimed films with powerful messages such as *Malcolm X*), minorities such as Blacks continue to be typecast as harmless distractions or as something to be laughed at, pitied, feared, or (on occasion) admired. This ambivalence towards minorities is reflected in the reluctance of white middle-class audiences to support films that feature all-black casts, with the possible exception of the 1996 film *The Preacher's Wife*.

Moviemaking is widely perceived to be the one medium with the potential to capitalize on minority experiences as a basis for narrative and character development. The industry is not dependent on advertising as a primary source of revenue, while its historical commitment to aesthetics should provide opportunities for innovation and exploration. Yet movies have fumbled the challenge of advancing an inclusive agenda, in part because of the corporatization of an artistic endeavour into a money-making machine that must pander to paying audiences and fidgety investors. The commercialization of the cinema has also had the effect of compromising its relationship with minority women and men, and this chapter explores the processes and reasons behind movie misrepresentations of minorities both in the past and at present. Particular attention is devoted to the often racist or Westocentric images of minority women and men in mainstream movies, together with why these relationships continue to exist despite improved levels of awareness and increased minority pressure. The chapter also demonstrates how "reel" mistreatment generates image problems that carry over into "real" life for people of colour and aboriginal peoples.

The argument is essentially straightforward: Films tend to reflect and reinforce the core values of society at large, while grappling with the contradictory articulations that pervade the mainstream media in general and moviemaking in particular. In embodying different dimensions, films are at once (or at least aspire to be) works of art; are inseparable from a profit-oriented society; offer snapshots of a reality both diverse and changing as well as uncertain and contested; and deliberately or inadvertently entail systems of persuasion. Insofar as films provide an important chronicle of who we think we are or would like to be, minority women and men have not figured prominently in establishing mainstream identity (except perhaps in the negative sense of who not to be), with the result that "celluloid" minorities continue to be put down, put in their place, or put up on an impossible pedestal (only to be pulled down again) (Cremen 2000). The chapter begins by providing a brief overview of film from a variety of different perspectives. Movie treatment of minorities is examined next, including a look at the stereotyping of minority women and men by a mediacentric movie industry. The chapter concludes by exploring the often negative relationship that Aboriginal peoples have had with the film industry.

Perspectives on the Cinema

Most of us enjoy seeing films or going to movies. In 1996, films earned a record $5.8 billion (U.S.) in gate receipts from Canada and the United States, with 12 films breaking the $100 million (U.S.) mark, led by *Independence Day* with $306.1 million and *Twister* with $241.7 million (*Globe and Mail,* December 30, 1996, C1). With another $427 million from world-wide sales (together with domestic sales), *Independence Day* had escalated into third place on the list of film grosses ($733 million), behind *Jurassic Park* ($915 million) and *The Lion King* ($755 million). By 1998, films earned $6.5 billion (U.S.) in ticket sales and another $86 million in Canada, thanks in part to the phenomenal success of the film *Titanic*, which currently stands as the all-time box office champ at about $1.1 billion (U.S.) in world-wide sales (*Star Wars* and *ET* rank a distant second and third, respectively). Such popularity has helped to consolidate the celluloid screen as the world's dominant form of cultural entertainment in the course of its first one hundred years, and its hold on centre stage in defiance of all probability bodes well for the second century (Puttnam 1996).

Films have been analyzed from different perspectives. Some see film as an expression of art: as an art form in a particular time and place, films tend to embrace the values and beliefs of an era in a manner that escapes print. Others prefer to regard movies as a business whose primary concerns are audiences and returns on investment. Still others dismiss motion pictures as a kind of propaganda in defence of national interests. Finally, cinema is viewed as a chronicle that documents and informs by providing audiences with a glimpse into the world at large. Each of these perspectives enlarges our understanding by casting light on different dimensions of the film industry.

I. Film as Art

Thomas Edison is credited with creating motion picture technology when he invented the kinetoscope in 1889 (Wilson and Gutierrez, 1995). The Lumière Brothers are thought to have shown the first film when they startled a Paris audience on December 28, 1895. Nevertheless, many believe the story line in *The Great Train Robbery* of 1903 endows it with the status of the first real film. Silents predominated until 1927 when the addition of sound in Al Jolsons's *The Jazz Player,* together with the inception of colour in 1932, launched the modern movie era. Over time, the culture of image and sound displaced the primacy of the printed word as the primary source of artistic expression, personal enrichment, and culture exchange. The best films say something about society and the often complex yet contradictory cultural values at the heart of contemporary human existence. Yet the 1977 blockbuster film *Star Wars* appears to have compromised the artistic by introducing a strident commercial mentality (from box office receipts to merchandising tie-ins) from which mainstream movies have yet to recover (Groen 1999).

The medium of film originated as an aesthetic expression that was distilled from a combination of theatre, literature, and painting. Initially, critics did not respond favourably to the cinema. At a time when opera was considered to be the apex of contemporary culture, film was disparaged as an insignificant novelty of use only as popular culture to distract the masses. This tension between film as aspiring art versus the commercial dictates of mass entertainment still pervaded the sensibility of film. As an art form, as well as a music hall novelty, film sought to establish techniques of logical story-telling and literary expression that reflected Victorian-era novels and popular nineteenth-century fiction and/or melodrama. Even into the mid-twentieth century, film remained bound in style by the conventions of linear story-telling and the premises of a literary culture, especially in Europe and in other world centres where film evolved a language and aesthetics of its own (Schepelern 1995). And to the surprise of no one, films from that golden era tend to rank highest on the list of "bests." Consensus suggests that Orsen Wells' *Citizen Cane* may be the best ever, followed by others from that era such as *Gone with the Wind, All about Eve*, and *Casablanca*. Of contemporary films, only the 1993 Holocaust epic *Schindler's List* makes it onto the list, thus reinforcing the shift from film as art to film as money.

II. Film as Hollywood Industry

Films are increasingly becoming big business whose bottom line is the bottom line. By the 1930s, Hollywood had emerged as the film capital of the world. As a dream factory par excellence, it had constructed a colossal entertainment and story-telling enterprise that linked stars and studios into a system that ensured profit both domestically and abroad. By the end of the Second World War, nearly 3 billion Americans went to the movies each year. These figures had plummeted dramatically to 920 million by 1970 because of the popularity of television, but crept back to about 1.3 billion in 1998 with the introduction of multiple-screen complexes and a spate of blockbuster films (Canadian Press 1999). Revenues continue to escalate, nearing $7 billion in the United States and about $1 billion in Canada—even though the number of tickets sold today is about one-fifth of the total of 90 million per week sold in the U.S. in 1946. Hollywood continues to churn them out, with 508 releases in 1998, up from 230 in 1980 and 483 in the golden days of 1950. Canada is no slouch either, at least on a per capita basis where 2 films are produced for every one million of population (the comparable figure for the United States is 2.6 films per one million people). However, Canadian production costs are minuscule compared to the United States ($3 million versus $55 million) while ticket sales from Canadian films (in some video shops Canadian films are categorized under foreign films) account for about 3 percent of the total box office receipts whereas American films account for 99 percent of the box office receipts in the United States (cited in the *Globe and Mail*, "How Canada Stacks Up," Feb 14, 1998). Much of the revenue generated by the film industry is linked with production for television or straight into video, in addition to merchandising, licensing, and spin-offs (Vivian and Maurer 1999).

Film today remains heavily driven by commercial imperatives. Films are expensive to make and, as costly investments, they need a large audience. Films routinely cost $40 to $60 million dollars to make (the average is $55 million), and another $22 million is set aside for marketing and advertisements (especially given the importance of opening week sales and subsequent word of mouth). Exceptions exist, of course, including the surprise hit *The Blair Witch Project*, which cost approximately $400,000 to produce while raking in millions. In contrast, the film *Godzilla* cost around $125 million to shoot with another $200 budgeted for marketing—proving once again that, in Hollywood at any rate, size does matter. Costs are further increased by the use of bankable film stars such as Demi Moore or Julia Roberts who earn $20 million per picture, while male stars such as Harrison Ford and Jim Carey earn closer to $25 million.

Escalating production and marketing costs ensure that investors have as much control over the final product as does an aesthetic sensibility. Private investors prefer bankable clones that will bring a following to the theatre rather than untested formulas or talents (Biggio and McKie 1999). As a result, the film industry has become increasingly risk aversive because of the increased corporatization of these artistic endeavours by bean counters and bottom line analysts (Eller 2000). Frances Ford Coppola, the director of such films as *Apocalypse Now*, writes to this effect when distinguishing Hollywood as a profit-oriented business from the creative licence implicit in serious films: "It's big business as much as any corporation. And in order to answer to a board of directors, they want products to be similar so they can be assured of the revenues being consistent. That is opposite to the artistic point of view in which you want each film to be something totally new and shed new light" (cited in Gerstel 1997, C7).

In light of these spiralling costs, as Mark Crispin Miller notes, the corporate need for immediate success on a grand scale makes it impossible to have movies that don't leave people laughing, crying, or applauding in the isles (cited in Horn 1996). And given that the main audience continues to be young people rather than adults (those between the ages of 16 to 24 constitute about one-half of the audience, with young men's craving for action, quests, and problem solving appearing to dictate movie tastes), catering to that market remains primary (Vivian and Maurer 1999).

III. Film as Chronicle

Films have long been used as a means of documenting the world around us. Unlike feature films that rarely correlate with the experiential world or historical past, films as chronicle play the role of civic educator for discussion and enlightenment (Roscoe 2000; Davis 2000). Tribal peoples were among the very first subjects of such documentaries. The multiple still images shot by Felix Regnault, which predated the work of the Lumière Brothers but were intended primarily for museum use, initiated an era of ethnographic filmmaking that continues into the present. Early depictions of primitive peoples were unflattering. Only in the early part of the twentieth century was an attempt made to present a positive slant by filming tribal peoples in the context in which they lived and from their point of view by exposing the underlying logic that governed their social and cultural organization (Marcus 1995). Much of the ethnographic impetus was focused on salvaging depictions of primitive peoples before they vanished in the struggle for survival. Nevertheless, the films continued to portray tribal peoples as "other," while bolstering the superiority of the West, the altruism of whites, the loyalty and devotion of some tribals to masters, and the romantic purity of indigenous lifestyles.

Consider one of the classics in chronicling diversity. The cinematic ethnography *Nanook of the North* first came out to glowing reviews in 1922. It provided audiences in Canada and abroad with a vivid and highly romanticized image of Inuit life, despite the harshness of the polar environment. The success of the film lay in Robert Flaherty's portrayal of a single Inuit family in dramatizing the challenges and enjoyment of everyday activities. Audiences were captivated by Nanook's good-natured manner and revelled in his resourcefulness in coping with Arctic rigours. (Ironically, the actor who played Nanook died of starvation two years after the filming.) The film also made it clear that the simplicity and virtue of Inuit culture, coupled with the happy-go-lucky nature of these noble savages, stemmed from their largely unacculturated status. The film convinced audiences that it was best to leave the Inuit alone in their natural environment (Marcus 1995).

Paradoxically, thirty years after the film, the Inukjuamiut and other Inuit were no longer being portrayed in benign terms, but increasingly as economically depressed people in overpopulated areas (Marcus 1995). Government officials were aware of Inuit poverty and starvation; many, however, were reluctant to act upon these concerns for fear of incurring costs and fostering additional dependencies. The Inuit problem was defined in terms of an unstable economy, poor health, and a pathological dependency on white society. The solution seemed simple enough: relocate the Inuit in a way that removed them as far as possible from the source of the problem. The relocation of the Inuit of Inukjuamit—the group that had been featured in the 1922 film *Nanook of the North*—was envisaged as a prototype for an ambitious plan to resettle Inuit throughout unoccupied regions of the high arctic (Marcus 1995).

How do contemporary chronicles of the "other" stand up? Diverse cultures and peoples are filtered through the simplistic perspective or superficial gaze of white eurocentrism as natural and normal, establishing in the process an "us" verse "them" discourse. Whiteness is equivalent to civilized, rational, and morally superior while the "other" is demeaned as inferior or irrelevant (Tator and Henry 2000). Cinematic depictions of the "other" in relationship to whites tend to revolve around several themes: (1) the superiority of the West; (2) the altruism of whites ("white man's burden"); (3) interethnic conflict upon contact; (4) loyalty and devotion to masters; and (5) the dignity/integrity/purity of indigenous lifestyles (Lyman 1990; Cowen 1991).

Portrayals that chronicle diversity present filmmakers with a host of dilemmas (Unspeakable Images 1991). What degree of cultural blandness robs a minority of their heritage and distinction? By contrast, how much ethnic characterization transforms minority women and men into a caricature? How does one determine an acceptable level of "minorityness" for characters across a broad spectrum of internal diversity? Will emphasizing their differences compromise their rights to equality? By the same token, will denial of differences erase their authenticity as a people and erode their leverage for recognition and reward? By what authority does a filmmaker have the right to depict a group? Or can only members of an ethnic group speak with authority about issues that concern that particular group? These dilemmas that focus on denying differences and/or denying similarities ("you're too much"/"not enough") are not easily resolved but surely the statement on inclusiveness by actress Lynn Whitfield deserves careful reflection: "We have to be careful of two things, excluding excellence based upon race, and expecting inclusion because of race" (quoted in the *Toronto Star*, March 25, 1996, B3).

IV. Film as Propaganda

It took little time for those in positions of authority to acknowledge the power of the media to persuade. The power of images to influence proved inviting for those who sought thought control in pursuit of national interests or personal goals. By World War One, film had become a political instrument of propaganda in the hands of European fascists whose blatant manipulation of the media for patriotic purposes did little to advance its aesthetic appreciation. Hollywood too responded with films that glorified democratic societies as symbols of courage and resistance in the face of the forces of evil. Currently, the use of film as propaganda is more subtle, yet no less real in effect if not intent. For example, the one-sidedness of Hollywood films as discourses in defence of the American way and tinseltown values may be interpreted as systemic propaganda. This whiff of systemic propaganda is put to the test in the following case study on the seemingly innocuous world of animation.

CASE STUDY: Disney—Wholesome or Hegemony?

Quick! A word association game: what image comes to mind when I say "wholesome"? A few would respond with "Walt Disney." Disney's animated films, from *Sleeping Beauty* and *Beauty and the Beast* to *Mulan* and *Pocahontas,* are endorsed as models of wholesome entertainment that extol family values while reinforcing the cultural values at the core of American greatness. But what Disney says or sets out to do is not necessarily what is best for all Americans. Beneath the glossy exterior of playful animation lurks a more disturbing discourse that, at best, reveals cultural naïveté or political insensitivity; at worst, it borders on sexism and racism, albeit in a subtle and disguised manner. Which is the correct interpretation? (see Giroux 1995 for a more intensive analysis).

Sexism

The women in Disney's animated world are almost completely defined by their relationship to males. Their lives are geared towards securing and supporting a man even if their sense of self and identity dissipates in the process of catering to patriarchal whims. Love with a man conquers all, and marriage with "Mr. Right" will ensure that both live happily ever after. In *Beauty and the Beast*, for example, Belle, the heroine of the film, is portrayed as a feisty and independent woman who resides in some remote French provincial village. To her credit, Belle rejects the advances of a male chauvinist pig named Gaston; however, she capitulates to the gruff charms of the Beast who holds her captive in hopes that her love for him will shatter a spell cast on him as a young man. Belle not only falls in love with the Beast; she also civilizes him by transforming this narcissistic tyrant into a sensitive new-age guy.

Some argue that Belle is a Disney feminist because she rejects a vain macho male. Others are not so sure. They see Belle as simply another woman whose life is valued primarily for her solving of a 1990s riddle between macho sensibilities and reformed sexism. The fact that she is forcibly kept and controlled speaks volumes about coercive love and male privilege. Other Disney animations such as *The Lion King* are even more openly sexist. All rulers in this animal kingdom are males, in effect reinforcing the message that patriarchal entitlement and high social standing confer independence and leadership. The animated version of *Pocahontas* drew a chorus of boos, not only for taking liberties with history, but also for its portrayal of the heroine as cute and curvaceous. Even in the film *Mulan*, the heroine might have saved the empire from the barbarians by virtue of her courage and intelligence, but instead remained despondent until noticed by the hero for her "feminine" qualities.

No one is accusing Disney of deliberate misogyny. But in manipulating consensus in defence of a patriarchal status quo, Disney discourses are hegemonic in consequence if not in intent. Disney films tend to celebrate a masculine kind of power that has the effect of reproducing an insidious type of gender stereotyping. Parents may think the denial of female agency and empowerment is essentially harmless; nevertheless, these subliminal images may have an extremely adverse effect on children because of the films' animation properties.

Racism

Even the magical world of Disney is not impervious to charges of racism (Byrne and McQuillan 1999). Disney has long had a problem with race and early films were notorious for their clumsy depiction of aboriginal people and people of colour as a basis for characterization and plot development. *The Jungle Book* lampooned Indians while *Frontierland* revelled in racist representations of members of First Nations as "redskins" or "injuns." Recent releases have also come under fire, including *The Lion King* for its racist stereotypes in promulgating the popular perception of Africa as nothing more than an animal kingdom. Even the portrayal of the evil lion as black in contrast with the light-coloured good lion reinforces colour-coded stereotypes while condoning the virtues of imperial rule over the realities of indigenous rabble (Coren 1994). The 1989 release of *Alladin* caused particular concern since it was one of the most important and celebrated of Disney releases. From the opening song, "Arabian Nights," with its depiction of Arabian culture with racist overtones and popular stereotypes, to its portrayal of supporting characters as violent or cruel, the film manipulated an audience already primed by the media portrayal of the Gulf War. Racism is also evident in racially coded language and accents. The bad Arabs speak in thick foreign accents, while Jasmine and Alladin speak in standardized English. In *The Lion King*, all members of the Royal Family speak in received British pronunciation while the style of Banzai and Shenzi resembles the nuances of inner-city gangs.

Cultural Time Out?

What do children learn from these racist depictions? Racism in Disney films is rarely conveyed by what is said, but by what is not said. Overtly negative representations are combined with the absence of complex characterization to create an impact that is racist in consequence if not always in intent. Through images and codes, children are taught that cultural differences outside the imprint of white middle-class culture are inferior, deviant, irrelevant, or threatening. Children of colour also learn to dislike who they are because of these depictions. A spokesperson for an American Islamic Association said this about the film *Alladin* (quoted in Giroux, 1995:40):

> All of the bad guys have beards and large, bulbous noses, sinister eyes and heavy accents, and they're wielding swords constantly. Alladin doesn't have a big nose; he has a small nose. He doesn't have a beard or a turban. He doesn't have an accent. What makes him nice is they've given him this American character.... I have a daughter who says she's *ashamed to call herself an Arab, and its because of things like this* (emphasis ours).

In short, Disney films are widely perceived as models of wholesome family entertainment. This is true in the sense that Disney endorses narrowly defined family arrangements consistent with the demands of Western patriarchal societies and Disney is working to improve its race and gender images (Byrne and McQuillan 1999). The reality is that Disney films embrace a subtext that may be difficult for young audiences to decode as part of the internalization process. Disney does not set out deliberately to demean women or people of colour. Rather, dissonance is created through the largely unintended consequences of seeing the world through Eurocentric and androcentric filters. Contradictions abound. For a corporation rooted in the propagation of family values, mothers are a remarkably scarce commodity; Belle, for example, is parented by a bumbling father. Moreover, Disney is criticized regardless of the images conveyed. For example, the film *Mulan* has been endorsed as one that teaches kids about honour, determination, courage, and devotion to family. In contrast, critics pounce on it for its political correctness in having the heroine succeed in a traditional male role while reinforcing the stereotype of males as "pigs" (Dewolf 1998). The character Pocahontas is praised by some as an attractive ambassador for multicultural relations, but condemned by others as an exercise in airbrushed imperialism. Perhaps the problem resides in the nature of the medium; that is, people tend to assume that with animated films (so like cartoons) they can relax by letting down their guard. Until people realize that there is no cultural free space or time out in a media-ted world, that if you aren't putting things in your head, then someone else is, the danger of succumbing to hidden agendas always exists.

***

Minorities in the Movies

Movies are a social construction; that is, they constitute human accomplishments created by individuals in contexts not necessarily of their own making. As social constructions, movies will invariably reflect the ideas and ideals that prevail at a particular point in time and place. Movies are ideological in two ways. First, as a discourse in defence of ideology, they tend to bolster mainstream perspectives at the expense of minority viewpoints. Second, movies are suffused with ideological assumptions about what is acceptable and desirable in society. This ideological dimension suggests that movie content may say more about the mainstream (the "us") than about minority women and men (the "other"). Such an observation is not intended to be carping insofar as movies are typical of all media as systemic propaganda. Nevertheless, such an indictment does provide insight into why the representational basis of movie-minority relations leaves much to be desired.

How do the media do their ideological work? Consider the degree to which action or adventure films tend to otherize minorities by drawing a rigid line between good and bad or "us" versus "them" (Croteau and Hoynes 2000). Race or nationality often serves as a boundary marker: whites are cast as civilized while minorities are disparaged as dangerous or deranged. The dangers of difference need to be vanquished and destroyed to make the world safe; alternatively, it must be domesticated by absorbing the "other" into the status quo. Historically, American Blacks and Asian-Americans have posed as threats to the social order. In more recent years, both communist and post-communist Russians have proven excellent foils, while Arabian Muslims continue to provide fodder for contrasting good with bad (Elmasry 1999).

Images of badness are inseparable from stereotypes. In the past, to cater to the broadest (and often uneducated) common denominator, films had to condense characters into a brief and homogeneous shorthand, and many bordered on being caricatures that seem openly insulting in retrospect. Minority women and men were cast in roles as victims, villains, or superheroes, even though many of them did not see themselves as symbols of evil, inspirational role models, or naïve innocents. Minorities were demonized while their cultural habits evoked images of danger or morbid fascination. Racial and ethnic minorities such as the Jews, Italians, Chinese, and Irish were compromised as sly or sleazy or dim-witted or pugnacious. When refracted through the "jaundiced" eyes of white filmmakers who reflected the popular Yellow Peril sentiments of the time, popular film characterized Asian-Americans

- as foreigners who cannot be assimilated
- as having no power or influence even when playing leading roles
- as restricted to clichéd or subservient occupations
- as having racial features or mannerisms that are inherently comical or sinister

- as playing supporting roles even in contexts that are unmistakably Asian or Asian-American
- as having sexuality that is negative or non-existent (for men)
- as having regressive speech patterns that compound low intellectual capabilities
- as having suicidal impulses in defence of honour, name, or country
- as model minorities, that is, overachievers but emotionally bankrupt
- as sources of magical or supernatural at odds with reason or science (adapted from http://janet.org/~manaa/.a.stereotypes.html. Also Hagedorn 1994; Parker 1997; and Fong and Shinagawa 2000).

By virtue of its innately spectacular and larger-than-life nature, films tend to fetishize whiteness (as well as youthfulness and beauty) while shunning minorityness as a source of profit in Hollywood. Yet this relationship between films and minorities has not developed without ambiguity, prompting Steve Parks to pounce on the movie industry for its one-dimensionality of Asians:

> We make up more than one half of the world's population, yet in spite of our numbers and contributions to the world, our images and perspectives are rarely seen. Our histories and cultures are obscured, overlooked, buried, or tokenized in a world dominated by Western classism. Our voices are seldom heard, our stories are left untold, and our realities are seldom presented by those who control the means and resources to name and shape a picture of reality. In spite of our diversity, in spite of our unique histories and cultures, we are often represented as a single homogenous group. Asians are the nearly silent, nearly invisible, majority of the world (Parks 1997, 7).

This stereotyping extends to gender differences. Consider how the exoticization of the "other" characterizes movie depictions of Asian women as objects of desire, servility, or suffering (Hagedorn 1994). As objects of desire for white men, Asian women exist to provide sex, colour, and texture in what is essentially a white man's world by rendering permissible on the screen what would otherwise be taboo.

The effects of such one-dimensional stereotyping is critical. Generally audiences tend to understand Asians and Asian-Americans only through stereotypical images that rarely flatter but often insinuate or insult (Fong and Shinagawa 2000). According to MANAA (Media Action Network for Asian Americans), caricatures of Asian-Americans (often played by white actors) become the standards by which real-life Asian-Americans are perceived, evaluated, and treated—thus reinforcing a perception that Asians are culturally incompatible and really don't belong in Canada or the United States (Robb 2000). A kind of "those people" mentality has not only reinforced their status as not-quite-human outsiders, but also discredited the legitimacy of their grievances and demands for justice while eroding their contributions to society. To be sure, as Michael Omi (1989) argues, there is no reason to believe that even the uneducated see these stereotypes as anything but distortions. Through constant repetition, however, these diminutions have assumed the mantle of real at least in consequence if not in intent. Moreover, initiatives to move beyond these negative images is fraught with ambiguity and uncertainty. After all, for images to work in media representations, they must resonate with meaning for audiences. To do this, they must be innovative enough to be "cool" or "hip" rather than conservatively stale or dated, yet not scare off audiences since people may recoil from anything too new (Nolen 2000).

Stereotypical images are a staple of the film industry because they simplify the filmmaking process. Media movers and shakers prefer to tap into a pool of minority stereotypes as a kind of convenient shorthand. Reliance on pre-selected images based on fantasies or fears creates readily identifiable frames (tropes) that may impose a thematic coherence to people or events to which audiences can relate (Taylor 1993). For in the final analysis, stereotyping sells. Consider the words by the lead investigator on a study of violence in music videos: "What sells is that which makes us feel secure in what we already believe—not films that make us think in new ways and question what we believe" (Krieger 1998, D9).

Nor should we ignore the wider context of stereotyping. Rather than an error in perception, stereotyping constitutes a system of social control through the internalization of negative images. Stereotypes are employed to keep aboriginal peoples in their place and out of sight. The colonialist discourse implicit in many films is used to impose Western perspectives and stereotypes while sanitizing the colonial conquest of aboriginal peoples by assuaging white guilt over exploitation (Churchill 1994). With stereotypes, it become progressively easier to disregard the humanity and status of aboriginal peoples as a distinct people. It also demonstrates how the often demeaning and patronizing images associated with stereotypes are so durable and pervasive that they form the basis of mainstream (and aboriginal) perceptions of First Nations. Negative stereotypes inflict a degree of symbolic and psychological violence on the lives of First Nations people. Their identity as a people is distorted by socially constructed images. Their sense of self-worth plunges through images that remind them of their status as a de-valued "other." Ironically, the internalization of even negative images serves to provide a degree of recognition, a basis for identity formation, and a source of collective empowerment. Such stereotyping may also contribute to white identities. Imaginary Indians are filtered through the prism of European prejudice and preconceptions, in the process projecting Euro-Canadian fears and fantasies. In other words, Europeans have long resorted to certain images of the "other" as a basis for collectively defining who they are in relation to themselves.

Filming First Nations

A flurry of excitement has greeted the recent distribution of films about aboriginal peoples. Many were produced in the United States, including *Dances with Wolves, Geronimo, Black Robe, Last of the Mohicans, Thunderheart, Oglala, Last of the Dogmen,* and *Pocahontas.* Others bore a Canadian label, namely, *Clearcut* and *Dance Me Outside.* And still others originated overseas, such as *Once Were Warriors* (New Zealand). Television has been no less active in tapping into this phenomenon: the critically acclaimed Canadian drama series *North of Sixty* stands alongside made-for-TV specials such as *Conspiracy of Silence*. The burgeoning interest in aboriginal issues reinforces the importance of taking stock of what is happening with regard to media representation of First Nations. After all, the mainstream media constitute a primary source of information about the world we live in. Movie portrayals have shaped the public image of aboriginal peoples while, in turn, influencing aboriginal images of themselves (Meadows 1993). Further distortions can only skewer our stock of knowledge with respect to the politics of aboriginal peoples' relations with Canada.

Mainstream media have come in for sustained criticism over representations of Canada's First Nations (see Meadows 1993). Depictions of aboriginal and Inuit peoples in film and television, as well as in magazines such as *National Geographic*, have historically reflected an image of aboriginal people as the "other"—a people removed in time and remote in space. This image of aboriginal peoples as the other has ranged in scope from their stereotyping as "noble savages" and "primitive romantics," to their stigmatization as "villains" or "pathetic victim of a proud races," with the label of "problem people" or "drunken welfare bums" sandwiched in between. What is common to each of these images is their propensity to be filtered through the prism of Euro-Canadian society and values (Blythe 1994). Most portrayals embrace a mythical image of an imaginary warrior who occupied the Great Plains region between 1825 and 1880 (Frances 1992). The standard for generic North American Indian could be packaged with ingredients from a so-called "Indian Identity Kit" (Berton 1975) that comprised the following items, few of which were even indigenous to aboriginal peoples prior to European settlement: wig with hair parted in the middle into hanging plaits; feathered war bonnet; headband (a white invention to keep actor's wig from slipping off); buckskin leggings; moccasins; painted skin tepee; and tomahawk and bow and arrows. This "one size fits all" (seen one, seen them all) image applied to all aboriginals, regardless of whether they were Cree or Salish or Ojibwa or Blackfoot. Cultural differences, locational adaptations, and diverse levels of development were of minor concern in the headlong rush to standardize these depictions. These images could be further broken down into a series of recurrent stereotypes, therby securing a "seen one Indian, seen em all" mentality.

Blood-Thirsty Barbarians

Aboriginal people have long been portrayed as dangerous and violent because of the brutal acts they commit in film. White-settler violence by contrast is rarely portrayed. Many films dwell on this theme of aboriginal peoples as savages. Most of us are only too aware of the classic confrontational pose, beginning with sinister smoke signals, followed by a boisterous attack on encircled wagon trains or military forts, and the torturing of prisoners who have had the misfortune of falling into such depraved hands. Their lack of subtlety—even open stupidity—

in thwarting white settlers and soldiers simply reinforced the notion of Indians as not-too-bright"others." Not all Natives conformed to this image. Some warriors were brave and courageous enough as individuals in their own right; rarely, however, did the same generous assessment apply when collective resistance was invoked. Finally a distinction was applied to "half-breeds" and "full bloods." According to Pierre Berton (1975), Hollywood tended to equate half-breeds with the Métis. Métis men were cast as villainous murderers, both degenerate and untrustworthy, while Métis women came across as hot-blooded temptresses with an irresistible weakness for white men. Indian women fell into two categories: the princess (Pocahontas) or the dishevelled "squaw." Full bloods were no less prone to primitive savagery, but this lapse in character was justified in their attempts to protect what little they possessed because of European contact.

Feisty Radical

There are several variations to the theme of aboriginal peoples as primitive pugilists. The radicalism of the 1960s appeared to have produced the feisty radical, best exemplified by the film *Billy Jack*. Young and angry, the aboriginal radical was resentful of white injustices and appalled by mainstream greed, and responded with individual acts of resistance or violence. Again, collective actions were generally unheard of; nor was there much interest in articulating the broader context of this defiance.

Indians with Attitude

Another unflattering image entailed the emergence of the borderline psychotic. Usually drunk and often out of control, these aboriginals with attitudes proved to be a thorn in the side of all law-abiding persons. Uncontrolled actions may be directed at acts of injustice (for example, in the film *Clearcut*); alternatively, this lack of control reflects an "Indian" who has simply given up on life and resorts to random acts of violence or self-abuse for coping with life.

The Noble Savage

Another variation in media stereotyping stems from the inclination to romanticize aboriginal peoples as gentle and compassionate, without naked ambition or materialist greed, and supposedly in tune with nature and with themselves. This image was spawned originally in European salons during the nineteenth century, where an "out of sight, out of mind" mentality prevailed. This noble savage image received a boost with the film *Nanook of the North*. Produced in 1922, it followed the lives and lifestyles of several Inuit ("Eskimo") families whose cheerful and gritty determination provided a perfect foil to the harsh environment. This film and many other documentary travelogues tended to romanticize aboriginal peoples as creatures from another time and place, whose noble but doomed existence is tottering on the brink. As noble savages, they are relegated to a victim status as people whose lives have been damaged by the loss of their hunting grounds and traditional lifestyle. In addition to being doomed and marginalized, aboriginal peoples are perceived as powerless because of colonialist forces beyond their control. The Kevin Costner film *Dances with Wolves* qualifies for this category.

Trusty Sidekick

Related to this image is the portrayal of Indians as faithful companions (Tonto). The trusty sidekick is able to apply "his" knowledge and expertise to salvage the white hero from imminent danger.

Mystic Indian

This image depicts an all-knowing and wise elder with one foot in the heavens and the other in a canoe. Even films that put down Natives often insert a token elder of deep wisdom—in part to accentuate the folly of the young or misguided.

Ecological Trustee

Recent films have reinforced long-standing images of aboriginal peoples as guardians of natural resources. Aboriginal lifestyles are portrayed as environmentally sound; by contrast, whites are portrayed as greedy and rapacious, with a corresponding threat to a sustainable environment. The Disney production of *Pocahontas* conveys this theme.

Problem People

Aboriginal peoples have long been portrayed as problem people. To convey this image of a problem people with an outdated lifestyle and immoral cultural values, movies have turned to aboriginal resistance to progress and prosperity, ranging in scope from nineteenth-century white settlements to twentieth-century resource extraction. Costs have escalated in efforts to bring this anti-progressive element under control and into the fold of civilization through force, education, or exposure to the arts of civilization. Even more problems are generated by aboriginal refusal to comply with white dictates or to abandon an irrelevant culture. Their contemporary predilection for making unprecedented demands for return of the land ("territorial repossession") and control over destiny ("self-determination") further contributes to this image of a problem people. The films *Oglala* and *Thunderheart* stand out as recent contributors.

Aboriginal peoples not only create problems, according to movie representations, they also have problems in need of costly solutions. They are often portrayed as wallowing in poverty and the misery that accompanies the demands of eking out an existence in bleak surroundings. Many are depicted as being hooked on welfare, with the pathological dependency this creates; others are physically dependent on alcohol or abuse substances as one way of escaping the despair and hopelessness of their lives. Government initiatives to deal with the problems of poverty and powerlessness are rarely appreciated, tend to be unsuccessful, and often cost a lot of tax-payers money.

Aboriginal peoples have been portrayed in many ways, but all portraits reinforce the notion of Indians as primitives (see also Berton 1975). Emphasis is on tribalism or entrapment in a backward culture, threats posed by aboriginal violence or outbreaks into white society, their role as failures and undisciplined rejects, as victims of whites, and as the first environmentalists (Jakubowicz et al. 1994). As primitives, aboriginal peoples are viewed as people who are remote in time and removed in space. The primitivity of the "other" (in contrast with Western civilization) can be a blessing or curse depending on which set of images are employed. For some, the primitiveness of First Nations is something to treasure or to aspire to if only to avert the destruction of our planet. Others tend to see this primitivity as something to avoid at all costs for the survival of a progressive and prosperous society.

Three main themes appear to characterize film representations of aboriginal peoples: aboriginal peoples as primitive and savage (wild, defiant and non-deferential, lawless); aboriginal peoples as primitive yet pastoral (picturesque, idealized, bucolic, and romantic); and aboriginal people as a problem because of their primitiveness (create problems and/or have problems). To be sure, one of more of these images may prevail during a single era and pervade a genre of film. Generally speaking, recent films have begun to invert the conventional stereotypes between whites and First Nations, with much greater emphasis on the beauty and nobility of the indigenous people of the land versus the rapacious greed of white-settler colonization. Alternatively, some or all can appear in a single film such as *Dances with Wolves*; that is, the Pawnee as the bad guys, and the Lakota Sioux as borderline saints. Collectively, these images reinforce the notion of First Nations as peoples from a different time and place, whose histories began with the arrival of the white man and whose reality only makes sense in terms of their interaction with whites. With images as powerful as they are, there is growing pressure for First Nations to wrest control over representations about who they are and what they want to be. The table below provides a summary statement of the three main images, in addition to the variants within each set of representations.

Table 7.1: Stereotyping Aboriginality—Recurrent Images

PRIMITIVE SAVAGES	PASTORAL PRIMITIVES	PRIMITIVE PROBLEM PEOPLE
blood-thirsty barbarians	noble savages	create problems
feisty radicals	mystic Indian	have problems
Indians with attitude	ecological guardians trusty sidekick	

RECASTING THE MOULD

The miscasting of minorities by mainstream media processes is widely acknowledged. Newscasting mistreats minority women and men by reducing diversity to discourses about negativity, conflict, and problems. TV programming remains locked into the formulaic and derivative, with a corresponding negative impact in depicting minorities. Advertising is only marginally better, notwithstanding improvements in the quantity and quality of minority representations, by virtue of its reliance on market-driven stereotyping as a basis for generating discontent while glamorizing consumption. And filmmaking is also subject to criticism for selling out minorities by refracting their realities through the prism of whiteness. Not surprisingly, the representational basis of media-minority relations continues to resonate with the language of concern over the status and role of minority women and men in a multicultural society.

This miscasting of minorities in Canada's mainstream media raises several important questions that need to be addressed. First, are there patterns or themes that can be extrapolated from the myriad of images of minority women and men in both print and electronic media? Second, can a classificatory scheme be produced that is narrow enough to make sense of this diversity yet broad enough to have validity across a wide range of minority images? Third, is it possible to account for this miscasting of minority women and men in a manner that is sociologically accurate? In other words, is this miscasting anchored in the institutional and systemic rather than personal and deliberate? Fourth, what if anything can be done to improve the representational bias of media-minority relations? Should differences be taken more seriously or is it best to ignore differences to ensure equitable treatment? Fifth, what is the best approach for achieving an inclusive and multicultural media—reform from within or establishment of separate minority media? Sixth, in what way are developments in improving media minority representations a case of two steps forward, one step back?

This section is organized around responses to these questions. We assert that patterns in the miscasting of minority women and men are systemic and structural rather than random or personal. We also contend that inclusiveness strategies for multiculturalizing the mainstream media have proven of some value in representing diversity. Nevertheless, media minority representations continue to be couched in compromise because of the structural and systemic barriers that continue to deny or exclude, both deliberately and inadvertently. True, not everyone will agree with the proposed analytical framework for understanding the representational politics of media-minority relations. Nor will people concur with our conclusions over what has been done and what still needs to be done. Nevertheless, our assessment and analysis is based on a careful and thorough reading of the situation that is consistent with what others are saying about media (mis)treatment of minority women and men.

The previous section examined the miscasting of minorities at specific institutional levels. Attention was devoted to the structural and systemic prompts behind the miscasting of minority women and men. This section moves beyond such specificity by seeking to extrapolate common themes that account for the politics of media misrepresentation of minority women and men, to isolate the causes behind such misrepresentation, and to explore the challenges associated with recasting the relationship. The challenges are two-fold: first, to understand the precise nature of media minority miscasting and, second, to propose solutions that are consistent with how the problem is defined. To date, the mainstream media have only been partially successful in accepting the challenge, largely because of the systemic and structural barriers that preclude any departure from the norm.

Chapter 8 begins by demonstrating how media minority representations can be classified into five basic categories or themes; that is, minorities as invisible, minorities as stereotypes, minorities as problem people, minorities as white-washed, and minorities as adornments. The chapter also attempts to account for the miscasting of minorities, with particular emphasis on institutional structures rather than personal pathologies. The chapter concludes by pointing out how the otherizing of minority women and men has the potential to erode minority concerns and contributions to society by erecting a barrier between the "us" and the "them." Chapter 9 addresses the organizational challenges of creating a multicultural and inclusive mainstream media. Attention is focused on what constitutes an inclusive institution and the kind of barriers that preclude inclusiveness. Initiatives to date have revolved around two sets of strategies. One is based on improving responsiveness to diversity by way of reforms from within; the other seeks to establish a parallel or separate media for ethnic minorities and aboriginal peoples. The final chapter, Chapter 10, provides an overview and assessment of changes to date. It contends that the representing of diversity continues to be couched in compromise despite gradual improvements in the quantity and quality of media minority representations. It also concludes that this compromised relationship will persist without a sociological understanding of the magnitude of the challenge that awaits a recasting of the mould.

CHAPTER 8

MISCASTING MINORITIES: PATTERNS AND CAUSES

Framing the Issue

Mainstream media have rendered a grave disservice to minority women and men. When not openly ignored as irrelevant or inferior, minorities have been reduced in status to stereotypes or problem people, thus reinforcing their status as the "other." Two mutually exclusive yet interlinked media messages tend to entrap minority women and men: a denial of difference on the one hand (if different, then inferior); and a trivialization of sameness on the other (if the same, then loss of authenticity) (Stam 1993). Their visibility, paradoxically, is reduced to an invisible status through underrepresentation in images and contexts that count. Conversely they are overrepresented through images that demean or marginalize—either consciously or inadvertently. These images tend to normalize or naturalize segregation—a kind of "cultural apartheid" (Douglas 1995, 80)—to the detriment of those who want to participate and contribute.

In a seemingly progressive society such as Canada, the mainstream media have faltered in positively engaging diversity. Repeated visual and verbal references to minorities as irrelevant, inferior, dangerous, or unmarketable has reinforced their marginality in society. Neglect of minorities in the mainstream media may be attributed to a variety of reasons, spanning the spectrum from hard-boiled business decisions that reflect market forces to a lack of cultural awareness and deep-seated prejudice among media personnel, to a bias so systemic that it escapes detection or scrutiny but reflects the organization of power within media institutions. Does media mistreatment of minorities imply the presence of personal prejudice or overt discrimination? Is it a case of unwittingly cramming minority realities into Eurocentric categories as a convenience for description or evaluation? (Shohat and Stam 1994). Or does it reflect a preference to act out of self-interest by pandering to the dictates of the marketplace? Is it a case of precluding minority input into media outputs, considering that minorities are rarely part of a "white boys" network as writers, producers, and directors, but are instead confined to questionable coverage by outsider perspectives?

Is it possible to make sense of both former and current minority portrayals? If a classification system is possible, how many categories are necessary to capture the nuances of these representational images without getting bogged down? Can the system of classification be applied to all media processes or must it be modified for each medium? Is it possible to account for patterns of miscasting that are respectful of the data yet sufficiently comprehensive to make analytical sense for comparative purposes? This chapter argues that media miscasting of minority women and men is amenable to systematic and rigorous analysis, resulting in a classification system that yields patterns in what at first glance might have seemed random and inchoate phenomena. Four recurrent themes appear to have characterized media (mis)casting of minority women and men; namely, minorities as invisible, as stereotypes, as problem people, white-washed and as ornaments. Such an assessment would appear true for all media processes, including newscasting, TV programming, advertising, and filmmaking, although each medium may vary in terms of a recurrent negativity. The chapter also looks at how media miscasting of minority women and men has had the effect of otherizing minorities as irrelevant or inferior. The chapter concludes by isolating the reasons behind media misrepresentation, arguing that these causes may not reflect individuals or attitudes per se, but are rooted in the structural and systemic logic of institutional processes.

Theorizing the Miscasting Process

Evidence suggests the prevalence of certain patterns in the analysis of the representational basis of media-minority relations. Five patterns prevail in the miscasting process: minorities as invisible, minorities as stereotypes, minorities as problem people, minorities as, and minorities as adornments/whitewashed. The cumulative effect of such media minority miscasting goes beyond simple inconvenience. Rather, minority women and men are otherized as different and marginal to society. To be sure, this five-fold scheme is not intended to be exhaustive or accurately reflect reality. The objective instead is to provide an ideal-typical framework for improving our understanding of a complex issue. Nor do we suggest that the mainstream media deliberately set out to otherize minority women and men. Nevertheless, the end result of such one-sided negativity has had the effect of diminishing the social status and stature of minorities while de-politicizing their contribution to society.

I.   Invisibilizing Minorities

Numerous studies have extolled what many regard as obvious. Canada's multicultural diversity is poorly reflected in virtually all sectors of the popular media (Fleras 1994). Visible minorities tend to be invisibilized through underrepresentation in areas that count, but overrepresented in areas that don't. Newscasting ignores minority women and men unless crime or conflict is involved; advertising has long relied on the maxim that "white sells," and TV programming has yet to provide a full complement of roles for minorities to emulate. Such diminished coverage sets a cycle into motion: white content attracts white consumers which in turn encourages more white-based coverage, and the exclusionary cycle continues.

Even substantial presentation in the media may be misleading if minority women and men are slotted into a relatively small number of programs, such as children's, or reduced to victim and/or assailant in reality-based programming. Nor is there much sign of improvement. In 1989, Robert MacGregor acknowledged the invisibility of visible minority women in Canada's national newsmagazine (*Maclean's*), measured by the quantity and quality of their appearances over a 30-year span. A follow-up study indicates that women of colour continue to be "couched in compromise" by virtue of mixed messages that concede improvements in quantity but not quality (Kunz and Fleras 1998). Or consider the plight of African-Americans on television. Of the 26 new shows scheduled by the four major U.S. networks in 1999, not a single one featured a minority lead, despite the fact that Blacks consume up to 70 hours of television per week (Allemang 1999). Programs that feature all-black casts are common enough, but most TV sitcoms continue to be segregated outside of a workplace setting. As a result there is a dearth of dramas built around black families or protagonists as a result of the belief that there is no sizeable demographic audience for such programming. Not surprisingly, black casting in prime time sitcoms remains stuck around the clownish or demeaning (MacDonald 1992; Cuff 1992). Finally, even audiences appear to be racially segregated in terms of programming preferences, reflecting a lack of cross-over appeal for films and TV programs (Steinhorn and Diggs-Brown 1999).

However extensive the invisibilizing process, it would be inaccurate to accuse the mainstream media of ignoring minorities. A "shallows and rapids" treatment is a more accurate appraisal. That is, under normal circumstances, minorities are ignored or rendered irrelevant by the mainstream press ("shallows"). Otherwise coverage is guided by the context of crisis or calamity, involving natural catastrophes, civil wars, and colourful insurgents ("rapids"). Mainstream news media only want visuals of emaciated children and rotting cattle carcasses, according to Susan Moeller, author of *Compassion Fatigue: How the Media Cover War, Famine, and Death*. Sadly, as she concludes, many aid agencies are often only too happy to provide graphic footage. When the crisis subsides or the story stales, media interest is suspended—until the next eye-popping debacle. Conflicts and calamities are common enough, of course, but almost exclusive coverage on "happenings" or "events" without concern for the historical or social context has had the effect of eroding minority needs, concerns, or aspirations. The flamboyant and sensational are highlighted to satisfy audience needs and sell copy, without much regard for the impact on the lives of those sensationalized. This distortion may not be deliberately engineered. Rather, the misrepresentation reflects media preoccupation with audience ratings and advertising revenues. The media may shun responsibility for their discriminatory impact, arguing that they are doing what is necessary to stay financially afloat. Nevertheless, such an exclusive focus has the effect of portraying minorities as unworthy of sympathy or equitable treatment. And in alternately denying, then exaggerating, minority presence both in Canada and abroad, mixed messages are circulated that simultaneously racialize antisocial behaviour while criminalizing ethnicity.

II. Stereotyping Minorities

Minorities have long complained of stereotyping by the mainstream media. Historically, people of colour were portrayed in a manner that did not offend prevailing prejudices. Liberties with minority depictions in consumer advertising were especially flagrant. In an industry geared towards image and appeal, advertisers insisted that their products be sanitized and bleached of colour for fear of losing revenue. Images of racial minorities were steeped in unfounded generalizations that emphasized the comical or grotesque. This stereotyping fell into a pattern: Blacks in prime time TV shows cavorted about as superhero/ athletes or sex-obsessed buffoons when not typecast in secondary roles such as those of hipsters or outlaws (Azam 2000). Latino males came across as banditos, greasers, and revolutionaries, while Latina women are all heat and passionate salsa (Stam and Miller 2000). And newscasting continues to stereotype. A survey of major Toronto dailies indicated some minorities were typecast as criminals by way of a racist discourse that overreported their problems but underreported their successes except as entertainers or athletes.

Consider how the mainstream media have historically stereotyped Canada's aboriginal peoples. The image of aboriginal peoples as the "other" has been refracted through the prism of a Eurocentric lens, spanning the spectrum from their eulogization as "noble savages" and "quixotic romantics" to their debasement as "villains" or "victims," with the stigma of "problem people" or "menacing subversive" sandwiched in between (Blythe 1994; Wall 1997). Images of tribalism and the quixotic continue to resonate with a spicy mixture of meanings, from backwardness to spiritual mysticism to ecological custodians (Jakubowicz et al. 1994). The net effect of this symbolic "emasculation" has ensured an image of aboriginal peoples as "safe, exotic, and somewhere else," as Philip Hayward writes with respect to the music industry's co-optation of aboriginal artists, and it is precisely these stereotypes that compromise the aspirations of aboriginal peoples in Canada (Switzer 1997).

In recent years, however, Muslims appear to have replaced other disadvantaged minorities as the most egregious victims of media stereotyping. Rather than treating the Islamic world as worthy of respect in its own right, media approach it in terms of its differences and clashes with the West. Both the news and entertainment media foster disparaging images of Muslims as backward or fanatic. Muslim women are portrayed as the antithesis of the progressive and liberated Canadian mainstream woman, whose practices and values reflect and reinforce stereotypes as belly-dancing exotic, hijabs-wearing repressed, and a gun toting militant-terrorist (Bullock and Jafri 2000). Muslim males are typecast as ruthless and greedy tyrants, often removed beyond the pale of rational politics and civilized values because of their religious fanaticism and seeming disregard for the value of human life and freedom (Canadian Islamic Congress 1999). By typecasting Muslims as sleazy bullies or tyrannical patriarchs, according to a six-month study by the Media Watch group of the Canadian Islamic Congress, the mainstream media have intensified discrimination against Muslims. Films, including *The Siege* and *True Lies,* feed into the stereotyping, with their typecasting of Muslims as warring and dangerous, while conflating religion with terrorism (Kutty and Youseff 1998; Waxman 1998; Elmasry 1999). In the process, an entire people and civilization are vilified by the actions of those who act outside the boundaries of normalcy as defined by the Muslim world. And since most Canadians rarely encounter minorities such as Muslims in daily life, what little they do know is derived at face value from mainstream media messages (Ali 2000).

III. Problematizing Minorities

Minority women and men are frequently singled out by the media as social problems, that is, as having problems or creating problems in need of political attention or costly solutions. As problem people, they are taken to task by the media for making demands that may imperil Canada's unity or national prosperity. Too often aboriginal peoples are portrayed as individuals whose relationship to Canada is mediated by conflict, welfare dependency, disruption and militancy, social pathologies, and excessive demands. Recurrent images define aboriginal peoples as (a) a threat to Canada's territorial integrity or national interests (debate over Nisga'a self-government as an unconstitutional infringement on existing political jurisdictions); (b) a risk to Canada's social order (violence between aboriginal peoples and lobster fishers at Burnt Church, New Brunswick); (c) an economic liability (the costs associated with settling massive land claims, restitution for righting historical wrongs such as that of residential schools, or recent proposals to constitutionally entrench inherent self-governing rights); (d) a thorn in the side of the criminal justice system (ranging from the wrongful imprisonment of Donald Marshall to police shootings of aboriginal people including the killing of Dudley George at Ipperwash, Ontario); or (e) unscrupulous manipulators who are not adverse to breaking the law (cigarette smuggling or rum running across borders) or swindling their own people while hiding behind the smokescreen of aboriginal rights and entitlements (reports of nepotism and graft in First Nations communities).

Time and again aboriginal people are depicted as "troublesome constituents" whose demands for self-determination and the right to inherent self-government are contrary to Canada's liberal-democratic tradition. Aboriginal activism tends to be framed as a departure from established norms regardless of the context or urgency, while protestors are frequently labelled as dangerous or irrational. Such a dismissal has a dual effect. The legitimacy of dissent is marginalized by trivializing aboriginal concerns, and audiences are distracted from the issues at hand by the criminalization of both actors and action. As a result, many news stories involving aboriginal assertiveness are couched as a conflict of interest between the forces of disarray (aboriginal peoples) and those of order, reason, and stability (mainstream society) (Abel 1997). Compounding this negativity are constant references to a pathological reliance on welfare, a predilection for alcohol and substance abuse, an inclination to laziness and lack of ambition, and a temptation to mismanage what little they have. In other words, the mainstream media portray aboriginal communities as insoluble nightmares of self-induced crime, pain, or failure (Ziervogel 1999). The combined impact of this negative coverage paints a villainous picture of Canada's first peoples, inasmuch as success stories are rarely reported, and those that do succeed are proof of exceptions to the rule.

Non-aboriginal minorities are also problematized by the media. People of colour, both foreign and native born, are subject to negative reporting that dwells on costs, threats, and inconveniencies. As individuals or as groups, minority women and men appear in a dazzling array of trouble spots: hassling police, stumping immigration authorities, cheating on welfare, or battling among themselves at community or family levels. Media reporting of refugees pounces on illegal entries and the associated costs of processing them and their integration into Canada. Immigrants are routinely cast as potential troublemakers who steal jobs from Canadians, cheat on the welfare system, manipulate educational opportunities without making a corresponding commitment to Canada, engage in illegal activities such as drugs or smuggling, and imperil Canada's unity and identity by refusing to discard their culture. This negativity may be coded in different ways, from content to positioning and layout of the story, length of article and size of type, content of headlines and kickers (phrases immediately following the headline), use of newspeak or inflammatory language, coded speech that reinforces negative messages, use of quotes, statistics, and racial origins (Tator and Henry 2000).

Admittedly, the mainstream media are not averse to problematizing anyone, white or non-white, given the tendency of media narratives to cram reality into a framework of conflict or negativity. But impacts differ: the institutionalized power at the disposal of the mainstream helps to deflect and diffuse the unflattering; in contrast, the impact of disparaging minority representation is sharpened because of their specific vulnerabilities. The consequences of this miscasting not only reinforces the wedge between the "minority them" and "mainstream us." Such miscasting also has a tendency to demonize an entire community for the actions of a few, in effect further marginalizing minority women and men.

IV. Ornamentalizing Minorities

Mainstream media tend to portray minority women and men as ornamental features of society. Rarely do they appear as average, normal, tax-paying Canadians with a broad range of opinions on subjects that extend beyond their race or community. Rather, minority women and men tend to be trivialized ("miniaturized") as tokens in sorting out who gets what in society. This ornamentalizing effect is achieved by casting minorities in roles that are meant only to amuse or embellish. Minorities are coupled with the exotic and sensual, invoked as congenial hosts for faraway destinations, enlisted as superstar boosters for athletics and sporting goods, or ghettoized in certain marketing segments related to rap or hip hop. For example, travel brochures tend to portray minority women and men as background equivalent to the flora and fauna of the locale—a soothing visual backdrop that reinforces a deference to whiteness while further otherizing minority women and men (Hoeschmann 1999). Most minority roles on television consist of bit parts, a kind of walking away from the camera as Canadian pianist Oscar Peterson once explained. Blacks on television are locked into roles as entertainers, criminals, or athletes, with little emphasis on their intellectual or professional prowess, and little recourse to positive roles to which youth can aspire outside of athletics or entertainment (Siddiqui 1999). Such a restriction may prove inherently satisfying to mainstream audiences, who historically have enjoyed laughing at Blacks when cast as comics or buffoons. Yet the de-politicizing of Blacks as "emasculated" cartoons has the effect of reassuring nervous audiences that minorities still "know their place" in the broader scheme of things, despite their resentment at being slotted into a single category or role in which they are expected to conform across a broad range of circumstances (Alia 1999).

V. Whitewashing Minorities

Mainstream media long revealed a reluctance to include people of colour in any meaningful fashion. Both Canadian and American cultures embraced an implicit hierarchy of racial desirability. Whiteness was normally associated with acceptability while non-whiteness evoked menacing images of danger, pollution, or "dirt" (Entman and Book 2000). Such an association in a colour-conscious society resulted in the near exclusion of people of colour from mainstream cultural products except as stereotypes. To the extent that minorities did appear, acceptance was conditional on "scrubbing" minorities clean of any unpleasantness or threat they might pose to society. Inclusion was contingent on *airbrushing* minority women and men of those minority blemishes deemed unacceptable. This whitewashing of minorities was especially flagrant in consumer advertising. In an industry geared towards the creation of visually appealing images that tap into the fears and fantasies of the targeted audiences, advertisers insisted that their products be sanitized and bleached of colour for fear of alienating their primary (white) consumers.

Mainstream media are increasingly inclusive of minority women and men. Minorities are routinely portrayed as leading and acceptable figures in film, TV programming, and advertising. Yet the representational basis of media-minority relations continues to be couched in compromise. Minority models may appear in print advertising or in a fashion spread, but only if their appearance conforms to white standards of race-neutral beauty (Kunz and Fleras 1998). The world of celebrity may be open to whites and non-whites alike, but only if there is cross-over appeal. The most recognizable faces in the world today include sports figures of colour, such as Tiger Woods and Michael Jordan. To this list we could add celebrities such as Bill Cosby but also the now (in)famous OJ Simpson. OJ Simpson's rise to celebrity status in the 1970s and 1980s was predicated on his absorption into a white corporate culture. His cross-over appeal lay in his cultivation of a careful image as a "colorless male supremacist" or a "white non-black" (Sabo and Jansen 1998). With his looks, athleticism, congenial personality, and assurance of a devoted family man, Simpson represented the acceptable face of blackness in the U.S., one that allowed everyone to feel good about race relations in America while sleeping safer in their homes at night. But acceptance proved conditional: his disgrace and decline as an accused murderer revolved around the playing of a race card by which he was "re-raced" in terms of a black racial identity. A similar fate befell Ben Johnson who also underwent a shift towards "blackness" when stripped of an Olympic Gold Medal for substance abuse. The otherizing of Ben Johnson shifted accordingly, from Canadian to Jamaican-Canadian to Jamaican, as the allegations of substance abuse gradually eroded his honorary white status.

The current situation may look different, but appearances are deceiving. On the one hand, minorities are increasingly foregrounded as subjects of acceptability in advertising, programming, and film. The overtly negative stereotypes of the past are no longer acceptable in a society that claims to be colour-blind and in which open discrimination is neither tolerable nor legal, with the result that improvements in representation are inevitable. On the other hand, subtle images that codify racial preference remain in circulation. Mainstream cultural products have only been partly transformed despite the higher visiblility of minority women and men in commercial media. Differences are rarely taken seriously; preferred, instead, is a kind of pretend pluralism that revels in surfaces rather than substance. People of colour are not fully accepted as equivalent to whites but as inferior or irrelevant in a society that endorses only an acceptable face of diversity. For example, consider how skin colour continues to matter: acceptance of racially different minorities is contingent on thier looking lighter and more "Causasion." Looking lighter ensures a higher level of acceptability by transforming minority women and men into "objects" that are less threatening or intimidating. Not surprisingly, lighter-skinned models promote products pitched at audience fantasies associated with higher-status goods, from cars to credit cards. Darker skin representations are linked with the more mundane necessities of life, from fast foods to street wear (Entman and Book 2000). In other words, when it comes to the representational basis of media-minority relations, the relationship between media and society is inseparable. Media messages, especially those of advertising, continue to reflect, reinforce, and reproduce the inequities of status and acceptance that underscore society at large.

Accounting for Exclusiveness

The push of media inclusiveness is not inseparable from the politics of misrepresentation. The challenge lies in creating more positive images of minority women and men by making the mainstream media more responsive to positive portrayals of minorities. Yet there is little consensus regarding what constitutes positive minority images, nor is there much agreement on whether the mainstream media can possibly accommodate the kind of changes articulated by minority women and men. The elusiveness of creating a multicultural and inclusive mainstream media is not personal but systemic because of its rootedness in institutional agendas, priorities, dynamics, processes, and imperatives. Four factors are thought to be foremost in precluding media institutional inclusiveness: (1) institutional (commercial) imperatives; (2) institutional dynamics (systemic stereotyping); (3) institutional logic (systemic bias); and (4) institutional values (discourses in defence of dominant ideology). Others, such as confusion or uncertainty, prejudice, and racism have been discussed.

I. Institutional (Commercial) Imperatives

Mainstream private media are commercial enterprises with a responsibility for the bottom line. Their goal is to foster those images and representations that generate revenue by maximizing the link between audience and advertising. Commercial media do not see themselves as agents of social change whose primary goal is to criticize, challenge, resist, or reform, even if they may have a social responsibility to do so. Nor do the media exist to inform or to entertain. As a rule they are not interested in solving social problems or in promulgating progressive social change unless consumer goods are directly involved. Mainstream media are first and foremost business ventures whose devotion to the bottom line revolves around generating advertising revenues by attracting the largest possible audience. This preoccupation with audience ratings and advertising revenues is pivotal in shaping the quality and quantity of media representations (Gray 1995). Financial pressures may compel media to curtail investigative journalism, reduce minority contacts, capitulate to more demanding deadlines, and resort to the formulaic as a preferred way of generating outputs. Fear of bad publicity or negative backlash to minority inclusion in advertising may be unfounded or exaggerated; nevertheless, it exists.

II. Institutional Dynamics: Systemic Stereotyping

Institutional dynamics are sharply animated by those patterned images known as stereotypes. Stereotyping may be defined as a process of codifying reality for the purposes of conveying information about the world "out there." As a conceptual shorthand that enlightens even as it restricts, stereotyping offers a simplistic explanation of the world that extends to all members of a category regardless of individual differences. To be sure, stereotypes are an indispensable component in processing everyday information. In a world of bewildering complexity, stereotypes reduce reality into manageable proportions as a basis for defining situations. Stereotypes only become a problem when they are used to justify behaviour that denies or excludes others by virtue of preconceived (and irrelevant) characteristics. And just as stereotyping is critical in processing everyday information, so too are media reliant on stereotypes for codifying reality for consumer consumption.

Thus, media stereotyping of minority women and men is not necessarily a perceptual problem involving individual prejudice by a misinformed industry. Rather, media stereotyping is intrinsic to the operational dynamic of an industry constructed around simplifying information for audiences to consume by tapping into a collective portfolio of popular and unconscious images, both print and visual, each of which imposes a readily identifiable frame or narrative spin. Because of limitations in time and space, the mainstream media are rarely in a position to develop complex or complicated interpretations of reality that capture the spectrum of human emotion, conflict, or contradiction. Not surprisingly, distortions through simplification are inevitable. Both print or electronic news are constructed around the transformation of events "out there" into frames that are intense, unambiguous, familiar, and marketable (Czerny et al. 1994). For example, newsworthiness is routinely sorted into a conflict frame, with clearly defined protagonists and clearly articulated positions—a process that may appeal to mainstream audiences but that compromises the complexity of minority realities. Programming is organized around the formula of keeping it safe, simple, and familiar for fear of alienating audiences or advertisers. And advertising is virtually unthinkable without a stock of preconceived and readily identifiable images for subliminally linking products with advertisers.

In short, stereotyping is a systemic aspect of media processes. Over time these stereotypes solidify into definitive statements about "reality," and while not "real" in the conventional sense, they become real in their social consequences. Although personal stereotypes reflect individual preferences and dislikes, institutional stereotypes persist without the element of consciousness or malevolent intent. These stereotypes are systemic in that they are intrinsic to normal institutional operations, rules, and rewards. Institutional stereotypes do not originate from conscious intent; they arise from the logical consequences of seemingly neutral priorities or procedures. Rather than an error in perception, in other words, stereotyping constitutes a system of social control through the internalization of negative images.

Media do not necessarily set out to control or stereotype. Nevertheless, the operational rules and processes are such that the media have the adverse effect of controlling minorities by virtue of largely one-sided typecasts. For example, critics have argued that stereotypes are employed to keep aboriginal peoples in their place and out of sight, thus sanitizing the colonization of first peoples by assuaging white guilt (Churchill 1994). With stereotypes, furthermore, it become progressively easier to disregard the humanity and status of aboriginal peoples as a distinct people. The racially coded discourses that comprise stereotyping not only tap into public fears but also intensify public hunger for tougher measures of social control. Admittedly, there is no evidence to suggest that sustained exposure to stereotypes will alter existing patterns of beliefs. Rather, stereotypes are likely to reinforce what people already think and believe (Krieger 1998). Nevertheless, the cumulative effect of such stereotyping may reinforce the peripheral status of aboriginal peoples by de-politicizing their concerns and contributions as active and meaningful members to society.

III. Institutional Logic: Systemic Bias

There is another type of institutional bias, both impersonal and unconscious, yet no less invidious or destructive. Its unobtrusiveness makes it that much more difficult to detect, let alone to isolate and combat. Systemic bias refers to this type of subtle yet powerful form of institutional discrimination entrenched within the structure (rules, organization), function (norms, goals), and process (procedures). Systemic bias can be defined as the unintended yet adverse consequences that result from evenly and equally applying seemingly neutral rules to unequal situations, but with dissimilar effects for the historically disadvantaged. Universal rules and ostensibly standards may be biased in practice, rather than principle, even if the actors are themselves free of prejudicial discrimination. Barriers that preclude full and equal participation may be unintentional but hidden in institutional procedures and reward systems that inadvertently penalize some individuals because of who they are, rather than what they can do. Policies, rules, priorities, and programs may not be inherently racist or deliberately discriminatory—that is, institutions do not go out of their way to exclude or deprive minorities. But rules that are evenly and uniformly applied may have the inadvertent but real effect of excluding or penalizing those who don't fit because of differences or disadvantage. With systemic bias, in other words, it is not the intent or motive that counts, but rather the context and the consequences since identical treatment in unequal contexts may cement the inequities.

The charge of systemic bias is applicable to contemporary media. Journalists and editors are not free of bias, according to Tator and Henry (2000) and Hackett and Zhao (1998), despite oft-quoted claims of objectivity or neutrality. The result is that racism continues to exist in the mainstream news media because of language and images that reflect racialized assumptions and beliefs. These continue to reinforce negative stereotypes or to construct minority women and men as social problems and outsiders that undermine Canadian society. Think of how minorities are miscast because of media preoccupation with style over substance, visuals over depth, adversity over co-operation. For the most part minorities as a group are ignored or rendered irrelevant by the mainstream media unless victimized by crisis or calamity involving natural catastrophes, civil wars and ethno-religious strife, or colourful insurgence. This obsession with coups, quakes, and body counts has the effect of "framing" minority peoples (especially in developing world countries) as volatile and prone to mindless violence with a minimal regard for the sanctity of human life. While such violence occurs and deserves coverage and criticism, the absence of balanced and contextualized coverage culminates in a singular and distorted image of minorities as pathological or impulsive.

The absence of diversity in creative positions within the media industry may account for the systemic bias. Despite some improvement, minorities are largely excluded from roles as producers, directors, editors, and screenwriters. Fewer still are destined to attain the upper levels of management where key decision-making occurs. One consequence of such exclusion is that minority realities are inevitably refracted through the prism of a white-controlled media. Conflicts of interest are inevitable: should media stress our similarities or our differences? For example, the interracial romances in *Ally McBeal* are praised by some as progressive for not bringing up the "race" issue, but criticized by others for ignoring the "race" dimension in any such relationship. For women of colour, the situation is even more deplorable. They are doubly jeopardized by "pale male" ideologies that devalue contributions, distort experiences, limit options, and undermine their self-confidence and identity as Canadians. In this type of situation, one might conclude, what is said by the media is just as significant as what is not.

IV. Institutional Values: "Ideologically Loaded"

Mainstream media constitute a socially constructed system of technologically driven communication that is anything but neutral or passive in delivery. As a social construction, the mainstream media contain a number of hidden agendas and dominant ideologies in advancing vested rather than common interests (ideology = ideas and ideals that sustain relations of power by privileging one point of view as natural, superior, and normal, and others as inferior or irrelevant). Mainstream media are loaded with ideological assumptions that bolster the ideas and ideals of a dominant discourse while precluding the values and views of those who challenge convention (Abel 1997). Mainstream news media are ideological in that they endorse (or normalize) certain points of view as normal and acceptable; other views are discredited as a threat or violation of the norm. Media messages combine to naturalize contemporary social arrangements as normal, necessary, and inevitable, rather than as self-serving social constructs.

For example, a dominant discourse shared by many Canadians is a commitment to the ideal of consensus and conformity. Such a perspective ensures that those protest actions contrary to social unity are framed accordingly, that is, as deviations from a norm that need to be eliminated for the common good or national interests. A clear dichotomy of good versus evil is inadvertently conveyed by this agenda-setting process, as images tend to punish minorities by racializing crime while criminalizing racial minority groups. However unintentional the consequences, the effects of privileging the ideological media are anything but inconsequential, resulting in the exclusion of alternate points of view, a reduction in dissent and disagreement, the creation of consensus and compliance with dominant ideologies, and the restriction of free debate. Mainstream media do set out to contain or control, but the systemic bias within media messages has a controlling effect on audiences by drawing negative inferences about minorities. The net result is the same in both cases: a one-sided interpretation of reality that normalizes even while it marginalizes.

V. Impact: Silences of the Media

Media misrepresentations of minorities have tended to lapse into the unacceptable. Minority women and men have been rendered invisible through underrepresentation in programming and images that count, have been visibly overrepresented in areas that don't count such as sports or as problems, and misrepresented because of stereotyping. This indiscretion extends to all media processes, including advertising, newscasting, TV programming, and filmmaking, each of which negativizes minorities either by intent or by systemic effects. Such cultural racism is not new to the mainstream media. Just as representations in English literature have long portrayed colonized minorities as barbaric and inferior, thus facilitating the cause of Western imperialism (Said 1978), so too do media messages convey a message that minority women and men are not like "us," but are a "them" in need of pity, condemnation, or indifference. The cumulative result of racializing minority women and men as the "other" has had the effect of reinforcing a perception of minorities as peripheral foreigners and alien outsiders (Hanamoto, 1995).

The otherizing of minorities can be defined as a process by which minority women and men are treated as falling outside the mainstream. Strongly implicit in this otherization is a diminution of minority differences as irrelevant and inferior. The otherization process implies a double bind, insofar as minorities are denied their difference as a basis for equitable treatment, yet are denied full equality and similar treatment because of their differences. This racialization of minorities as the "other" may not be openly articulated, but so culturally embedded and tacitly accepted as to render this inferiorization both natural and normal (O'Barr 1994). Such an otherizing process cannot be considered accidental or unfortunate but systemic and controlling; that is, reflecting a process that is integral to media operations rather than peripheral to how media business is conducted. To be sure, media images of whites can be equally demeaning in light of a ratings-driven commitment to sensationalize or trivialize. Yet the impact of mainstream miscasting cannot compare in consequence, given the dearth of positive minority representations to counterbalance negative depictions. As a result, this otherizing process can be read backwards and forwards. Media representations about the "other" often say more about the "us" than the "them." Media depictions of "others" as socially constructed images reflect and reinforce mainstream perceptions, fears, and anxieties of minority women and men, and only rarely examine minority lives and concerns on their own merit (Hanamoto 1995).

The cumulative impact of media otherizing bodes poorly for Canada. The rhetoric of otherizing minorities as different and undeserving has resulted in the belittling of minority women and men, thus simplifying the process of exerting control while minimizing the complicating emotions of guilt or remorse (Churchill 1994; Riggins 1997). The mainstream is portrayed as the norm and standard by which to judge or accept. In contrast, minority women and men come across as "creatures" beyond the pale of normalcy, with lives that seem to revolve about their "defining" status of race or religion to the virtual exclusion of other attributes. This miscasting also has the effect of de-politicizing the concerns and contributions of minority women and men in Canadian society. Images of "them" as "those people" are filtered through the Eurocentric prism of preconceptions and priorities, and in the process mainstream disdain towards minorities or mainstream yearnings are projected because of unresolved desires to emulate the "other." For example, the social stigma resulting from the linkage of religion with suspected acts of terrorist violence not only insults minority women and men but also endangers their physical and social being, while violating core Canadian precepts that oppose the incitement of hatred against an identifiable religious and ethnic group. The scapegoating of minorities as dangerous, irrelevant, or inferior has also had the effect of victimizing minorities in their being the brunt of public resentment over unpopular social changes. Differences that are threatening or dangerous are "contained, controlled, normalized, stereotyped, idealized, marginalized, and reified—in effect driving a psychological wedge between minorities and the rest of Canadian society.

What kind of messages are conveyed by these negative depictions? What difference do they make? Imagine if the only information foreigners received about Canadians consisted of news clips about Paul Bernardo, the misconduct of Canadian soldiers in Somalia, and the beating death of Reena Virk by Canadian teenagers. On the basis of such skimpy and selective coverage, Canadians would come across as violent and barbaric with a callous or indifferent disregard for human life. Yet such a portrayal hardly squares with the reality experienced by most Canadians and its routine ranking as the world's best country to live in (St. Lewis 1996). A similar line of reasoning should apply to media representations of Canada's minorities. Through images and codes, minority women and men are taught that cultural differences outside the imprint of white middle-class culture are inferior, deviant, irrelevant, or threatening. Overtly demeaning representations are combined with the absence of complex characterization and balanced coverage to instil an inferiority complex. In short, no one should underestimate the negative effects of media mistreatment on minority lives and life-chances. Negative portraits inflict a degree of symbolic and psychological violence through the internalization of hateful images that trivialize or demean. Any sense of self-worth plunges because of images that devalue minorities to the status of the "other"—to be pitied, despised, or shunned as dictated by the context. References to ethnocentrism and white superiority may not be openly articulated in media "whitewashing," yet the Eurocentric standard by which the other is judged and impugned are tacitly assumed and deeply ingrained. How then do we deal with such miscasting madness in a society that is anchored around the principles of multiculturalism and institutional inclusiveness?

Conclusion

Canada's mainstream media have been accused of harbouring a love-hate relationship with minority women and men. To one side, media rely on minorities as a source of content for narratives, an angle for spicing up a story, a foil for sharpening the attributes of mainstream heroes, a catalyst for driving plot lines or character development, or a token dash of colour to an otherwise pallid cultural package. To the other side, minorities are subject to media "hate" by the playing of the "race card." Media representation of minority women and men has reflected a remarkably narrow range of images whose cumulative effect has been to diminish or demean minorities as positive contributors to Canadian society. By asserting mainstream values and beliefs as natural or universal—the tendency for people to see the world through their own experiences and cultures as a starting point for comparison or analysis is inescapable—whiteness becomes the norm that judges minorities for what they are not (not white) rather than for what they are (Artiles 1998). Such an ambiguous state of affairs raises a critical question: Why do particular types of images dominate the public domain while others are ignored or dismissed as part of the public agenda? Answers invariably are about power; after all, media images of minorities are not direct reflections of an objective or empirical reality. Rather than something natural or normal "out there," media minority representations constitute a social construction created by individuals within particular social and political contexts that plug into the existing distribution of power and resources (see Croucher 1997).

CHAPTER 9

"Multiculturalizing" the Media

Framing the Issue

Canada's mainstream media have come under pressure to become more inclusive. Multicultural minorities and aboriginal peoples are posing some tough questions of the popular media regarding their failure to engage constructively with Canada's diversity. Both aboriginal peoples and minority women and men are bombarded with messages that rarely reflect their realities, says Gary Farmer, founder of Aboriginal Voices (cited in *Ottawa Citizen*, 12 February 12, 1997). This miscasting by the mainstream media makes it doubly important for minorities to control images about themselves if they hope to take control of their lives and life-chances. Responsible coverage of minority interests and concerns is predicated on the need to stop (a) selective and sensationalistic accounts, (b) images and words that demean and malign, (c) portrayals that are biased and unbalanced while lacking any sense of context, and (d) stereotyping that incites hatred, fear, or indifference. The challenge lies in multiculturalizing the media by making it more responsive to minority realities.

Proposals for establishing an inclusive media include the following demands: (a) the incorporation of minority perspectives into the media process, (b) multicultural programming, (c) balanced and impartial newscasting, and (d) sensitivity training for journalists and decision-makers (Abel 1997). Alternative arrangements include the creation of parallel or even separate media outlets for enhancing minority input into media processes and outcomes. The objective of these demands goes beyond simply increasing the number of minorities in print or on the screen. Emphasis instead is on wielding sufficient power so that media representations have a better chance of reflecting, reinforcing, and advancing minority concerns and ambitions.

At the heart of minority demands for an inclusive and multicultural media is the need for improving the representational basis of media-minority relations. Such a commitment is understandable in light of the power exercised by contemporary mainstream media. The world we inhabit is pervaded by, resonates with, and is transformed through media images (or representations). Proliferation of these representations makes it impossible to distinguish fantasy from reality, according to Angus and Jhally (1989), especially since the "real" is so thoroughly media-ted that any distinction between reality and media images is rendered futile except for analytical purposes. Not surprisingly, the control of knowledge and its dissemination through media images is fundamental to the exercise of power in society. Media images are critical for conveying shared cultural beliefs and underlying assumptions about how a society is defined, constructed, and organized. These images not only assist in the identification and construction of what is acceptable or desirable in society. After all, media images about "others" may say more about the perceptions of those who construct them than anything about the realities of minority women and men. Images also serve as "windows" that routinely interpret social reality from a certain point of view as natural and normal while dismissing other interpretations as inappropriate. Such ideologically loaded images are not without consequence for minority women and men, proving both a strength or a weakness depending on who's holding the levers of power. With images as powerful as they are in shaping social agendas, the timing is right for minority women and men to reclaim control over representations about who they are and what they want to be. Yet a conflict of interest is inevitable: To the extent that the mainstream media have proven capable of moving over and making cultural space, despite some degree of reluctance or difficulty, the prospect for multiculturalizing the mainstream media is not to be casually dismissed.

Yet establishment institutions seldom willingly surrender even a portion of their power and privilege. A "push" is usually necessary as a proactive measure to ensure more inclusive standards and delivery of culturally sensitive services through the removal of discriminatory barriers. Nowhere is this more evident than with the mainstream media, who historically disdained having to move over and share power. Mainstream commercial media do not see themselves as reform agencies to promote progressive change or "engage" diversity, even though they may have a social responsibility to do so. Their raison d'être is disarmingly simple: to make money by connecting an audience to advertisers through ratings. Institutional practices that once worked to generate revenues (for example, stereotyping) will be retained, and those that do not will be discarded. Such a bottom-line mentality has not been conducive to minority demands for more inclusive coverage, given media preference for "bitability" over context, the flamboyant over the nuanced, conflict over co-operation, and personalities over issues (see Atkinson 1994).

This chapter is concerned with exploring trends in re-defining the representational basis of Canada's media-minority relations. The chapter focuses on the challenges associated with establishing a more inclusive mainstream media by comparing institutional ideals with the realities of implementation. It also emphasizes the accomplishments to date in improving the quantity and quality of media minority images in line with Canada's multicultural commitments. The chapter begins by examining the concept of institutional inclusiveness in terms of principles, practices, and barriers to attainment. This is followed by a discussion of what is involved in multiculturalizing the mainstream media. To one side are those reforms aimed at mainstreaming diversity by improving the institutional responsiveness of existing media institutions. To the other side, the creation of separate aboriginal and ethnic media has allowed minority women and men to take greater control of how they are portrayed. In both cases, the challenges of fostering an inclusive and multicultural media have proven to be daunting, and the success stories that exist serve to remind us of how much more needs to be done before putting multiculturalism to work in re-making mainstream media.

Institutional Inclusiveness

It is one thing to encourage the multicultural diversity of Canada in principle. It is another thing to promote a multiculturalism that endorses the reality of diversity as a legitimate component in Canadian society building. It may be something altogether different to transform these principles into institutional practices in a way that makes an appreciable difference. Institutions can no longer afford the luxury of remaining aloof from the demographic and cultural revolutions taking place in Canada. Conventional ways of doing things—from working with others to delivery of a service or a product—are less acceptable than in the past. The combination of minority pressure and government edicts has compelled many institutions to re-define themselves in ways that are more inclusive and equitable. Barriers continue to plague the transformation process since those in positions of power dislike the prospect of relinquishing privilege. Institutional subcultures and organizational procedures may not lend themselves to inclusive change. Yet doing nothing is neither a solution nor an expression of neutrality. Dangers lurk everywhere for those impervious to the demands of a diverse, changing, and uncertain world. Consider the damage to personal careers and institutional reputation. Or, imagine the potential for social chaos unless minority women and men are convinced that they have a stake in Canadian society. The theme of putting multiculturalism to work at institutional levels revolves around the challenges of engaging with diversity in ways that balance inclusiveness with the realities of organizational dynamics.

I.   Defining Inclusiveness

What is meant by an inclusive institution? The concept goes beyond a simple incorporation of minority women and men into an institution. It also transcends the insertion of bits of ethnic symbols into the corporate setting. Inclusiveness is about fostering the full and equal participation of everyone regardless of their difference by creating space and sharing power through adjustments in structures, values, and practices. For our purposes then, *institutional inclusion* can be defined as a process by which institutions proactively and positively engage with diversity as different yet equal by way of structural arrangements that provide a basis for working together with our differences.

Inclusiveness is about the acceptance and promotion of differences as necessary, normal, and beneficial without ignoring the need to address disadvantages that minorities confront. It begins with the "radical" assumption that all persons are equally valued members of Canada's institutions, and it is worthwhile to do whatever it takes to include everyone as different yet equal. As Joan Wallach Scott points out in her article "Campaign against Political Correctness," the concept of inclusiveness entails a process of responding appropriately to an institution's diversity mix—keeping in mind that diversity is not a state of separate being in which predetermined classes of people are slotted into a pre-existing category. Rather, diversity is properly thought of as differences that are hierarchically arranged in relations of power and inequality, undergoing constant evaluation and adjustment in response to social changes. In other words, diversity is not a thing but a relationship, and that makes it doubly important to understand how these constructed relations are expressed, sustained, challenged, and transformed. Failure to understand the dynamics of these often unequal and contested relations glosses over the challenges of living together with our differences.

There are good reasons why institutions should become more inclusive, especially at a time when society is increasingly diverse and demanding. For service organizations, a commitment to diversity can reap institutional dividends by easing workplace tensions, generating creative synergies, facilitating community access, and improving the quality of service delivery. For private companies, positive and proactive engagement with diversity may be good for business. Methods of wealth creation have changed from mass-produced goods and one-size-fits-all service to a growing reliance on meeting the multicultural needs of ethnically driven niche markets, both domestically and internationally. Diversity connections can provide a platform for internationalizing domestic businesses and improving competitive advantage in global markets, as Bill Cope and Mary Kalantzis point out in their 1996 book *Productive Diversity: A New Australian Approach to Work and Management.* In an era of expanding global markets yet sharpened local needs, institutions increasingly rely on the language skills, cultural knowledge, life experience, and international connections that people of diversity bring to the workplace. The languages and cultural heritage of multicultural minority communities have the potential to assist in priming partnerships that are required for institutions to internationalize. An inclusive institution is able to capitalize on an expanded pool of talent, foster more co-operative working relations, promote a positive corporate image, and secure open lines of communications with diverse communities.

II. Operationalizing the Concept

An inclusive institution is anchored around three conceptual levels (Cox Jr. 1993). First, inclusiveness must be directed towards employees, who are expected to act in a non-discriminatory manner in discharging their obligations to colleagues or customers. Of particular note is the need to modify personal attitudes towards differences, from its perception as inferior or irrelevant to its acceptance as normal, necessary, and beneficial. Second, groups and subcultures within institutions have been singled out as potential problem areas. Informal groupings that exist within all organizations not only exercise control over their members' behaviour; these groups also have the ability to facilitate or subvert the implementation of management diversity initiatives. Third, emphasis must be devoted to organizational structures and corporate cultures. Institutions have a tendency over time to become ends in themselves and to satisfy only their own criteria for excellence. Resistance to reforms and accommodation are not situational but structurally embedded, and this makes it important to dislodge structural and cultural barriers. The interplay of these three levels is intended to minimize disadvantage for minority employees and service receivers; it is also expected to maximize potential advantages for all stakeholders.

Five components would appear uppermost in specifying the attributes of inclusive institutions: workforce representation, organizational rules and operations, workplace climate, service delivery, and community relations. First, an institution's workforce should be representative, that is, relatively proportional to the composition of the regional labour force—taking into account both social and cultural factors as extenuating circumstances. Canada's Employment Equity Program is based on the hiring of workers of colour in federally regulated workplaces in numbers consistent with Canada's labour diversity patterns (Beeby 1998). Such a numerical accommodation applies to entry-level jobs; it also extends across the board to include all levels of management. Second, institutional rules and operations cannot hinder the recruitment, selection, training, promotion, and retention of minority personnel. This commitment to root out systemic bias demands a carefully scrutiny of company policy and procedures. Third, the institution must foster a working climate conducive to minority health and productivity. At a minimum, such a climate cannot tolerate harassment of any form; at best, diversity is actively promoted as normal, even beneficial, to effective functioning. A central element of this engagement is ensuring that managers are sensitive to cultural differences as valuable in their own right and a key asset in managing the bottom line. Fourth, an inclusive institution promotes delivery of a service that is community based and culturally sensitive. This multicultural commitment to culturally sensitive services entails a willingness on the part of the organization to engage in genuine dialogue and negotiate in partnership with the community at large. Outcomes must be based on bilateral decision making rather than be unilaterally imposed. Fifth, and finally, institutions do not operate in a social or political vacuum. They cannot hope to remain outside community control and public accountability if open and productive lines of communication are to be secured.

In short, institutional inclusiveness is all about compromise. The organizational structure, management process, and corporate culture of monocultural organizations neither acknowledge the strength of diversity nor capitalize on its potential. By contrast, as Taylor Cox argues, multicultural institutions endorse and promote diversity as a strength and opportunity rather than as a weakness or annoyance. In seeking to facilitate the shift from a monocultural to a multicultural institution, a commitment to inclusiveness goes beyond the realm of celebrating diversity or promoting minorities per se. It involves more than sensitizing managers to differences in hopes of defusing workplace conflict. Multicultural institutions deal with creating institutions by way of structural and systemic arrangements that respond to diversity as legitimate and integral without abdicating their traditional role of service delivery, institutional coherence, and bottom-line profitability. This is particularly true of the media where the politics of media representations continue to challenge or perplex. A dual focus is required to foster a media both representative of and accessible to minorities, as well as equitable in treatment and culturally sensitive. The adjustment process must occur at the level of institutional structure as well as within individual mindsets. It must also concentrate on the relationships within (the workplace environment), in addition to relationships without (clients). Fostering an inclusive media institution requires the careful calibration of rules, procedures, and outlooks. After all, underemphasizing the relevance of differences when needed is as discriminatory as overemphasizing them when uncalled for. The end result may prove an elusive and enigmatic balancing act, but critical in securing co-operative work relations.

III. Barriers to Inclusiveness

Numerous barriers exist that interfere with the inclusion process. Stumbling blocks include the presence of people, hierarchy, bureaucracy, corporate culture, and occupational subcultures. People as institutional actors are a prime obstruction. People in general tend to be ethnocentric; that is, they have a tendency to interpret the behaviour of others on the basis of what they would have done under similar circumstances. But such a rationale will prove problematic. Appeals to inclusion may fall on deaf ears when people do not understand what is going on and why. Resistance to inclusiveness is sharpened when individual self-interest is threatened. That revelation should come as no surprise; unless convinced or compelled, few individuals are inclined to relinquish power or share privilege—especially with those once perceived as inferior or irrelevant. The dimension of hierarchy will also inhibit inclusive adjustments. Those in higher echelons may be highly supportive of institutional change for a variety of reasons, ranging from genuine concern to economic expediency, with an eye towards public relations in between. Yet those in position of power may be long-winded on platitudes but short-minded on practice or implementation. Middle and lower management may be less enthusiastic about changes, preferring to cling to traditional authority patterns instead, since this level of management is most likely to be affected by institutional adjustments. Those at the bottom of the employment pecking order may be least receptive to accommodating diversity and change—even to the point of ignoring or sabotaging such directives.

Bureaucratic structures can also inhibit institutional inclusion. Larger systems operate on bureaucratic principles of hierarchy and rational control. Such a controlling imperative is not conducive to adjustment and accommodation, especially if the reform process interferes with the "business as usual" syndrome. Institutional cultures are no less inimical to change. The operational philosophy encompassed by corporate cultures may not be conducive to adjustment when it is perceived to be a threat to the bottom line or the "way things are done around here." Finally, institutional subcultures may derail the best of intentions in "inclusivizing" institutions. Subcultural values of front-line workers may differ from that of management because of differences in experience or expectations. This slippage may prove disruptive to the inclusion process.

An array of personal and social barriers confront the engagement with diversity at institutional levels. Institutions are filled with people who are resolutely opposed to and resist change at all costs. The structural embeddedness of barriers make it difficult to move over and make space. An official policy on inclusiveness will not necessarily translate into practice in any consistent fashion, with the result that decisions concerning promotion or recruitment may be clouded by prejudice, nepotism, patronage, and the "old boys network" (Travis 1998). While nothing of significance may happen without pressure from the top, similarly nothing happens on the ground without the support of the rank and file. Advances in this field are further complicated by those who advocate change without much thought for the complexities involved. Implementing institutional changes is not like installing a new computer technology; institutions are complex, often baffling landscapes of domination and control as well as resistance and sabotage whose unflinching resistance to planned change is both structural and individual. Conservatives and progressives are locked in a struggle for power and privilege. Conventional views remain firmly entrenched as vested interests balk at discarding the tried and true. Newer visions are compelling yet lack the singularity of purpose or resources to scuttle traditional ways of "doing business." The interplay of these juxtapositions can be disruptive as the institution is transformed into a "contested site" involving competing world views and opposing agendas.

Inclusivizing the Media

Mainstream media are powerful agencies with the capacity to dominate and control. In some cases, the exercise of power is blatant; in others, media power is sustained by an aura of impartiality, objectivity, and balance, yet is no less powerful in its impact. An ability to frame issues and set agendas in ways that bolster the status quo reinforces the notion of media as thought control in democratic societies. This agenda-setting property also reinforces a view of the media as discourses in defence of dominant ideology. Not unexpectedly, minority perception of media misrepresentation is informed by institutional racism and firmly locked within a Westocentric framework (Meadows 1996). Despite their status as hegemonic thought control, the mainstream media are not monolithic structures with conspiratorial designs, nor are they impervious to the challenge of change. Mainstream media as institutional structure and culture embody a complex and multifaceted assemblage of logic, values, imperatives, symbols, and norms that, collectively, serve a host of diverse interests and agendas. Put baldly, the mainstream media represent a contested site, a kind of ideological battleground where different interests struggle for control over media agendas. It is precisely the openings in this area of the "in between" that is pivotal in exploring the politics of media inclusiveness. To date, moves to re-define the representational basis of media-minority relations have focused on institutional responsiveness through mainstreaming minority women and men, or, alternatively, the establishment of parallel and separate media institutions that reflect, reinforce, and advance minority interests and aspirations. That each of these patterns of institutional inclusiveness is reaping dividends without wholesale success is indicative of the politics at the heart of multiculturalizing Canada's mainstream media.

I. Institutional Responsiveness: "Mainstreaming Diversity"

Media institutions have explored the possibility of internal reform in a way that ensures a level playing field and equal starting blocks. Reform is premised on the assumption that media structures and values are fundamentally sound and only require cosmetic changes to ensure equitable treatment. Proposed changes include the incorporation of minority perspectives into the media process, multicultural programming, removal of discriminatory barriers, balanced and impartial newscasting, and sensitivity and anti-racist training for journalists and decision-makers (Abel 1997). Responsible coverage of minority interests and concerns is predicated on the need to stop (a) selective and sensationalistic accounts, (b) images and words that demean and malign, (c) portrayals that are biased and unbalanced while lacking any sense of context, and (d) stereotyping that inflames hatred and fear. Such coverage is not simply to increase or improve the portrayals of minority women and men. Rather the focus is on sharing power so that minority representations reflect, reinforce, and advance minority concerns and ambitions. Yet a conflict of interest is inevitable unless changes are seen as bolstering the bottom line of a commercially driven yet conservatively oriented institution.

Some progress is evident in delineating a more positive and realistic portrayal of minority women and men. Reforms within the CBC include sensitivity training for program and production staff, language guidelines to reduce race and role stereotypes, and the monitoring of on-air representation of racial minorities. Abusive representations of individuals on the basis of race, ethnicity, age, gender, religion, or disability are no longer openly tolerated. The *Broadcasting Act* of 1991 has firmly endorsed the concept of "cultural expression" by expanding air time for ethnic communities. As well, the CRTC has made it known that broadcasters will be evaluated on the basis of employment-equity hiring upon renewal of licences. These initiatives are consistent with the premise that positive minority depictions will follow when minorities share power and make decisions. They are also consistent with the provisions of the *Multiculturalism Act*, with its expectation that all government departments and Crown agencies will improve minority access, equity, and representation. In addition, the *Employment Equity Act* of 1986 requires annual progress reports on minority hiring and equity goals from federally regulated agencies such as the CBC. To date, formal sanctions for non-compliance are largely symbolic.

The concept of mainstreaming is critical to securing institutional inclusiveness. Under a mainstreaming diversity approach, efforts are made to improve the quantity and quality of minority images within the existing institutional framework. Such inclusiveness makes good business sense in view of the increasing economic clout of minority-group members. Equally critical is the notion of ensuring that minorities have a say in the kind of images that appear in newscastings, advertising, or TV programming. In Southern Ontario, the multicultural channel (CFMT) delivers a much-needed service. Serving 18 cultural groups in 15 languages, CFMT has proven pivotal for those who want to cash in on the ethnic market, not only in producing 23 hours of original programming per week, but also because 60 percent of the programming is non-French or non-English (Quill 1996). Vision TV also hosts about 30 programs, largely about different religious faiths and practices. Inroads are also evident in the private sector, where, since 1984, multicultural issues have been addressed by Toronto's CITY-TV through two large blocks of non-English, non-French programming. Toronto is served by six ethnic radio stations, two closed circuit audio services, an ethnic television station, three ethnic specialty services, and another six channels accessible with special receiving equipment (Lawton 1998). On-air programming, such as the critically acclaimed but now cancelled series *North of Sixty* and *The Rez*, is also pushing the frontier of acceptance. In the field of advertising, minorities are appearing more frequently across a broader range of products and services. Companies that utilize diversity are now perceived as sophisticated and cosmopolitan as compared to their all-white counterparts who come across as archaic. Demographics may be pushing these changes: when people of colour comprise over 30 percent of the population in Vancouver and Toronto, the media have little choice except to improve the quantity and quality of representation.

One of the more successful stories is the creation in 1999 of an indigenous channel as part of basic cable package. The Aboriginal Peoples Television Network (APTN) has been called one of the most significant events in recent aboriginal history, providing aboriginal peoples with a creative outlet rather than incorporation into someone else's agenda (Clark 1999). The rationale behind APTN was clearly defensible, given the miscasting of aboriginal peoples on the screen. Biroux (1999, 4) captures their marginalization and demeanment: "Throughout the '50s and '60s, when westerns were at their peak, Indians were routinely depicted as bloodthirsty savages to be gunned down by singing cowboys in white stetsons. Only Jay Silverheels, from the Six Nations reserve in southern Ontario, maintained some dignity as the Lone Ranger's stoic sidekick." Challenging these stereotypes has amplified the need for APTN to become the world's first national public aboriginal television network. In the words of APTN chair Abraham Tagalik, "The only time we get to see ourselves in the mainstream media is in the stereotype situation. We want to show that we aren't the stereotypes by entertaining, enlightening, and breaking down the barriers" (cited in Rice 2000). Much of the initial programming is based on previously produced content from Television Northern Canada—an aboriginal network that has been broadcasting in the north since 1991 as a cultural response to the intrusion of southern television signals in the 1970s. In time, however, APTN is expected to use its annual budget of $5.9 million to provide a full range of services, including programs in English, French, and a dozen aboriginal languages.

II. Aboriginal and Ethnic Media

How well the does the present broadcasting system serve Canada's minority communities, especially in light of demographic changes and given that 80 percent of the immigrants who arrived in Canada between 1991 and 1996 spoke a mother language other than French or English? (Zerbisias 1999). In general, both ethnic minorities and aboriginal peoples have subscribed to the view that mainstream media images are racist, negative, and offensive, and this dissatisfaction has resulted in the creation of media institutions that operate alongside of the mainstream (Meadows 1995). The proliferation of ethnic presses is an important factor in serving the minority community. For example, the Indo-Canadian community in Vancouver is serviced by up to 19 publications, with about half in English (Howard 1999). In the greater Toronto area, ethnicity is well served: there are six radio stations, one black-owned FM station, two closed circuit audio services, one ethnic TV station, three ethnic speciality channels, and six SCMOs (specialized audio services that work on FM frequencies) (Zerbisias 1999). There are at least eight non-English dailies in Toronto: three in Chinese, two in Korean, and one each in Italian, Polish, and Spanish. Each reports on news from "home" as well as on current affairs in Canada. Evidence suggests that ethnically owned media perform several major functions. Heritage-language papers create safe havens for ethnic cultures to flourish, while simultaneously fostering newcomer adaptation to the new cultural environment. They also facilitate the integration of immigrants into society by serving as a buffer and agent of socialization. Others concede that ethnic newspapers may isolate the ethnic community through emphasis on heritage-culture values and links with the home country (Black and Leithner 1988). Expanding the amount of ethnic broadcasting may also make it easier for the mainstream media to renege on its responsibilities for inclusiveness.

Equally significant have been advances in aboriginal media. Canada remains the world leader in Aboriginal media: there are several hundred local aboriginal radio stations, 11 regional radio networks, 6 television production outlets, including Television Northern Canada, and a lively if uneven print media

(Alia 1999). With the introduction of Anik satellites in the early 1990s, northern aboriginal communities acquired the resources to blunt the electronic distortions of southern radio and/or TV programming. As a result, aboriginal-owned media are currently in a position to assert their own cultural values in a way that reflects their needs, concerns, and aspirations—in contrast with Eurocentric constructions of aboriginality where power, technology, ideology, and institutionalized racism come together to produce images that function to "silence" people (Cohen 1996). Being plugged into the world has also enabled northern communities to break out of their isolation and to align themselves with the politics of indigenous peoples elsewhere. Politicizing aboriginal awareness through the exposure of comparable movements in the area may prove the most long-lasting benefit of aboriginal media. The following case study provides deeper insight into how the Inuit of Canada have wrested control over the local media, in large part by appropriating satellite technology to meet their social and cultural needs. However, as Valerie Alia reminds us, it is not how the messages are conveyed that is important, but rather what kind of messages are sent and by whom.

CASE STUDY: Empowering the North

Media in Canada have long been viewed as key components of society building. The CBC has been mandated to include all Canadians as part of its society-building process. Difficulties have been encountered in this commitment to Canada as a community of communities in areas that are isolated and sparsely populated. Without access to media, it becomes difficult for indigenous Canadians to establish a sense of national identity within the framework of Canada. Such is the situation for the indigenous peoples who occupy the barren lands near the Arctic Circle (Quasser 1998). The fact that many Inuit communities are now serviced by a media that reflects their interests and priorities rather than those of the south is encouraging in its own right. Yet despite Canada's reputation as a world leader in both northern and aboriginal communications, each increase of progress, both small scale and ad hoc or ambitious and far reaching, has been succeeded by relapses and cutbacks, thus jeopardizing Canada's leadership position (Alia 1999).

The CBC began operating a northern television service for some communities as far back as 1958 (radio broadcasting arrived in the north in the 1930s). However, the objectives of this northern service were derived from a southern perspective (Raboy 1990), and they tended to reflect political interests related to establishing Canadian sovereignty during the Cold War. Economic interests pertaining to industrial expansion were also important. However, the service proved to be a commercially unfeasible proposition because of distances and isolation—at least until the early 1970s with the availability of satellite technology. Passage of the *Telsat Act* in 1969 made Canada the first country to establish a domestic satellite transmission policy (Roth 1995). With the launch of Canada's domestic satellite in 1973, Anik B, all but the most remote Inuit communities were eventually connected by satellite services in terms of radio, telephone, and television. For example, the 4,000 members of the community of Iqaliut on the southern tip of Baffin Island can subscribe to 20 channels from mainland Canada and the United States (Quasser 1998). The availability of popular entertainment was attractive; yet indigenous communities remained dependent on CBC funding for its survival. TV programming also posed a problem in the reconciliation of traditional values with the modern images conveyed by broadcasting. Many feared the introduction of television would result in the loss of time-honoured pursuits and social interactions, as well as accelerate a growing generation gap. This made it even more imperative for the Inuit to gain control over television messages and images.

The Inuit Broadcasting Corporation (IBC) was instituted in 1981 with the express purpose of controlling the airwaves through Inuit-produced programs about themselves, in the language of their ancestors (Meadows 1996). The IBC promised a balance of CBC programming and Inuit-language programming that reflected the realities and concerns of the local communities. The northern broadcasting policy promised a significant measure of Inuit participation in programming and regulation, with funds to create a limited amount of Inuit-produced programs about issues that dealt with language, culture, and society (Raboy 1990). IBC currently produces five hours of original programming per week that is non-violent, family oriented, and respectful of Inuit traditions. Surveys indicate that 90 percent of the Inuit watch from one to three hours of IBC programming, including *Takuginai* (Look Here) a kind of Inuit *Sesame Street* and *Kippinguijautit* (Things to pass time by) for showcasing Inuit talent and story-telling (Bergman 1996). Funds were also set aside to re-dub CBC programming into Inuit. The introduction of this northern service proved that modern technology, when locally owned, community based, and culturally sensitive, could be used to preserve indigenous language and culture.

The CRTC implimented Canada's current Aboriginal Broadcasting Policy in 1990 although a Northern Native Broadcasting Access Program was established in 1983, with a budget of $4.5 million (Meadows 1995). A Television Northern Canada consortium had argued for programming that reflected northern rather than southern interests. First Nations people wanted diversity in programming, yet their expectations differed from southern audiences. Communications was endorsed as a powerful tool to ensure cultural survival, with the result that programming had to mirror the social, cultural, and linguistic realities of the Far North. Aboriginal programming was defined as any program about some aspect of Native life that was directed towards an aboriginal audience or a program involving one of the indigenous languages. Limitations were also imposed on the kind and amount of advertising on Aboriginal radio and television. The inception in January 1992 of TV Northern Canada, a transArctic aboriginal TV network (comprising a consortium of government and private interests), firmly secured access to northern airwaves while reducing dependency on the CBC (Alia 1999). Primarily an aboriginal network with an audience base of 100,000, TV Northern Canada proposed to produce one hundred hours per week of programming for 94 communities in 13 different indigenous languages. Its rationale was straightforward: if aboriginal society was to survive, it was imperative to foster a sharing of ideas and experiences between dispersed communities from the Arctic Inuit to the Cree-Ojibwa of Northern Ontario.

This exercise in local self-determination enhanced Inuit pride and identity by reflecting Inuit values and survival skills. It also empowered Inuit communities through control over the electronic media by filtering southern realities through Inuit sensibilities while countering non-indigenous constructions that continue to dominate the mainstream media. Primary attention is directed at indigenous youth, with programming directed at skills enhancement, language and culture preservation, and entertainment through music videos (including aboriginal artists), talk-back shows hosted by young people, and magazine-style programs. Finally, indigenous broadcasting has served to politicize northern peoples by aligning and drawing Inuit awareness to human rights issues as viable alternatives in other parts of the world. Knowledge that the concerns and challenges confronting the Inuit are similar to those of other indigenous peoples has united otherwise disparate Inuit communities into a more globally aware and progressive society.

The emancipatory potential of local media has altered our perception of traditional mass media. Commodity-driven mass media tend to obliterate identity in an avalanche of American-style programming, yet local productions may assist in locating or consolidating a collective affiliation. However, even these efforts will fail unless indigenous peoples can gain local ownership over programming and a sense of community commitment and involvement. This appears to be the case with TV Northern Ontario and IBC. Local programming has elicited high levels of interest in TV and radio programs; the popularity of shows related to language learning, skills acquisition, and northern exposure to regional organizations also indicates a bright future. To be sure, cutbacks in funding have led to uncertainty and increased reliance on the government with its potential to compromise the integrity of indigenous cultures. For example, the federal government cut the IBC budget by 36 percent between 1990 and 1995 ($2.6 million to $1.6 million) even though it was dependent on federal spending for 65 percent of its operating budget. The Northern Native Broadcasting Access Program saw its budget slashed from a high of $13.2 million in 1989 to around $9 million by the mid-1990s. Nevertheless, despite contradictions that both give advantage to yet disadvantage media coverage of aboriginal peoples, evidence suggests that there will be no turning back—even with cutbacks—as Canada's indigenous people re-establish their rightful place in an inclusive media network.

***

CHAPTER 10

RE-PRIMING THE RELATIONSHIP

Framing the Issue

Mainstream media in contemporary society have become central to the social construction of identity. Both print and electronic media provide the material out of which individual and national identities are developed around the reference points of race, ethnicity, identity, power, and "us" versus "them." Both minorities and majorities depend on images of the "other" to define themselves, yet the mainstream is often ignorant of the racist assumptions employed in defining others as less than normal. Images of minorities are socially and historically constructed from this dominant perspective, thus reflecting a reality that says more about the mainstream than anything about minority experiences and realities (Ross 1996).

There is little doubt that Canada's mainstream media once resonated with an attitude of indifference or hostility towards minority men and women. Minorities were diminished and disparaged by both the quantity and quality of images that, cumulatively, had the effect of invisibilizing, stereotyping, problematizing, and ornamentalizing minority women and men. How accurate is this assessment at present? Responses vary. To one side, it is obvious that media have "become more inclusive of minority women and men since the days when soap ads portrayed black children being scrubbed in a tub with the slogan: 'If you can get this skin clean, think what our products can do for your white complexion.'" To the other side, minority women and men are so routinely incorporated in certain media processes that the question is not about inclusiveness per se, but about how much and in what way. Between these poles is a convoluted range of perceptions and images that exemplify the ambiguities in dismantling a racist past for an inclusive future. These links between media discourse and racial discrimination are complex and multifaceted, according to Tator and Henry (2000). Yet they are part of the intricate network of social relationships in which power and control play a central role. Mainstream media certainly shape perceptions and an understanding of reality. However, these media definitions are not constructed in a social vacuum but within the context of power and privilege. To be sure, public expectations may be unrealistic; after all, the mainstream media are rarely at the cutting edge of change, are poorly equipped to constructively engage diversity, and may resist the inclusion of minority voices if profits are jeopardized. Nevertheless, criticism and resistance are challenging the mainstream media to usher in transformations in the portrayal of minority women and men.

The representational basis of media-minority relations can best be described as complex and contested, often contradictory or inconsistent, and perpetually fraught with double standards or inadvertent hypocrisy. This contestation is particularly evident in debates over integrating minority women and men into the mainstream media without arousing accusations of paternalism, cultural theft, or tokenism. Consider the no-win situation that confronts the mainstream media: Positive minority role models are encouraged, yet the mainstream media come under fire for portraying unattainable success stories that foster resentment or feelings of inadequacy among those less fortunate (think of *The Cosby Show*). Exclusion of minority women and men is denounced as racist, yet inclusion may be dismissed as little more than a cynical publicity ploy that oversimplifies complex problems. Critics pounce on the media for focusing on the negative and the confrontational, yet are equally critical of excessively upbeat coverage that glosses over reality. Networks that devote one night a week to primarily black casts are criticized for promoting either segregation or integration, while separate radio stations for Blacks or aboriginal peoples are rejected as much-reviled towers of Babel or endorsed as fabled pathways to understanding. Bewildered and taken aback by criticism of their efforts, regardless of what they do, the mainstream media have tip-toed cautiously in engaging diversity, with good outcomes competing with bad outcomes, and a host of outcomes in between.

The Good

Demographic changes and shifts in intellectual fashion have ignited a broader debate over the worth and authenticity of diversity as refreshingly different, in contrast to the past when differences were routinely dismissed as inferior or irrelevant. Newscasting is making an effort to avert blatant racism, for example, by reducing the number of disparaging references to minorities through the "race tagging" of crime stories where race is immaterial in tracking suspects. Advertising, including that of Benetton, is increasingly supportive of diversity as something to be positively marketed, while the marketing industry in general is increasingly more responsive to diversity—if only to curry favour with the public as bastions of good corporate citizenship (Franklin 2000). TV programming is more inclined to portray minorities in a positive light by acknowledging people of colour across a broad socio-economic spectrum. While proof is inconclusive, such a shift would appear to foster (a) increasing interracial familiarity, (b) the shattering of stereotypes, (c) the fortifying of the comfort zone, and (d) the expansion of the number of minority role models. Films are also leading the charge by challenging conventional stereotypes between whites and non-whites. Black lead actors from Richard Rountree's *Shaft* to Samuel Jackson's millennium *Shaft* are increasingly common (Cremen 2000), while black female actors such as Whoopi Goldberg are among Hollywood's leading money-makers.

Nowhere are changes more evident than in media representations of aboriginal peoples. The portrayal of aboriginal peoples following the 1990 epic *Dances with Wolves* has improved, with much greater emphasis on the courage or durability of indigenous people in contrast with the rapacious greed of white-settler colonization. TV programming such as *North of 60* has expanded a multicultural mindset towards aboriginal peoples: According to Linda Wortley in her article "The Mountie and the Nurse" (1999) positive aboriginal programs provide (a) a view of aboriginal peoples as individuals living in a community where problems are explored and solutions negotiated rather than as passive players in sensationalized stories; (b) insights into the sources of social and personal problems, thus putting issues into context in contrast to the de-politicized coverage of the past; (c) affirmation of the continuity in culture and its dynamics (rooted in history but not stuck in the past); and (d) a glimpse into the lives of enterprising aboriginal people. Yet even this critically acclaimed series is not exempt from snipes since its lack of humour and perpetual crisis mentality is perceived as a serious distortion and a significant disservice.

Opinion within the media industry is equally upbeat. Media workers have expressed a cautiously optimistic outlook over recent developments in media responsiveness to minority women and men. In a series of interviews conducted in 1996 by one of this book's co-authors (Jean Lock Kunz) with key officials from major television stations in southern Ontario, a largely buoyant mood of inclusiveness was conveyed without acknowledging that more work was needed. Nearly all the interviewees agreed with the following points:

1. There is a need for the mainstream media to reflect the multicultural mindset and realities of an increasingly diverse Canada. As one official put it, "Our audience is changing, society is changing, and programming has to match this change."

2. Improvement in the representations of minorities in the mainstream media cannot be denied, especially in newscasting and drama programming.

3. Much of this change is motivated by commercial imperatives since incorporating minority women and men "makes good business sense" when in pursuit of the "almighty dollar." This bottom-line outlook acknowledges changes in the ethnic composition of Canadian consumers.

4. Advertising was deemed by most as the media process least likely to be accommodating because they "are so ingrained in the old value system."

5. Confusion remains regarding the focus on multiculturalism with respect to media inclusiveness; that is, should a multicultural commitment emphasize our differences or our similarities? This ambiguity is captured in the words of one respondent who explained, "On the one hand we celebrate cultures, on the other hand we isolate cultures."

6. There is even greater disagreement on how to represent minorities within an inclusive and multicultural institution, namely, to integrate minorities into the mainstream or to segregate minorities by way of ethnic-specific channels and programs.

7. More attention is currently being paid to budget cuts than to improving representation of minorities. As one respondent put it, "There's not much effort going on. In fact, we are into cuts."

This synopsis indicates that media personnel (with several exceptions related to advertising which we believe is at the cutting edge of change) are reinforcing much of what this book has argued. Changes in the representational basis of media-minority relations are necessary, timely, and overdue. And to a large extent some mainstream media processes have complied. Others have not.

The Bad

Improvements notwithstanding, there is much to the adage that the more things change, the more they stay the same. Improvements in some areas are undermined by stagnation in others. Minorities may appear in a greater number and variety of positive roles in mainstream media, yet updated versions of century-old stereotypes continue to circulate—as symbols of success as well as failure—with the result that representations resonate with ambiguity and contradiction. Mainstream media depictions continue to have the effect of portraying minorities as the "other," as social oddities compared with the mainstream, and in the process reinforce negative stereotypes. Appearances are deceiving: improvements in the quantity of minority representations are not the same as quality of representations, prompting Robert Stam (1993) to pose the following questions:

> How much space do they occupy in the shot? Are they seen in closeups or only in distant long shots? How often do they appear compared with the Euro-Canadian characters and for how long? Are they active, desiring characters of only decorative props?... How do character positionings communicate social difference or differences in status? How do body language, posture, facial expression communicate social hierarchies, arrogance, servility, resentment, pride? Which community is sentimentalized? Is there an aesthetic segregation whereby one group is haloed and the other villainized?

Newscasting remains a medium of the negative, with minority men and women continuing to be framed as people who have problems or create problems. Print news continues to squeeze minorities into a limited number of roles as athletes, entertainers, or criminals, according to a host of recent studies in Canada's English print media (Siddiqui 1999). A pervasive institutional monoculturalism persists within newscasting, resulting from a dearth of minority staffing, budgetary constraints, and difficulty of accessing minority spokespersons (Abel 1997). Mainstream news coverage of minority women and men remains meagre or inconsistent and subject to double standards in the same way that media coverage of the poor suffers from comparison with the affluent. News items involving minority women and men (as well as the poor) continue to be ignored until their actions are loud and public. Subsequent coverage of minorities remains distorted and misleading, and revolves around contradictory messages of minorities as failures, as undeserving, as threats to core values, with only themselves to blame. The end result? A public perception that being a problem constitutes the entirety of minority existence.

TV programming is no less ambivalent. Television appears to be content to offer sponsors the least jarring entertainment for drawing the largest possible audiences. Decision-makers are petrified of making a mistake by stepping on a cultural landmine that could detonate into negative publicity, offend sponsors, sacrifice ratings, or incite a consumer boycott. Talk of inclusiveness is one thing, but the failure of the four major U.S. networks in 1999 to include minority main characters is indicative of a timidity in engaging any topic that might strike a discordant note in the formulaic and derivative. Visibility may not be the same as power, but invisibility is definitely disempowering, most notably in TV series such as *Mad about You*, which is set in New York City but generally lacks any minority presence. Both advertising and TV programming may be exploring new dimensions yet neither are averse to cloning variations on minority stereotypes for connecting with audiences. For example, while minorities are making headway in U.S. network dramas, comedies and sitcoms continue to rely on stereotypes as a source of jokes. The rise of positive images is undercut by continued emphasis on Blacks as victims or villains—eliciting feared and loathing in white audiences. With several exceptions, such as *ER* and *North of 60*, TV programming remains segregated into predominantly white casts or minority casts, especially in those sitcoms that are set outside a workplace, with the result that the world of television remains nearly as segregated as it did in the colour-deflating days of *Amos 'n Andy*.

Even acceptance in filmmaking is conditional. With financial stakes as high as they are, Hollywood movies must appeal to massive audiences for profit. This process induces producers to play it safe by resorting to type-casting—on the premise that if minority characters behave as audiences think they should, people will not be offended. The incorporation of minority women and men is more likely if they conform with an allegedly race-neutral but preferred Eurocentric image. As a result, the mainstream media are drooling over beautiful young actors with "olive" complexions (from Jennifer Lopez to Ricky Martin) whose wholesomeness is easy to market.

The In-Between

Few minorities have experienced as much media ambivalence as aboriginal peoples. The situation for Canada's first peoples is increasingly grim as growing aboriginal assertiveness is matched by increased media hostility over their "uppityness." Despite the visibility of aboriginal peoples on the big and small screen, the all-too-commodified images of aboriginal life appear to feed into a white consumer hunger for the exotic to enliven the "dull dish that is mainstream white culture." Alternatively, the media seem only too anxious to portray aboriginal peoples as problem people whose greed and irrationality are pushing

Canada to the brink. Not surprisingly, the goal of positively engaging aboriginality has a long way to go before parity sets in, according to Maurice Switzer, a member of the Elders' Council of the Mississaugas of Rice Lake First Nations at Alderville, Ontario:

> The country's large newspapers, TV and radio news shows often contain misinformation, sweeping generalizations and galling stereotypes about natives and native affairs. Their stories are usually presented by journalists with little background knowledge or understanding of aboriginals and their communities. As well very few so-called mainstream media consider aboriginal affairs to be a subject worthy of regular attention.

Portrayal of minorities as the "other" typically entails a cultural Catch-22: they are criticized for being too different yet may be chided for not being different enough; they are taken to task for aspiring to be the same yet vilified when they falter or refuse; and they are expected to pick up the slack in making a contribution to society yet are criticized as too pushy if too successful (Hanamoto 1995). Paradoxically, while the mainstream media are critical of other institutions for not living up to their multicultural obligations, they appear reluctant to criticize those industry standards and institutional practices that contribute to aboriginal miscasting and media racism. Or as Brian Maracle puts it, the mainstream media are so steeped in Eurocentric values (including liberal pluralism and universalism) that this bias may elude detection without constant reminders to that effect. The fact that media bias exists is not the problem; after all, all social constructions reflect the values, agendas, and priorities of those who create them. Rather problems arise from the refusal to admit this bias exists while hiding behind a smokescreen of neutrality, fairness, and objectivity.

What do minorities want from the mainstream media? While responses will vary given the diversity of minority opinion, certain patterns appear to be constant, including:

1. A media that reflects the multidimensionality of their lives as full and equal members of society as well as respected members of their ethnic community.

2. A media that appreciates their cultural differences as valuable in their own right as well as being positive contributions to society without denying their status as normal and integral members of the community.

3. A media that depicts their concerns, realities, needs, and experiences within a broader political, historical, cultural, and social framework.

4. A media that approaches minorities as individuals who live in meaningful cultural communities that are respectful of the past but not to the point of precluding full and equal participation in society.

5. A media that expresses inclusiveness, insofar as possible, and makes accurate coverage of minority lives and concerns the rule rather than exception.

This wish-list could be expanded but a pattern is discernible. Minority women and men want to be part of Canada but also want Canadians to acknowledge the legitimacy of their diversity by taking differences seriously without losing their right to fit in or get on. But minority aspirations are one thing; the question of whether the mainstream media can deliver may be quite another, given its nature as a profit-driven industry that is both formulaic and derivative, reflective of increased corporatization of the process and product, and anchored in systemic biases as a basis for persuasion. Again, consensus is difficult. Still, certain attributes suggest formidable barriers before a truly inclusive and multicultural media can be established, including the following:

1. Mainstream media are mediacentric, that is, reality is routinely and automatically portrayed from the perspective of the mainstream as normal, natural, and superior, while other perspectives are approached as inferior or irrelevant. Is it possible for a discourse in defence of dominant ideology to engage positively with minority women and men from their perspective?

2. Minorities don't want to be stereotyped, yet stereotyping is central to the creation of images that resonate with meaning or menace with mainstream audiences. Is it possible for a system that must distil and convey vast amounts of complex information in visually appealing sound bites to move beyond generalities about others?

3. Minorities don't want to be cast as problem people yet media are inseparable from narratives anchored in conflict and confrontation between readily identifiable protagonists. Is it possible for the mainstream media to transcend conflict narratives as the basis for story-telling in news, TV programming, or filmmaking without boring an audience that has been force-fed a diet of jiggles, jolts, and jokes?

4. Minorities don't want to be typecast as ornaments yet the mainstream media have little choice but to cater to whiteness as the prime audience and primary source of revenue. Is it possible for the commercial media to reconcile the competing interests of many without alienating the support of all?

5. Minorities don't want to be stereotyped as problem people. Is it possible to introduce a neutral way of reporting negative events about minority women and men that informs without feeding into prejudices?

6. Minorities don't want to be otherized. Yet the mainstream media are caught in a tension between unity and differences. Can minorities afford a broad range of images, from positive to negative, without compromising a public stance of unity? Does a commitment to a unified minorityness come at the cost of denying growing internal differences? Can minorities afford to "air their dirty laundry" without fuelling stereotypes or eroding power, social legitimacy, or cultural visibility?

7. While inclusiveness makes good business sense for the media, it can only be accomplished internationally. Globalization and marketability of media product are the driving forces for including minorities in television programming. The United States is the biggest client for

Canadian television products. The social climate south of the border will definitely have an impact on television programming in Canada. This is evident in the increasing presence of Blacks and aboriginal peoples in Canadian television shows.

8. The media should reflect the mindset and the reality of Canadian society. This leads to the question of who really controls the media: the audience or the elite? Although it has long been established that the mass are seeing what they are supposed to see as decided by the media elite, the change in demographic structure and the increasing social and economic power of minority groups appear to have an impact on media programming. Yet, if media are consumer-driven, why would content lag behind reality in representing cultural diversity?

The Hopeful: A Last Word

The minoritization of minority women and men continues. Many are rendered invisible through underrepresentation in areas that count; conversely there is visible overrepresentation in areas that don't count, including tourism, sports, international relief, or entertainment. Improvements in positive media imaging of minority women and men tend to be neutralized by representations that continue to marginalize, deny, or demean, with the result that the representational basis of media-minority relations tends to send mixed signals—to the detriment of all Canadians. Yet this ambiguous state of affairs cannot be tolerated much longer. We live in a world that is pervaded by and transformed through images. The control of knowledge and its dissemination through media images is fundamental to the exercise of power in society. Media images are critical for conveying shared cultural beliefs and underlying assumptions that organize people's understanding about society in terms of entitlement, social actors, and their relations. These images not only assist in the identification and construction of ourselves as social beings, but they also serve as "windows" that provide insight into the social patterns and cultural values of society. As Bannerji writes, "Visual images in that sense are congealed social relations, formalizing in themselves either relations of domination or those of resistance. The politics of images is the same as any politics; it is about being the subjects not the objects of the world that we live in" (Bannerji 1986, 20).

The proliferation of images makes it impossible to distinguish fantasy from reality, according to Angus and Jhally (1989), especially since the "real" is mediated through images while social representations constitute a basis for formulating social identities (Gillespie 1996). This dialectical interplay between structure and agency has proven to be both a benefit and a cost in challenging the representational basis of media-minority relations.

The world we inhabit is a world of representation. Media do not merely present a reality that exists "out there"; nor do they simply reproduce or circulate knowledge. As active producers of knowledge, media construct and constitute the very reality of our existence (Goldman 1992; Fiske 1994; McAllister 1995). Direct access to the so-called real world is not humanly possible, much less an earned right or acquired skill; the "real" world is filtered through a prism of prevailing messages, symbols, and representations. Mainstream media reduce everyone to prisoners of image, but visible minority women and men are more susceptible to social and psychological damage through the internalization of hateful images that trivialize or reject. These complex articulations not only de-politicize the concerns and aspirations of women of colour. Their realities and contributions to society are trivialized through their placement in an environment where stereotypes define reality without offering alternatives. Such misrepresentations are not simply a mistake in perception, but rather a system of social control. Of course, the mainstream media do not set out to control, but the cumulative effect of these one-sided messages is controlling by consequence if not necessarily by intent.

Not surprisingly, then, the control of knowledge and its dissemination through media images is fundamental to the exercise of power in society. The representational basis of media-minority relations constitute relationships of power and inequality; this makes it even more imperative that we understand how these unequal relations are congealed around the symbolic representations of minorities. However, knowledge is empowerment, and reclaiming control over media representations of minority women and men can serve as a countering force to the privileged discourse that functions as a strategy of ideological control and containment. Isolating and challenging the misrepresen-tational basis of media-minority relations through direct action is a complex and demanding undertaking (George and Sanders 1995; Lee 1995). Yet until media minority representations are acknowledged as expressions of power, and dealt with accordingly, any moves to escape this psychic imprisonment are destined to falter in establishing an inclusive media and a multicultural Canada.

REFERENCES

Abel, S. 1997. *Shaping the news: Waitangi Day on television.* Auckland: Auckland University Press.

Abercrombie, N. 1995. *Television and society.* London: Polity Press.

Adams, M. 1997. *Sex in the snow. Canadian social values at the end of the millennium.* Toronto: Penguin.

Ali, M. 2000. Canadian comedy sketch re-inforced "terrorist" stereotype of Muslims. *The Silhouette* (McMaster University publication; 3 February).

Alia, V. 1999. *Un/Covering the north: News, media, and aboriginal people.* Vancouver: UBC Press.

Allemang, J. 1999. Sitcom stereotypes nothing to laugh at. *The Globe and Mail* (26 January).

Andersen, R. 1996. *Consumer culture and TV programming.* Boulder, Colo.: Westview Press.

Angus, I., and S. Jhally. 1989. *Cultural politics in contemporary America.* N.Y.: Routledge.

Angus Reid Group Inc. 1991. *Multiculturalism and Canadians: Attitude study, 1991.* National survey report submitted to the Department of Multiculturalism and Citizenship.

Annual Report. 2000. *Multiculturalism: Respect, equality, diversity.* Annual Report on the Operations of the Canadian Multiculturalism Act, 1998-1999. Ottawa: Canadian Heritage, Multiculturalism.

Artiles, A.J. 1998. The dilemma of difference: Enriching the disproportionality discourse with theory and context. *The Journal of Special Education* 32(1).

Atkinson, J. 1994. The state, the media, and thin democracy. In *Leap into the dark: The changing role of the state in New Zealand since 1984,* edited by A. Sharp (pp.146-177). Auckland: Auckland University Press.

Avery, D.H. 1995. *Reluctant hosts: Canada's response to immigrant workers 1896-1994.* Toronto: McClelland and Stewart.

Ayers, W. 1999. To the Bone: Reflections in black and white. In *Racism explained to my daughter,* edited by T. Ben Jelloun (pp.138-173). N.Y.: New Press.

Ayn Rand Institute. 2000. Multiculturalism and diversity—The new racism. http:// multiculturalism.aynrand.org/

Azam, S. 2000. Festival brings black reality to silver screen. *Toronto Star* (26 April).

Bannerjee, S.B., and G. Osuri. 2000. Silences of the media: Whiting out aboriginality in making news and making history. *Media, Culture, & Society* 22: 263-284.

Bannerji, H. 2000. *The dark side of the nation: Multiculturalism, nationalism and gender.* Toronto: Canadian Scholars Press.

Bauder, D. 2000. When is a TV show black or white? *The Globe and Mail* (4 July).

Beier, J.M. 1999. Of cupboards and shelves: Imperialism, objectification, and the fixing of parameters on Native North Americans in popular culture. In *Indigenous Constructions and Re/Presentation,* edited by J.N. Brown and P.M. Sant (pp.244-256). Commack, N.Y.: Nova Science Publishers.

Beiser, M., and M. Truelove. 2000. Toronto Star receives CERIS award. *CERIS* 4(1).

Ben Jelloun, T. 1999. *Racism explained to my daughter.* N.Y.: New Press.

Bergman, B. 1996. TV that protects the north from the south. *Maclean's* (21 January).

Berry, J., R. Kalin, and D.M. Taylor. 1977. *Multiculturalism and ethnic attitudes in Canada.* Ottawa: Ministry of Supply and Services.

Berton, P. 1975. *Hollywood's Canada.* Toronto: McClelland and Stewart.

Beverley, J. 1999. *Subalternity and representation.* Raleigh, N.C.: Duke University Press.

Bissoondath, N. 1994. *Selling illusions: The cult of multiculturalism.* Toronto: Stoddart.

Black, J., and C. Leithner. 1987. Patterns of ethnic media consumption: A comparative examination of ethnic groupings in Toronto. *Canadian Ethnic Studies* XIX(1): 21–39.

———. 1988. Immigrants and political involvement in Canada: The role of the ethnic media. *Canadian Ethnic Studies* XX(1): 1–20.

Bledsloe, G. 1989. The media: The minorities still fighting for their share. *Rhythm and Business Magazine* (March/April): 14–18.

Blythe, M. 1994. *Naming the other. Images of the Maori in New Zealand film and television.* Metuchen, N.J.: Scarecrow Press.

Bolaria, B.S., and P.S. Li. 1988. *Racial oppression in Canada.* 2d ed. Toronto: Garamond Press.

Bonilla-Silva, E. 1996. Rethinking racism: Toward a structural interpretation. *American Sociological Review* 62: 465-480.

Bottomley, G., M. de Lepervanche, and J. Martin. 1991. *Intersexions: Gender/race/culture/ethnicity.* Sydney: Allen & Unwin.

Bourette, S. 2000. Black, aboriginal groups looking for voice on radio. *The Globe and Mail* (31 January).

Brazier, C. 2000. Africa united: Not hopeless, not helpless. *New Internationalist* 326 (August): 9-13

Breton, R. 1984. The production and allocation of symbolic resources: An analysis of the linguistic and ethnocultural fields in Canada. *Canadian Review of Sociology and Anthropology* 21(2): 123-140.

———. 1988. The evolution of the Canadian multicultural society. In *Canadian mosaic, essays on multiculturalism*, edited by A.J. Fry and C. Forceville (pp.25-47). Amsterdam: Free University Press.

Brioux, B. 1999. Birth of a station. *National Post* (17 February, p.4).

Britton, N.J. 2000. Examining police/black relations: What's in a story? *Ethnic and Racial Studies* 23(4): 692-711.

Bullock, K.H., and G.J. Jafri. 2000. Media (mis)representations: Muslim women in the Canadian nation. *Canadian Woman Studies* 20(2): 35-40.

Burnet, J., and H. Palmer. 1988. Coming Canadians. In *An Introduction to the History of Canada's People.* Toronto: McLelland and Stewart, in conjunction with the Multicultural Directorate within the Secretary of State.

Byrne, E., and M. McQuillan. 1999. *Deconstructing Disney.* Sterling, Va.: Pluto Press.

Canadian Advertising Foundation. 1992. *Visible minorities in advertising: Focus groups/CEO survey results/national consumer survey.* Research report for Race Relations Advisory Council on Advertising. Toronto.

Canadian Islamic Conference. 1999. *Anti-Islam in the media.* An executive summary. Waterloo, Ont.

———. 1999. *Anti-Islam in the media: A six month case study of five top Canadian newspapers.* Waterloo, Ont.

Canadian Press. 1999. Movie attendance up for sixth straight year. *The Globe and Mail* (25 August).

Cardozo, A., and L. Musto, eds. *Battle over multiculturalism: Does it help or hinder Canadian unity.* Ottawa: Pearson-Shoyama Institute.

Carey, E. 2000. City's diversity key to Olympic sales pitch. *Toronto Star* (1 September).

Carter, G. 1999. Fair trial a just dessert. *The Lawyers Weekly* (26 February, p.3, 5).

Caws, P. 1994. Identities: Cultural, transcultural, and multicultural. In *Multiculturalism: A critical reader*, edited by D.T. Goldberg (pp.371-387). Oxford, U.K.: Blackwell.

Cernetig, M., and R. Matas. 1997. Swords in the temple. *The Globe and Mail* (25 January).

Chambers, G. 1997. The hypertextual sea change. *NZ Education Review* (9 July).

Churchill, W. 1994. *Indians are us? Culture and genocide in Native North America.* Toronto: Between the Lines.

Clark, A. 1999. An election meeting place. *Maclean's* (6 September, pp.60-61).

Cohen, H. 1996. Introductory essay. *Australia-Canada Studies* 14(1/2): 1-7.

Cowen, T. 1999. Cashing in on cultural free trade. *National Post* (24 April).

Cremen, C. 2000. That old black magic. *The Weekend Australian* (28-29 October).

Croteau, D., and W. Hoynes. 2000. *Media society: Industries, images, and audiences.* 2d ed. Thousand Oaks, Calif.: Sage.

Croucher, S. 1997. Constructing ethnic harmony. *Urban Affairs Review* (January).

Cryderman, B., A. Fleras, and C. O'Toole. 1998. *Policing, race, and ethnicity: A guidebook for the policing services.* 3rd ed. Markham: Butterworths.

Cuff, J.H. 1992. Cos' and effect: A mixed message. *The Globe and Mail* (30 April).

————. 1996. Black TV requires more than black actors. *The Globe and Mail* (9 September).

Curran, J., and M. Gurevitch. 1994. *Mass Media and society.* London: Edward Arnold.

Czerny, M., J. Swift, and R.G. Clarke. 1994. *Getting started: Social analysis in Canada.* Toronto: Between the Lines.

Darling, C. 2000. You call this reality TV? *National Post* (2 August).

Das Gupta, T. 1994. Multiculturalism policy: A terrain of struggle for immigrant women. *Canadian Woman's Studies* 14(2): 72-76.

Das Gupta, T., and F. Iacovetta. 2000. Whose Canada is it? Immigrant women, women of colour, and feminist critiques of "multiculturalism." *Atlantis* 24(2): 1-4.

Dates, J.L., and W. Barlow. 1990. *Split images: African-Americans in the mass media.* Washington: Howard University Press.

Davis, N.Z. 2000. *Slaves on screen: Film and historical vision.* Toronto: Vintage Publishing.

DeWolf, R. 1998. Disney forever facing criticism. *Toronto Star* (15 July).

Dow, B.J. 1996. *Prime-time feminism: Television, media culture, and the Women's Movement since 1970.* Philadelphia: University of Pennsylvania Press.

Duncan, P., and G. Cronin. 1997/98. Behind the rise of Maori sovereignty. *Revolution*: 15-21.

Duncanson, J. 1999. Police woo minority recruits. *Toronto Star* (6 March).

Ecologist. 1999. Beyond the monocultural: Shifting from global to local. *Ecologist* 29(3).

Eisenstein, Z. 1996. *Hatreds: Racialized and sexualized conflicts in the twenty-first century.* New York: Routledge.

Eller, C. 2000. Formula flicks for dull summer. *Toronto Star* (11 August).

Eller, J.D. 1997. Anti-anti-multiculturalism. *American Anthropologist* 99(2): 249-260.

Ellul, J. 1965. *Propaganda.* New York: Knopf.

Elmasry, M. 1999. Framing Islam *K-W Record* (16 December).

————. 2000. Islam exploited for political gain. Letter to Editor. *Toronto Star* (26 June).

Farli, P. 1995. TV "ghetto" has last laugh on Blacks. *Guardian Weekly* (29 January).

Fish, S. 1997. Boutique multiculturalism, or why Liberals are incapable of thinking about hate speech. *Critical Inquiry* (winter): 378-394.

Fiske, J. 1994. *Media matters.* Minneapolis: University of Minnesota Press.

Fleras, A. 1994. Walking away from the camera. In *Ethnicity and culture in Canada: The research landscape,* edited by J.W. Berry and J. Laponce (pp.340-384). Toronto: University of Toronto Press.

————. 1995. Please adjust your set: Media and minorities in a post-multicultural society. *Communications in Canadian Society,* edited by Benjamin Singer (pp.281–307). 4th ed. Toronto: Nelson.

————. 1998. Working through differences: The politics of posts and isms in New Zealand. *New Zealand Sociology* 13(1): 62-96.

————. 2001. *Social problems in Canada: Constructions, conditions, and challenges.* Scarborough: Pearson Education.

Fleras, A., and J.L. Elliott. 1999. *Unequal relations: An introduction to race, ethnic and aboriginal dynamics.* Scarborough: Prentice Hall.

Fleras, A., and P. Spoonley. 1999. *Recalling Aotearoa: Indigenous politics and ethnic relations in New Zealand.* Melbourne: OUP.

Frances, D. 1992. *The imaginary Indian. The image of the Indian in Canadian culture.* Vancouver: Arsunal Pulp Press.

Franklin, C. 2000. The need to look beyond Black History Month. *Advertising Age* (28 February).

Frederickson, G.M. 1999. Mosaics and melting pots. *Dissent* (summer): 36-43.

Friedman, Thomas.L. 1999. *The Lexus and the olive tree: Understanding globalization.* (New York: Farrar, Straus & Giroux).

Garth, J., and V. O'Donnell. 2000. *Propaganda and persuasion.* 3rd ed. Thousand Oaks, Calif.: Sage.

Gillespie, M. 1996. *Television, ethnicity, and culture change.* London: Routledge.

Giroux, H. 1994. Insurgent multiculturalism and the promise of pedagogy. In *Multiculturalism: A critical reader,* edited by D.T. Goldberg (pp.325-343). Cambridge: Blackwell.

———. 1996. *A fugitive culture: Race, violence and youth.* N.Y.: Routledge.

———. 1997. *Channel surfing: Race talk and the destruction of today's youth.* Toronto: Canadian Scholars Press.

Gitlin, T. 1995. Prime time ideology: The hegemonic process in television entertainment. In *Television: The cultural view,* edited by H. Newcombe. N.Y.: OUP.

Goldberg, D.T. 1994. Introduction: Multicultural conditions. In *Multiculturalism: A critical reader,* edited by D.T. Goldberg (pp.1-44). Oxford, U.K.: Blackwell.

———., ed. 1994. *Multiculturalism: A critical reader.* Cambridge, Mass.: Blackwell.

Goot, M. 1993. Multiculturalists, monoculturalists and the many in between: Attitudes to cultural diversity and their correlates. *Australia and New Zealand Journal of Sociology* 29(2): 226-254.

Granzberg, G. 1989. Portrayal of visible minorities by Manitoba television: A summary of findings. *Currents* 5: 25.

Gray, H. 1995. *Watching race: Television and the struggle for "blackness."* Minneapolis: University of Minnesota Press.

Graydon, S. 1995. The portrayal of women in the media: The good, the bad, and the beautiful. In *Communications in Canadian society,* edited by B.D. Singer (pp.143-171). Toronto: Nelson.

Groen, R. 1999. The neverending story. *The Globe and Mail* (31 December).

Grossman, D., and G. DeGaetano. 1999. *Stop teaching our kids to kill.* N.Y.: Crown Publishing.

Gunew, S. 1999. Colonial hauntings: The (post) colonialism of multiculturalism in Australia and Canada. *Australian-Canadian Studies* 17(2): 11-31.

Gwyn, R. 1994. The first borderless state. *Toronto Star* (26 November).

Ha, T.T. 2000. Multiculturalism, Canadian-style, lauded. *The Globe and Mail* (4 August).

Hackett, R.A. 1992. Coups, earthquakes, and hostages? Foreign news on Canadian television. In *Critical studies of Canadian mass media,* edited by M. Grenier (pp.313-328). Toronto: Butterworths.

Hackett, R.A., and Y. Zhao. 1998. *Sustaining democracy? Journalism and the politics of objectivity.* Toronto: Garamond.

Hall, S., et al. 1980. *Culture, media and language.* London: Hutchinson.

Hanamoto, D. 1995. *Monitored peril: Asian Americans and the politics of representation.* St. Paul, Minn.: University of Minnesota Press.

Hannerz, U. 1992. *Cultural complexity: Studies in social meaning* (p.26). New York: Columbia University.

Hannon, G. 1999. Snow on your TV. *The Globe and Mail* (2 March).

Harles, J. 1998. Multiculturalism, national identity, and national integration: The Canadian case. *International Journal of Canadian Studies* 17(spring): 217-248.

Harris, D.W. 1993. Colonizing Mohawk women: Representation of women in the mainstream media. *RFD/DRF* 20(1/2): 15-20.

Harris, F. 1995. *Multiculturalism from the margins.* Westport, Conn.: Bergin and Harvey.

Harrison, R. 1999. Borrowed images. *The Canadian Forum* (September; p.24-25).

Helly, D. 1993. The political regulation of cultural plurality: Foundations and principles. *Canadian Ethnic Studies* XXV(2): 15-31.

Henry, F., and C. Tator. 1999. State policy and practices as racialized discourse: Multiculturalism, the Charter, and Employment Equity. In *Race and ethnic relations in Canada,* edited by P.S. Li (pp.88-115). 2d ed. Toronto: OUP.

———. 2000. *Racist discourse in Canada's English print media.* Toronto: Canadian Race Relations Foundation.

Henry, F., C. Tator, W. Mathis, and T. Rees. 2000. *The colour of democracy.* 2d ed. Toronto: Harcourt.

Herman, E., and N. Chomsky. 1988. *Manufacturing consent: The political economy of the mass media.* New York: Pantheon Books.

Hesse, B. 1997. Its your world: Discrepant multiculturalisms. *Social Identities* 3(3): 375-394.

Hiebert, D. 2000 Immigration and the changing Canadian city. *The Canadian Geographer* 44(1): 25-43.

Hoeschmann, M. 1999. Cited in B. Turnbull. Lecturer takes on racism and the media. *Toronto Star* (18 March).

Holdaway, S. 1996. *The racialisation of British policing.* N.Y.: St Martin's Press.

Holland, J., and J.W. Gentry. 1999. Ethnic consumer reaction to targeted marketing: A theory of intercultural accommodation. *The Journal of Advertising* 28(1): 65-78.

hooks, b. 1992. *Black Looks: Race and representation.* Boston: South End Press (p.21).

———. 1995. *Killing rage.* Boston: South End Books.

Howard, C. News for the niches. *National Post* (10 November).

Hubbard, C. 1998. General introduction: Ethnicity and media democratization within the nation-state. In *A richer vision: The development of ethnic minority media in Western democracies,* edited by C. Husband. Paris: UNESCO.

Hudson, M.R. 1987. Multiculturalism, government policy and constitutional enshrinement—A comparative study. In *Multiculturalism and the Charter: A legal perspective,* edited by the Canadian Human Rights Foundation (pp.59–122). Toronto: Carswell.

Huff, R. 1999. What's black and white and watches different shows on television? Originally in *New York Times Daily,* reprinted in *National Post* (4 February).

Infantry, A. 1999. Vagueness of police sketch puts Blacks under suspicion. *Toronto Star* (17 September).

———. 1999. "Inadvertent" racism seen in the media. *Toronto Star* (18 September).

Innis, H.A. 1951. *The bias of communication.* Toronto: University of Toronto Press.

Isajiw, W., ed. 1997. *Multiculturalism in North America and Europe: Comparative perspectives on interethnic relations and social incorporation.* Toronto: Canadian Scholars Press.

Jakubowicz, A., et al. 1994. *Racism, ethnicity, and the media.* Sydney: Allen & Unwin.

Jaworsky, J. 1979. *A case study of Canadian federal government's multicultural policies.* Unpublished M.A. thesis. Political Science. Ottawa: Carleton.

Jhally, S., and J. Lewis. 1992. *Enlightened racism: The Bill Cosby Show, audiences, and the myth of the American dream.* Boulder, Colo.: Westview Press.

Jiwani, Y. 1992. In the outskirts of empire: Women of colour in popular film and television. *Aquelarre* (fall): 13–17.

Johnson, P. 1999. Network news remains domain of white men. *USA Today* (17 March).

Johnston, P.M.G. 1994. Examining a state relationship: "Legitimation" and Te Kohanga Reo. *Te Pua* 3(2): 22-34.

Jones, L. 1995. Waking up to the colour of money. *Style* 27 (August): 10-12.

Jones, V.C. 2000. Black models need not apply. *Now* (10-16 February).

Kallen, E. 1982. Multiculturalism: Ideology, policy, and reality. *Journal of Canadian Studies* 17: 51-63.

———. 1987. Multiculturalism, minorities, and motherhood: A social scientific critique of Section 27. *Multiculturalism and the Charter: A legal perspective,* edited by the Canadian Human Rights Foundation (pp.123–138). Toronto: Carswell.

Kaplan, W., ed. 1993. *Belonging: The meaning and sense of citizenship in Canada.* Montreal and Kingston: McGill-Queen's University Press.

Kelly, J. 1998. *Under the gaze: Learning to be black in white society.* Halifax: Fernwood Publishing.

Kim, K.S., and Y.G. Kim. 1989. Who reads an ethnic language newspaper, and why? *Multiculturalism/e* XII(1): 28–30.

Kobayashi, A. 1999. Multiculturalism and making difference: Comments on the state of multiculturalism policy in Canada. *Australian-Canadian Studies* 17(2): 33-3.9

Krieger, L.M. 1998. Stereotypes pervade music videos, study finds. New York Times Services, reprinted in *The Globe and Mail* (8 April).

Kunz, J.L. 1997. Associating leisure with drinking: Current research and future directions. *Alcohol and Drug Review.* 16(1): 69-76.

Kunz, J.L., and A. Fleras. 1998. Women of colour in mainstream advertising: Distorted mirror or looking glass? *Atlantis* 22(2): 27-38.

Kunz, J.L., A. Milan, and S. Schetagne. 2000. *Unequal access: A Canadian profile of racial differences in education, employment, and income.* Report prepared for the Canadian Race Relations Foundation. Toronto.

Kutty, F., and B. Youseff. 1998. Hollywood's view of Arabs and Muslims. *Toronto Star* (21 September).

Kymlicka, W. 1995. *Multicultural citizenship: A liberal theory of minority rights.* Oxford: Clarendon Press.

———. 1998. *Finding our way: Rethinking ethnocultural relations in Canada.* Toronto: OUP.

Lam, L. 1980. The role of ethnic media for immigrants: A case study of Chinese immigrants and their media in Toronto. *Canadian Ethnic Studies* XII(1): 74–90.

Li, P.S. 1999. The multiculturalism debate. In *Race and ethnic relations in Canada,* edited by P.S. Li (pp.148-177). 2d ed. Toronto: OUP.

Levitt, C. 1997. The morality of race in Canada. *Society* (July/August): 32-37.

Longley, K. 1999. Beyond multiculturalism: Australia and Canada. *Australian-Canadian Studies* 17(2): 75-83.

MacDonald, F.J. 1992. *Black and white TV: African-Americans in television since 1948.* Chicago: Nelson-Hall.

MacGregor, R. 1989. The distorted mirror: Images of visible minority women in Canadian print advertising. *Atlantis* 15(1): 137–143.

Mackey, E. 1999. *The house of difference: Cultural politics and national identity in Canada* (p.6). London: Routledge.

Mander, J. 1991. *In the absence of the sacred: The failure of technology and the survival of the Indian.* San Francisco: Sierra Books.

Maracle, B. 1996. One more whining Indian tilting at windmills. In *Clash of Identities,* edited by J. Littleton. Scarborough: Prentice Hall.

Marcus, A.R. 1995. *Relocating Eden: The image and politics of Inuit exile in the Canadian Arctic.* Hanover, N.H.: The University Press of New England.

McGregor, J. 1996. *Dangerous democracy: News media politics in New Zealand.* Palmerston, North N.Z.: Dunmore.

McRoberts, K. 1997. *Misconceiving Canada: The struggle for national unity.* Toronto: OUP.

Meadows, M. 1995. Northern exposure: Indigenous television developments in northern Canada. *Media International Australia* 78: 109-118.

———. 1996. Making cultural connections: Indigenous broadcasting in Australia and Canada. *Australia-Canada Studies* 14(1/2): 103-118.

Mietkiewicz, H. 1999. Colour coded casting. *Toronto Star* (1 March).

Miller, J. 1998. *Yesterday's news: Why Canada's daily newspapers are failing us.* Halifax: Fernwood.

Modood, T., and R. Berthoud, eds. 1997. *Ethnic minorities in Britain: Diversity and disadvantage.* London: Policy Studies Institute 14(2): 41-46.

Moeller, S.D. 1998. *Compassion fatigue: How the media sell disease, famine, war, & death.* N.Y.: Routledge.

Mura, D. 1999. Explaining racism to my daughter. In *Racism explained to my daughter,* edited by T.B. Jelloun (pp.90-137). N.Y.: Free Press.

Nelson, A., and A. Fleras. 1998. *Social problems in Canada: Conditions and consequences.* 2d ed. Scarborough: Prentice Hall.

Nolen, S. 2000. The adman's best friend. *The Globe and Mail* (10 August).

Okin, S.M., ed. 1999. *Is multiculturalism bad for women? (with respondents),* (pp.7-26). Princeton: Princeton University Press.

Palmer, H., ed. 1975. *Immigration and the rise of multiculturalism.* Toronto: Copp Clark Publishing.

Parekh, B. 1996. The united colours of inequality. *New Statesman* (13 December): 18-19.

———. 1999. Political theory and the multicultural society. *Radical Philosophy* 95: 27-32.

Pearson, D. 1995. Multi-culturalisms and modernisms: Some comparative thoughts. *Sites* 30 (fall): 9-30.

Pearson, S. 1999. Subversion and ambivalence: Pacific Islanders on New Zealand prime time. *The Contemporary Pacific* 11(2): 361-388.

Peter, K. 1978. Multi-cultural politics, money, and the conduct of Canadian ethnic studies. *Canadian Ethnic Studies Association Bulletin* 5: 2-3.

Pevere, G. 1998. Violence is at the heart of media storytelling. *Toronto Star* (28 March).

Poole, R. 1996. National identity, multiculturalism, and aboriginal rights: An Australian perspective. *Canadian Journal of Philosophy* 22 (Supplement): 407-423.

Postman, N. 1985. *Amusing ourselves to death.* N.Y.: Pantheon.

Potter, W.J. 1999. *On media violence.* Thousand Oaks, Calif.: Sage Publications.

Qualter, T. 1991. Propaganda in Canadian society. In *Communications in Canadian society,* edited by B.D. Singer (pp.200-212). 3rd ed. Scarborough, Ont.: Nelson Canada.

Quasser, P. 1998. Technology links the Arctic to the world. *Aboriginal Voices* (December): 32-33.

Quill, G. 1996. CFMT: The world in miniature. *Toronto Star* (19 May).

————. 2000. They shall overcome. *Toronto Star* (20 August).

Raboy, M. 1990. *Missed opportunities: The story of Canada's broadcasting policy.* Montreal and Kingston: McGill-Queen's University Press.

Reuters/Variety. 2000. Blacks on TV "ghettoized" to Monday and Friday sitcoms, U.S. study shows. *National Post* (28 February).

Rice, H. 2000. Don't touch that dial. *Voices*: 26-29.

Rich, F. 1997. Bill Cosby unplugged. *The Globe and Mail* (30 January).

Schlesinger, A., Jr. 1992. *The disuniting of America: Reflections on a multicultural society.* New York: WW Norton.

Shohat, E., and R. Stam. 1994. *Unthinking Eurocentrism: Multiculturalism and the media.* New York: Routledge.

Siddiqui, H. 1998. "Muslims unfairly labelled" by the Toronto Star Ombudsoffice. *Toronto Star* (10 January).

————. 1999. Wave the flag for Canadian mosaic. *Toronto Star* (1 July).

————. 1999. Damming indictment of racism in the media. *Toronto Star* (26 September).

————. 1999. How the media report crime news. *Toronto Star* (30 September).

————. 1999. Media need to catch up to audience. *Toronto Star* (3 October).

Skea, W.H. 1993/94. The Canadian newspaper industry's portrayal of the Oka crisis. *Native Studies Review* 9(1): 15-27.

Spoonley, P., and W. Hirsch. 1990. *Between the lines: Racism and the New Zealand media.* Auckland: Heinemann Reed.

Spotlight. 1999. Minority roles in U.S. movies, TV dip in 1998. *Toronto Star* (4 May).

Stam, R. 1993. From stereotype to discourse: Some methodological reflections on Racism in the Media. *Cineaction* 32 (29 October).

————. 2000. Introduction: Permutations of difference. In *Film and theory: An anthology,* edited by R. Stam and T. Miller (pp.661-668). Oxford: Blackwell Publishers.

Stam, R., and E. Shohat. 1994. Contested histories: Eurocentrism, multiculturalism and the media. In *Multiculturalism: A critical reader,* edited by D.T. Goldberg (pp.296-324). Cambridge, Mass.: Blackwell.

Stam, R., and T. Miller. 2000. Black America cinema. In *Film and theory: An anthology,* edited by R. Stam and T. Miller (pp.236-256). Oxford: Blackwell Publishers.

Steinhorn, L., and B. Diggs-Brown. 1999. *By the color of our skin: The illusion of integration and the reality of race.* N.Y.: Dutton.

St. Lewis, J. 1996. Identity and black consciousness in North America. In *Clash of identities: Essays on media, manipulation, and politics of the self,* edited by J. Littleton (pp.21-30). Scarborough: Prentice Hall.

Sugunasiri, S. 1998. How to kick multiculturalism in its teeth. Toronto: Canadian Scholars Press.

Switzer, M. 1997. Indians are not red, they are invisible. *Media* (spring): 21-22.

————. 1998. Media indulgence on aboriginal issues a myth. Letter to the Editor. *The Globe and Mail* (4 November).

————. 1998. The Canadian media have declared open season on Indians. *Aboriginal Voices* (December; p.8).

Taras, D. 1991. *The newsmakers*. Toronto: Nelson.

Task Force on the Participation of Visible Minorities in the Federal Public Service. 2000. *Embracing change in the federal public service*. Treasury Board. Catalogue No. BT22-67/2000.

Tator, C., and F. Henry. 2000. South Pacific perspective based on denigrating stereotypes. *Toronto Star* (3 January).

Taylor, C. 1992. The politics of recognition. *Multiculturalism and the politics of recognition*, edited by Amy Gutman (pp.25–74). Princeton: Princeton University Press.

Thobani, S. 1995. Multiculturalism: The politics of containment In *Social Problems in Canada Reader*, edited by A. Nelson and A. Fleras (pp.213-216). Toronto: Prentice Hall.

Toughill, K. 2000. Burnt Church Natives reject lobster deal. *Toronto Star* (10 August).

Ujimoto, K.V. 1999. Studies of ethnic identity, ethnic relations, and citizenship. In *Race and ethnic relations in Canada*, edited by P.S. Li (pp.253-290). 2d ed. Toronto: OUP.

Vasta, E., and S. Castle. 1996. *The teeth are smiling. The persistence of racism in multicultural Australia*. Sydney: Allen & Unwin.

Wall, M. 1997. Stereotypical constructions of the Maori "race" in the media. *New Zealand Geographer* 53(2): 40-45.

Waxman, S. 1998. Muslim fury as The Siege hits screen. *Washington Post*, cited in the *NZ Sunday Star-Times* (15 November).

Walker, J.W. St. G. 1998. *"Race": Rights and the law in the Supreme Court of Canada*. Waterloo: WLU Press.

Weatherell, M., and J. Potter. 1993. *Mapping the language of racism. Discourse and the legitimation of exploitation*. N.Y.: Columbia U. Press

Webber, J. 1994. *Reimaging Canada: Language, culture, community, and the Canadian Constitution*. Montreal and Kingston: McGill-Queen's University Press.

Weintraub, J. 2000. Where's Bill Cosby when you need him? *National Post* (24 July).

Wente, M. 2000. Asper, mogul and a half. *The Globe and Mail* (1 August).

Wilson, C. III., and F. Gutierrez. 1995. *Race, multiculturalism, and the media: From mass to class communication*. Thousand Oaks, Calif.: Sage.

Wilson, V.S. 1993. The tapestry vision of Canadian multiculturalism. *Canadian Journal of Political Science* XXIV(4).

———. 1995. Canada's evolving multicultural policy. In *Canada's century: Governance in a maturing society*, edited by C.E.S. Frank et al. (pp.165-195). Montreal and Kingston: McGill-Queen's University Press.

Winter, J. 1997. *Democracy's oxygen: How corporations control the news*. Montreal: Black Rose Books.

Young, I. 1990. *Justice and the politics of difference*. Princeton: Princeton University Press.

Zerbisias, A. 1994. Media accused of inflaming conflicts of language and race. *Toronto Star* (30 May).

———. 1999. "Third language" TV policy review. *Toronto Star* (1 February).

Ziervogel, K. 1999. Airwaves of a different colour. *Voices* (spring): 24.

GLOSSARY

Agenda setting. Agenda setting is the ability of the media to influence people's perception of what is important, acceptable, or desirable by drawing attention towards certain aspects of reality and away from others. This capacity to shape priorities may be secured deliberately or be inadvertently attained by the cumulative and controlling effect of one-sided media messages. See also *Propaganda*.

Contested site. The concept of a contested site suggests that any domain (from society to institutions) may be viewed as a battleground involving a struggle between conflicting visions. New ideas and unorthodox agendas compete to gain ascendancy over conventional ways of doing or thinking. The end result of this struggle is a social reality that is continually challenged, emergent and evolving, and subject to negotiation and compromise. Also implied by this notion is the idea that minority groups may find openings by which to challenge, resist, or transform.

Cultural relativism. The doctrine of cultural relativism asserts that the worth and value of all cultures or cultural practices are relative to a particular time and place. Such an assertion is not the same as saying that all cultural practices are legitimate expressions of the human experience. Rather, all cultural practices must be approached *as if* they were equally good and valid for purposes of study and understanding, but not necessarily as a basis for living.

De-construction. Based on the assumption that social reality is constructed by individuals who make choices, albeit in contexts not of their making, the process of de-construction involves unpacking those assumptions and the underlying logic that created the product in the first place. Reality is treated as any kind of text that can be exposed in terms of those biases and premises that went into the construction.

De-politicize. The process of taking something that resonates with danger and subversion and transforming ("neutralizing") this potential potency into something that is relatively harmless, marginalized, and "neutered."

Discourses. A discourse can be simply defined as a distinctive approach to reality in terms of (a) looking at it, (b) thinking about it, (c) experiencing it, and (d) talking about it. This socially constructed outlook involves an internal logic and a set of an underlying assumptions, the most important of which is a belief that an objective reality does not exist but only perceptions and ways of talking about this reality. As a result, discourses about the world "out there" are constructed in the same way as literary texts and are relative to a particular position rather than reflecting rightness or goodness. The totality of a discourse is embued with more meaning than what might be gleaned from approaching the constituent elements in isolation from each other.

Discrimination. Discrimination refers to any action that has the intent or effect of denying or excluding someone from equitable treatment because of membership in a particular racial or ethnic group. See also *Racism*.

Diversity. For many, diversity is widely seen as a mixture of items characterized by differences and similarities. Diversity evokes images of fixed and distinct cultures that persist in states of separate being. Individuals, in turn, are slotted into these pre-existing cultural categories without much option or choice and outside of any historical or power context. However, diversity goes beyond hermetically sealed classifications. Instead, it entails relations between groups in contexts of unequal power, reflecting the signification of individuals into categories that are both contested and evolving. Any reading of diversity must go beyond the cultural and discursive to embrace political economy at the level of hierarchically constructed relationships.

Dominant ideology. Dominant ideology is those ideas and ideals that are commonly used to justify and rationalize the prevailing patterns of what is acceptable and desirable in society. See also *Ideology*.

Ethnicity. Ethnicity can be defined as a shared awareness of inherited commonalities as a basis for recognition, reward, and relationships. This shared awareness provides a rationale for organizing ethnically related people into activity to protect, preserve, or advance social and cultural interests.

Ethnocentrism. Ethnocentrism is the tendency to automatically and routinely interpret reality from one's own perspective as normal or superior and to assume that others would do so as well if given half a chance, while dismissing other perspectives as inferior or irrelevant.

Eurocentrism. Eurocentrism is a belief or position that asserts the moral or evolutionary superiority of Anglo-European values as the standard by which others are measured and evaluated and found to be deficient.

Frames. Framing is the process of imposing a preferred meaning ("framework") on an event. See *Mediacentrism*.

Hegemony. Hegemony refers to a process of "thought control" in which people's attitudes are changed without their being aware that this change is occurring. Consent over the prevailing distribution of power and resources is secured through consensus rather than coercion. Dominant beliefs and ideals become so normalized and deeply ingrained as part of the natural order that they are (a) taken for granted as normal and necessary, (b) rarely questioned or subject to challenge, and (c) to be defended at all costs.

Ideology. Ideology can be defined as a set of ideas and ideals that provide an explanation for a particular community. Ideology can also be defined in more political terms as a set of ideas and ideals that justify the prevailing distribution of power, resources, and privilege in society. Media are ideological in two ways: they are loaded with ideas and ideals that reflect and reinforce unequal power relations in society, and they convey ideas and ideals that legitimize the patterns of inequality that empower some and disempower others.

Inclusion. In its most basic sense, the concept of inclusion refers to the incorporation of minority individuals and differences into a pre-existing institutional framework. A more sophisticated notion of inclusion acknowledges the need to restructure values and systems to ensure full and equal participation for minority women and men.

Institutional inclusiveness. Institutional inclusiveness claims that institutions must move over and make space if they are to reflect the reality of diversity while taking advantage of differences as a potential asset. Inclusiveness goes beyond the slotting of minorities into existing institutional structures and values. More importantly, it entails the modifying of rules and procedures related to access, equity, and participation in ways that are workable, necessary, and fair. Examples may include employment equity initiatives.

Liberal pluralism. A liberal approach to diversity, liberal pluralism argues for the universality of humanity. That is, what we have in common as rights-bearing and equality-seeking individuals is much more important than what divides us as members of a group, the content of our characters is more important than the colour of our skin, and what we do and accomplish is more important than who we are. A commitment to liberal pluralism makes it difficult to take differences seriously.

Mainstreaming. Mainstreaming is a process whereby minorities are moved from the margins of institutional life ("sidestream") into the centre ("mainstream"). Minority women and men are approached as integral and legitimate components of institutional life. See also *Inclusion*.

Mass communication. This process involves a predominantly one-way flow of standardized information from a centre to a largely undifferentiated audience, with limited feedback. In recent years, technology has taken the mass out of mass communication, with the result that media communication tends to be customized and two-way.

Media. The concept of media (pl.) has proven difficult to define, given that definitions of media may focus on the structure, functions, or process of both new media and mass media. Generally speaking, media may be defined as those institutions of persuasion involving the rapid transmission of "standardized" information to a relatively large audience through some mechanized channel ("medium"). See also *Ideology*.

Mediacentrism. Mediacentrism is derived from the concept of androcentrism or Eurocentrism. These concepts acknowledge the fact that reality is never interpreted objectively but tends to be routinely and automatically interpreted from the point of view of those in positions of power (white males, those of European tradition, those in positions of authority) as natural and normal, while other perspectives are dismissed as irrelevant or inferior. Mediacentrism refers to the process of understanding social reality through the imposition of "frames" that impose a certain meaning or cultural frame of reference on the world.

Media racism. Unlike a racist media that openly asserts the normality or superiority of the mainstream by routinely interpreting reality from a majority perspective, media racism involves those structures and values that continue to inadvertently and unconsciously deny or exclude the "other" while naturalizing the norms of those in positions of power and privilege and its inevitability.

Minority. Sociologically speaking, the concept of minority refers to any socially defined category of persons who are defined as different and treated in a discriminatory or exclusionary manner. Minority does not necessarily mean numerically inferior but encompasses those individuals whose disproportionate access to resources stems from a lack of power or opportunity.

Multiculturalism. Multiculturalism can be broadly defined as a constructive engagement with diversity as different yet equal. Other definitions will vary with the level of meaning that is employed; that is, multiculturalism as fact, as ideology, as policy, as practice, and as critique.

Othered. See *Otherizing*.

Otherizing. The process by which minority women and men are portrayed as people who are removed in time, remote in space, marginal to society, and undeserving of equal treatment because of their inferiority or irrelevance. Also othered or othering.

Policy. Policy can be defined as a formal set of specific initiatives (including laws, rules, and practices) designed to solve an acknowledged problem. Policy can also be defined as an ideological framework that justifies the creation and implementation of specific initiatives to solve problems.

Postmodernism. Generally speaking, postmodernism is associated with a rejection of modernism as a set of principles and outcomes. Postmodernism refers to a way of thinking and talking about the world (discourse) that denies the modernist claim for a unified and organized body of "totalizing" knowledge from a fixed and objective perspective. Also rejected is the idea that there is a rational core of meaning at the centre of society with a compilation of myths and symbols that secures unity and identity. Endorsed instead is a perspective that embraces the notion of reality as a series of discourses, a relativism that embraces diversity, the perception of identities as fluid and multidimensional, and resistance to conventional patterns.

Power. Power can be defined in many ways, but the term normally refers to the capacity of some to make others do what they usually would not do under normal circumstances. Power may be openly wielded or reside in agendas that are hidden but no less powerful ("hegemony"). Power should not be thought of as a thing or in absolute terms but as a process that is inherent in relationships and varies with particular contexts.

Prejudice. Prejudice refers to generalized pre-judgements about others that are derived from incomplete and inflexible information. It is based on irrational and unfounded assumptions that preclude the ability to treat others as individuals. From a sociological perspective, prejudice is not a psychological phenomenon but is interpreted as a social construction created by those in positions of power to justify and entrench the prevailing distribution of resources in society.

Problematizing. In problematizing a social issue, the objective is to make transparent ("expose") the socially constructed nature of the phenomenon under study to determine why it is defined as problematic, by whom, how, on what grounds, and with what implications. By de-constructing ("problematizing") the social construction, sociologists hope to reveal as clearly as possible the issues, agendas, politics, pressures, and arbitrariness that combine to construct this aspect of reality. See *Social construction*; also *De-construction*.

Propaganda. Propaganda can be defined as a process of persuasion by which ideas and symbols are organized in such a way as to ensure that the few influence the many. Systemic propaganda may also be defined as a process of persuasion rather than explanation or enlightenment. Unlike propaganda per se, systemic propaganda eliminates the conscious and deliberate dimension by arguing how the cumulative impact of largely one-sided messages may have had a controlling effect on audiences. See also *Systemic racism*.

Official multiculturalism. Official multiculturalism refers to an institutionalized set of policies and practices for integrating minority women and men into the institutional framework of society. The underlying logic of an official multiculturalism is to acknowledge differences without losing sight of national interests related to unity, identity, and prosperity.

People of colour. See *Visible minorities*.

Racial minorities. See *Visible minorities*.

Race. Race encompasses the belief that people's behaviour is determined by biology. It also reflects the belief that humanity can be classified into categories on the basis of fixed attributes, arranged in an ascending and descending order of superiority or inferiority, and treated accordingly. Most social scientists deny the existence of races as discrete and determinative classes of people. The lack of scientific validity has not precluded race from exerting significant social importance as a social construction.

Racialized. This concept refers to the assigning of racial connotation to the activities of minority women and men. For example, crime may become racialized by virtue of its association with a particular minority group. The term can also be used in the sense of describing race relations. That is, there is no such thing as race relations but only relationships that are conferred with a racial meaning by those in positions of power.

Racism. Racism can be approached in different ways, in part because of different dimensions (racism as biology, as culture, as power), and in part because of different types (interpersonal racism, institutional racism, societal racism). For our purposes, racism is defined as that constellation of ideas and ideals that asserts the superiority or assumes the normalcy of one group over another on the basis of biological or cultural characteristics, together with the power to put these racialized beliefs into practice in a way that has the intent or effect of denying or excluding those who are perceived as different or disadvantaged.

Racist media. A racist media is one that openly encourages discriminatory bias towards minority women and men, or, alternatively, a racist media does not do anything to prevent or deal with racial discrimination. See also *Media racism.*

Representational basis of media-minority relations. This term refers to the relationship between mainstream media and minority women and men at the level of how minorities are visually and verbally portrayed in newscasting, TV programming, advertising, and filmmaking.

Representations. Representations are the construction of mental images of some aspect of reality. These images often say more about those producing them than about the objects that are being projected through symbols, codes, and meanings.

Social construction. A popular perspective in sociology, the concept of social construction argues that there is nothing natural or normal about the world we inhabit. Rather, social reality is created by individuals to reflect certain interests in a world not necessarily of their making.

Socially constructed. See *Social construction.*

Stereotyping. Stereotyping refers to a process of information processing. Reality is codified in a simple and often simplistic manner for making generalizations about groups of people on the basis of limited information. As a conceptual shorthand, stereotyping tends to attribute similar properties to everyone within that particular category. To the extent that media are heavily dependent on stereotyping as a basis for codifying reality for audiences, the concept of systemic stereotyping captures the often unconscious process of slotting individuals into pre-existing categories as a basis for thought or action. See also *Systemic racism.*

Systemic propaganda. See *Propaganda.*

Systemic racism. Systemic racism can be defined as a largely inadvertent bias that is built into the institutional framework of society. In contrast to deliberate and conscious expressions of denial or exclusion, systemic racism refers to the subtle yet powerful form of discrimination that is entrenched within institutional structures, cultures, processes, and outcomes. Institutional standards, rules, and rewards may appear to be universally applicable and colour-blind, yet they have the unintended effect of excluding those who fall outside the mainstream while consolidating the pattern of power and privilege of a racialized social order.

Symbol. A symbol is something that stands for something else in which there is no direct relationship between signifier and the signified.

Theorizing. Theorizing is the process of defining general principles that can be employed as a basis to explain the relationship between seemingly unconnected patterns.

Visible minorities. Visible minorities is a popular term used to describe people of colour or racial minorities. The term itself refers to an official government category of persons who are native or foreign-born, non-white, and non-Caucasoid, including Chinese, Africans, and so on. In the 1996 Census, 11.2 percent of Canada's population identified themselves as or were identified as visible minorities.

INDEX

Abel, S., *48, 52, 70, 152, 157, 174*
Abercrombie, N., *52*
aboriginal peoples, *80-83, 145*
    as 'problem people," *136, 145*
    in film, *133-137*
    Inuit Broadcasting Corporation, (IBC)
    168
    APTN, *166-169*
Adams, M., *27*
advertising, *58, 103-119*
    and the prism of whiteness, *113-115*
    crisis in, *109-111*
    criticism of, *104*
    deconstructing, *107-109*
    dynamics of, *105-107*
    minority women, *115-117*
Alia, V., *147, 167*
Asian Americans, *131*
Assimilation, *13, 24*
Ayn Rand Institute, *33*
Benetton, *111-113*
Berry, J., *11*
bicultural focus, *13*
Bissoondath, N., *26*
Blacks, *97*
    "mammy syndrome," *99*
    Star Trek, 96
    television, and, *93-98, 143*
    see also The Cosby Show, *97-99*
Brazier, C., *68, 69*
Breton, R., *11, 12*
Burnt Church, *81*
Cardozo, A., *11, 14*
CFMT, *165*
celebrating differences, *13-14*
Charter of Rights and Freedoms, the, *15*
Chomsky, N., *48*
Citizenship Act, *13*
City-TV, *165*
civic multiculturalism, *15*
consensus multiculturalism, 20-21
couched in compromise, *172-178*
critical multiculturalism, *19-21*
cultural relativism, *11*
demographics, *see* ethnicity; multiculturalism
depoliticizing, *20-21*
developing world minorities, *67-70*
discourses,
    of resistance, *20*
    multicultural, *26*
    of whiteness, *43*
Disney films, *128-129*

distinct society, *25*
double standards, *83*
    see also mediacentrism
Elliott, J.L., *see also* Fleras
equity multiculturalism, *14*
ethnic multiculturalism, *13*
ethnic media, *166-167*
ethnicity, *7-10*
    see also multiculturalism
ethnocentrism, *46, 54*
Eurocentrism, *43, 46, 54*
    see also mediacentrism
exclusiveness, *148-154*
films, *121-137*
    aboriginal peoples, and *134-137*
    Disney, *128-130*
    Inuit, *126-127, 135*
    minorities, and *122, 132-133*
    perspectives on, *123-128*
Fleras, A., *3, 4, 24, 36*
framing, *79*
    see also newscasting
gender, *115-117*
ghettoized, *24*
Gray, H., *47, 93-96*
Gunew, S., *26*
Harles, J., *3, 12*
Henry, F., *30, 34, 44-46, 85, 146, 171*
Holdaway, S., *34*
Hooks, B., *35, 37*
Hughes, R., *11*
ideology
    in defense of, *49, 129*
    dominant, *52*
    institutional, *152*
    multiculturalism and, *10-11*
immigrants, as "problem people," *146*
immigration, *9-11*
    inclusiveness, *15-16, 157-169*
    institutional, *viii, 6, 157-159*
    media, and, *163-169*
    politics of, *viii*
operationalizing *160*
    barriers to, *162-163*
institutional accommodation, *14-15*
    see also inclusiveness
institutional inclusiveness, *159-163*
    barriers to, *162-163*
    definition of, *159-160*
    operationalizing, *160-161*
Inuit, *126-127, 167-169*
Inuit Broadcasting Corporation, *168*

Jakubowicz, A., *71*
Jaworsky, J., *13*
Kobayashi, A., *12*
Kunz, J.L., *32, 143, 147, 173*
Kymlicka, W., *16*
mainstream media, *30, 47-61*
    as inclusiveness, *163-164*
    deconstructing, *50-51*
    developing world, and, *70*
    effects of, *56-61*
    ideology, and, *52-53*
    violence and, *56-57*
    see also multiculturalizing the media
mainstreaming diversity, *164-166*
McRoberts, K., *13, 14*
media responsiveness, *173-177*
media minority miscasting, *ix, 63-64*
    developing world minorities, *67-79*
    Third World news, *71*
media-minority relations, *48*
media racism, *ix, 41-46*
mediacentrism, *54-55, 83-85*
    double standards, *83-86*
miniaturizing, *viii, ix, xiii, 91, 178*
    minority women, *115-117*
    invisiblizing, *142*
    ornamentalizing, *147*
miscasting minorities, *139-140, 141-155*
    accounting for, *148-154*
    theorizing, *142-148*
misrepresentation, *ix*
movie-making, *see* film
multiculturalism, *viii*
    assessment of, *25-27*
    conceptualization of, *4-6*
    criticism of, *6-7*
    levels of meaning, *7-16*
    national attitudes, *21-24*
    perceptions of, *21-22*
    practices, *17-24*
    United States, and, *19-21*
Multiculturalism Act, *15*
multicultural minorities, *8-10, 18-19*
    see also ethnicity; multiculturalism
multiculturalizing the media, *157-169*
    see also mainstreaming media
Muslims, *144*
newscasting, *58, 65-86*
    as social construction, *71-72, 76*
    love-hate relationship, *60*
    defining news, *70*
    corporatization, *73*
    bias, *72-78*
    minorities, *78-85*
    television, *77*
official multiculturalism, *3, 16*
    see also Multiculturalism Act
otherizing, *63*
    minorities, *152-154*

paradox, *viii, 23*
Parekh, B., *10*
Pearson, D., *24, 25*
policy, *11-16*
    see also multiculturalism
politics, *17-18, 24*
positive programs, *173*
prism of whiteness, *113-115*
problematizing, *145-146*
propaganda, *128*
    see also systemic
Quebec, *13, 22*
Quiet Revolution, *13*
racialize, *xiii, 35*
racism, *29-46, 129*
    definition, *33*
    dimensions of, *33-36*
    media and, *29-32, 41-46*
    typology of, *37-41*
recasting the mould, *139-140, 147-148, 171-172*
representational images, *104*
    redefining, *157-169*
repriming the relationship, *171-179*
reverse racism, *31*
Satzewich, V., *32*
shallows and rapids, *78*
    see also newscasting
Siddiqui, H., *84*
stereotyping, *31, 144-145, 151*
stereotype, *x*
    aboriginal peoples, 133-137
    gender role, *116*
    minority women, *115-117*
    systemic, *149-150*
Stam, R., *48, 141*
Steward, N., *67*
subliminal racism, *39-41*
systemic, *149-150*
    bias, *150, 151*
    propaganda, *xii, 49, 53, 55*
    racism, *38-39*
Tator, C., *31, 44-46, 49*
television programming, *87-102*
thought control, *see* systemic
Toronto Star
    Beyond 2000, *86*
Trudeau, P.E., *11*
Vasta, E., *3, 4, 24*
visible minority, *8*
    distribution of, *9*
violence and the media, *56-59*
Westocentric, *viii*
    see also Eurocentric, *43, 46, 102*
    ethnocentrism, *46, 145*
white stream, *xiii*
whitewash, *147-148*